IN THE HEART OF AMERICA

AND OTHER PLAYS

Naomi Wallace

THEATRE COMMUNICATIONS GROUP
NEW YORK

In the Heart of America and Other Plays is published by
Theatre Communications Group, Inc., 355 Lexington Ave.,
New York, NY 10017–6603.

This publication is made possible in part with public funds from the New York State Council on the Arts, a State Agency.

Page 5: "The Flea" by John Donne, *The Complete Poetry and Selected Prose of John Donne*, Charles M. Coffin, ed., The Modern Library (A Division of Random House), New York, 1994; *Mother Courage* by Bertolt Brecht, Grove Press, New York, 1991. Page 81: *Music of the Human Flesh: Poems of the Palestinian Struggle* by Mahmoud Darwish, Heinemann, London, 1980. Page 282: *Love's Philosophy* by Percy Bysshe Shelley, Dial Books for Young Readers, New York, 1992.

TCG books are exclusively distributed to the book trade by Consortium Book Sales and Distribution, 1045 Westgate Dr., St. Paul, MN 55114.

LIBRARY OF CONGRESS CATALOGING-IN-PUBLICATION DATA

Wallace, Naomi.
In the heart of america, and other plays / Naomi Wallace.—1st ed.
p. cm.
ISBN 1-55936-186-7 (pbk. : alk. paper)
I.   Title.
PS3573.A42688 I5 2000
812'.54—dc21   00-037756

Book design and composition by Lisa Govan
Cover art by Bruce McLeod
Cover design by Lisa Govan
Author photo by Kathleen Cei

First edition, June 2001

PS
3573
.A42688
I5
2001

Special thanks to my two irreplaceable agents, Rod Hall and Carl Mulert; to my three ever-present, rebellious, Club-Cobra girls—Nadira, Caitlin and Tegan; and to Bruce McLeod, my comrade—my work would be far less than it is, without his love and encouragement.

CONTENTS

ONE FLEA SPARE

1995

This play is for my children, Nadira, Caitlin and Tegan

PRODUCTION HISTORY

One Flea Spare was commissioned by the Bush Theatre in London, and opened there on October 18, 1995. It received its American premiere at the Humana Festival of New American Plays at the Actors Theatre of Louisville on February 27, 1996, and was awarded the 1996 Susan Smith Blackburn Prize, the 1996 Fellowship of Southern Writers Drama Award and the 1996 Kesselring Prize.

One Flea Spare opened February 25, 1997, at The Joseph Papp Public Theater/New York Shakespeare Festival. The director was Ron Daniels, the scenic design was by Riccardo Hernandez, the costume design was by Paul Tazewell, the lighting design was by Scott Zielinski, the sound design was by Stuart J. Allyn, the original music was composed by Michael Rasbury, the production dramaturg was Mervin P. Antonio and the production stage manager was C. A. Clark. The cast was as follows:

MR. WILLIAM SNELGRAVE	Jon de Vries
MRS. DARCY SNELGRAVE	Dianne Wiest
BUNCE	Bill Camp
MORSE	Mischa Barton
KABE	Paul Kandel

CHARACTERS

MR. WILLIAM SNELGRAVE, a wealthy, elderly man
MRS. DARCY SNELGRAVE, an elderly woman, his wife
BUNCE, a sailor, in his late twenties
MORSE, a girl of twelve
KABE, a watchman and guard

TIME

1665.

PLACE

A comfortable house in Axe Yard, off King Street,
Westminster, London.

SETTING

A room that has been stripped of all its fine furnishings,
except for a couple of simple, though fine, wooden
chairs. One small window upstage.

A cell or a room of confinement.

The street below the window of the Snelgraves' house.

Oh stay, three lives in one flea spare,
Where wee almost, yea more than maryed are.
This flea is you and I, and this
Our mariage bed, and mariage temple is;
Though parents grudge, and you, w'are met,
And cloysterd in these living walls of Jet.
Though use make you apt to kill mee,
Let not to that, selfe murder added bee,
And sacrilege, three sinnes in killing three.

—John Donne

Corruption is our only hope.

—Bertolt Brecht

ACT I

SCENE ONE

Morse locked in an empty room or cell. Alone. She wears a dirty, tattered, but once fine, dress. She stands center stage with the dress pulled up to hide her face. She is wearing a torn pair of boys britches or long underwear under her dress. She is just barely visible in the dim light. She repeats the words that her interrogator might have used earlier.

MORSE: What are you doing out of your grave? *(Beat)* What are you doing out of your grave? *(Beat)* Speak to me.

(We hear the sound of someone being slapped, but Morse remains still and does not react.)

Speak to me, girl, or you'll stay here 'til it's known.

(Another sound of a slap, harder. Morse still does not move.)

What happened to the gentleman?

(Another slap.)

What happened to his wife?

(Another slap.)

Whose blood is on your sleeve? *(Beat)*

(Morse drops her dress down to reveal her face.)

The blood of a fish. Is on my sleeve. Because. The fish. The fish were burning in the channels. Whole schools of them on fire. And the ships sailing and their hulls plowing the dead up out of the water. And the war had begun. The war with the Dutch had begun. *(Beat)* It was March. No, it was later. In summer. A summer so hot vegetables stewed in their crates. The old and the sick melted like snow in the streets. At night the rats came out in twos and threes to drink the sweat from our faces. *(Beat)* And it had finally come. *(Beat)* The Visitation. We all went to sleep one morning and when we awoke the whole city was aglow with the fever. Sparrows fell dead from the sky into the hands of beggars. Dogs walked in the robes of dying men, slipped into the beds of their dead masters' wives. Children were born with the beards of old men. *(Beat)* They were locked in their own house, the two of them. All the windows, but one, nailed shut from the outside. They'd waited out their time of confinement. Three more days and they could escape.

But then we came. In through the basement and across the roofs.

One of us died. In that room. Two of us died. *(Beat)* It was night. Yes. At night. He moved as though invisible. Gliding through the empty streets.

(Bunce, making a fair amount of noise, tumbles into the cell, which has now become the Snelgraves' room. He stands facing into a corner.)

He came in through the cellar. He thought the house was empty and so he made himself at home.

(Snelgrave and Darcy enter their bare room.)

But his timing was off. Mr. and Mrs. Snelgrave caught him in the act of relieving himself into one of their finest vases.

(Morse joins the scene, but hides in the corner. Everything freezes. Then lights go up on Bunce in the Snelgraves' house. Bunce is looking over his shoulder at the Snelgraves, who remain in the shadows, almost invisible.)

BUNCE *(Producing the vase, with a genuine embarrassment)*: Thought I'd. Save my piss. It's got rum in it. Might be the last I'll have for weeks.

SCENE TWO

Lights up on the Snelgraves' room. Morse is still hiding. Snelgrave and Darcy jump back, terrified of contact with Bunce.

BUNCE: I'm a poor man looking for shelter.
SNELGRAVE: My God! Lord have mercy on us!
BUNCE: I thought everyone died in this house.
SNELGRAVE: Help! Someone help us!
BUNCE: Shhh. I mean no harm.
DARCY: He's relieved himself. In my vase.

(Bunce holds out the vase, offering to give it back to her.)

Get out of our house.
SNELGRAVE: He has the infection!
BUNCE: Not I.
SNELGRAVE: He's lying. He stinks. And sick. Look at his eyes.
BUNCE: I'm not sick. Just hungry.
SNELGRAVE: The guards. What if they saw you enter?
DARCY: They have no mercy; it's the law.
SNELGRAVE: Open your shirt. Stay! Open! Prove there's no marks on you.

(Bunce opens his shirt. With his cane, Snelgrave pokes at Bunce, moving the shirt this way and that to have a better

look. We see a bandage around Bunce's waist and a spot of blood.)

What? There's blood. My God! Blood!

BUNCE: It's years old.

SNELGRAVE *(Brandishing his cane)*: Get back! Get back!

BUNCE: Still bleeds.

SNELGRAVE: Your arms, then. Show us your arms!

(Bunce pulls up his sleeves and Snelgrave examines his arms.)

No other marks. He's clean.

(Morse comes out of hiding. All three of them jump back.)

MORSE: I am Morse Braithwaite.

SNELGRAVE: There's another! God have mercy.

MORSE: Sole daughter to Nevill and Elizabeth Braithwaite.

SNELGRAVE: Back, vile trespasser!

DARCY: Sir Nevill Braithwaite and his wife. We know them.

SNELGRAVE: Dead of the plague last Tuesday. Man, wife and daughter.

MORSE: It's true my father fell on me in a fit of fever, and there I lay beneath him for two nights and a day. It's terrible to smell such things from a father. But I finally dug my way from under him and up on the roofs I went. To hide. To hide from the plague. I saw no light in this house. I came in through the window. I'm not a thief.

SNELGRAVE: Open your collar. Let's see your neck.

(Morse opens her collar.)

DARCY: Sleeves.

(Morse pulls up her sleeves and the Snelgraves examine her.)

SNELGRAVE: Shame. Shame on you both. You could have infected this house.

(Banging at the window.)

Both of you. Quickly! Crawl back out of this house, whatever way you came in. Hurry. Hurry! Before you're known.

(Banging at the window again. Morse and Bunce hide. Kabe, the guard, peers in, thrusting half his body through the small window.)

KABE: Good morning, Mr., Mrs. Snelgrave. Have a good sleep, did you? It stinks in here, it does.

SNELGRAVE: We've washed the floors with vinegar.

KABE: And stripped the room bare, I see. Well, the less the nasty has to hide in.

SNELGRAVE: We've boarded up the other rooms, except for the kitchen.

KABE: Ah. Shame it is. Such fine rooms, some of the finest in town maybe, empty but for stink. Bit cramped this one though?

DARCY: This is the only room where someone hasn't died.

KABE: Ah yes. Two maids and a houseboy, carted and pitted. And the canary too, Mrs. Snelgrave? *(Makes the sound of a canary)* Shame. *(Beat)* Will you be needing any provisions from the market this morning, madame? Plenty of corn but cheese there's none. Butter, none. Some fruit but it's got the hairs.

DARCY: No, thank you, Kabe. That will be all.

KABE: The whole town's living on onions. You can smell it in the evenings. It's all that farting that's killed the birds.

(Sound of hammering on boards.)

DARCY AND SNELGRAVE: Kabe?

KABE: Sorry. Fellow across the way saw you let in a couple of guests last night.

DARCY: No. No.

SNELGRAVE: You can't do this. You can't—

DARCY: Please. Kabe. We beg you.

KABE: Can't have that. They might be carrying.

SNELGRAVE: They broke in. They were uninvited.

KABE: We're doubling up the boards.

DARCY: We are innocent.

SNELGRAVE: We have good health.

DARCY: We've held out in here alive.

SNELGRAVE: Alive, damn you, for almost four weeks! We are clean!

KABE: Sorry.

BUNCE *(Appearing)*: Then why didn't you lot try and stop us?

KABE: Not our job. We're just the guards. We make sure no one gets out. If they get in, well, that's just luck. So, twenty-eight days again for the lot of you. Just enough time to get snug. I don't mind. I like this house. Pretty as a bird, it is, heh, Darcy? *(Tweets again)*

DARCY: How dare you!

KABE: Does stink, though. I get paid twice as much to guard a proper house like this.

Could I have one of your gloves today, Mistress? Won't you show us your pretty white hands?

(Kabe shrieks with laughter.)

SNELGRAVE: I'll have you in the stocks when I'm out of here, Kabe.

KABE: I've been wanting to ask her that for years. Never could 'til now. *(To Morse)* Why don't you ask her? Ask her to show you her pretty, white neck! *(Sings)*

One o'clock, two o'clock, three o'clock, four,
here's a red cross for your door.
Where's my enemy?
Flown to the country!
Never mind that, coz . . .

DARCY: Someone should shoot him.

KABE *(Continues singing)*:
One o'clock, two o'clock, three o'clock, four,
I've got the key to your locked door!

(Kabe shrieks again with laughter and is gone.)

SNELGRAVE: Come here, child.

(Morse approaches him. Snelgrave slaps her.)

You would have been better off if you'd stayed put.
Sir Braithwaite's daughter doesn't climb over roofs.
Sir Braithwaite's daughter doesn't enter uninvited.
Your father is dead. Give me your hand. In the
Snelgrave house, we behave like Christians. There-
fore, we will love you as one of our own.

MORSE: Why?

*(Darcy takes the girl's other hand and the three of them
stand together. Bunce stands alone.)*

DARCY: Because you're one of us.

SCENE THREE

*Bunce sitting alone in the bare room. A key turns in the lock, and
an apple rolls across the stage toward him. He picks it up, smells
it with ecstasy. Snelgrave enters.*

BUNCE: I haven't seen one of these in weeks.

SNELGRAVE: Something special I have Kabe bring in now
and then.

BUNCE: The three of you in the kitchen?

SNELGRAVE: For the time being.

(Bunce holds up the apple, admires it, then begins to eat.)

I'm not a cruel man, Bunce. But even under these
conditions I can't just let you walk about. This is my
home. Under my protection. The problem is you
have the only suitable room in the house because it
has a door that I can lock and now we must sleep on
the kitchen floor. *(Beat)* And you smell awfully.

BUNCE: It's the tar, sir.

SNELGRAVE: Ah-ha! A sailor. I knew it! It keeps the water out, the tar. And your buttons, of cheese or bone?

BUNCE: Wood, sir.

SNELGRAVE: That's unusual. I know a bit about the waters myself. I work for the Navy Board, just down the lane, on Seething. My friend Samuel and I, we control the largest commercial venture in the country, hmm. The Royal Dockyards.

BUNCE: They're as good as closed, sir.

SNELGRAVE: That's the curse of this plague. It's stopped all trade. There's not a merchant ship that's left the main port in months. Rats eating at the silks, damp at the pepper. You fellows out of work, selling spice and nutmeg on the streets. And starving. The lot of you.

(Bunce eats the apple core as well.)

BUNCE: I sailed three cats and a hag before we unloaded at the main port. Half of the crew got sick and died. A crowd set fire to three flys unloading beside our rig. They said the ships were carrying the plague. The crew had to swim to shore. Those that weren't burned.

SNELGRAVE: What were your routes? Did you ship to Calcutta? Bombay?

BUNCE: Green waters of the Caribbean and back, mostly. Green water, green islands, green air, and all the colors of Port Royal.

SNELGRAVE: Port Royal. They say the women there are masculine and obscene.

BUNCE: Salt-Beef Peg.

SNELGRAVE: Your wife, certainly?

BUNCE: Not married.

SNELGRAVE *(Enjoying this)*: Shameful.

BUNCE: She had nothing on Buttock-de-Clink Jenny.

SNELGRAVE: Not in this house.

BUNCE: Old Cunning-finger Nan. As sweet and sour as . . . ah well. Sorry, sir. There's not a lot of good memories a sailor has, and them he has he carries tucked deep in.

SNELGRAVE: I've heard the stories at the coffeehouse. You know, I often dream of the sea but if I step my foot in a boat, the world goes black before my eyes. My body can't abide it, but my heart. Well. *(Beat)* I'm a rich man, Bunce, and you a common sailor yet— look at the two of us—we have the sea between us. The struggle, the daring, the wrath. Cathay's lake of rubies. The North-West passage. Ice monsters fouling the sea—that angry bitch that'll tear you limb from limb. Man against the elements.

BUNCE: Mostly for us sailors it was man against the captain.

SNELGRAVE *(Begins to rock back and forth, eyes closed, living in the moment of a sea story)*: And the winds, how they blow like a madness and the sea leaps up like a continuous flame. The hideous, howling wilderness that stabs at the hull, that would rend flesh from bone. Sea spouts the size of cities. The cargo shifting and tumbling below deck and water casks rolling from side to side. One terrible cry after another pierces the air as the crew is swept overboard.

(Snelgrave motions for Bunce to stand beside him and rock back and forth with him. After some initial hesitation, Bunce does so.)

To lessen the resistance to the fiendish wind and keep her from capsizing, three of our best crawl on deck with axes and climb aloft to cut away the fore topmast and the bowsprit ropes.

BUNCE: And as they hack at the mast, a monstrous wave, three times the size of the rig, whacks the starboard and snaps the foremast like a stick, and carries it with one of the sailors into the sea. The second is crushed . . .

SNELGRAVE *(Continues for Bunce)*: . . . between the mast and the side of the ship.

BUNCE: The third is hung by his boot in the ratline.

SNELGRAVE: The sea has no mercy and smashes all who try to rule her beneath her foul and lecherous waves.

BUNCE: Smashing, smashing.

SNELGRAVE: . . . Smashing the small vessel like eggshells against a stone. Oh death, death, death.

(Snelgrave whacks his stick on the floor furiously a few times.)

And scurvy. Did you get the scurvy?

BUNCE: Many a time.

SNELGRAVE: Knots. You can do knots? *(Takes out a piece of rope and knots it)* What's that?

BUNCE: That's a bowline. But your tail's too short.

SNELGRAVE: Is it?

(Bunce takes the rope and reties the knot.)

Hmmm. Show me another.

(Bunce does a series of knots, one after the other, as they speak.)

BUNCE: Butterfly knot.

SNELGRAVE *(Indicating a scar on Bunce's neck)*: How'd you get that scar? Spanish Main pirates?!

BUNCE *(Another knot)*: Lighterman's hitch. *(Meaning his neck)* Sail hook.

SNELGRAVE: In a drunken brawl?

BUNCE: We were a short ways outside Gravesend. Our fly was carrying sugar and rum. The press gangs were looking for fresh recruits and boarded us just as we came into port. *(Another knot)* Half hitch with seizing. *(Beat)* To keep from the press, sometimes we'd cut ourselves a wound and then burn it with vitriol. Make it look like scurvy. They wanted whole men, so I stuck myself in the neck with a sail hook. They passed me over when they saw the blood.

(Snelgrave hands Bunce some nuts. Bunce eats. Snelgrave watches him eat.)

SCENE FOUR

Morse, Bunce, Darcy and Snelgrave in their room. Darcy reads, but more often just stares. Snelgrave sits with an unopened book. Morse sits and stares. Bunce sits in the corner on a dirty mat, making himself small. A sense of boredom, tedium, inside a house where no one can leave.

SNELGRAVE: Did you vinegar the corner, under your mat, as well, Bunce?
BUNCE: Yes I did, sir.
SNELGRAVE: Right.

> *(Long silence.)*

The chairs as well?
BUNCE: Yes, sir.
SNELGRAVE: Right.
MORSE *(Sings)*:
> Over and across the tall, tall grass
> They lay my love in the dirt
> He was just a kid and myself a lass
> If it'd bring him back, I'd reconvert.

> *(Snelgrave whacks his cane.)*

SNELGRAVE: Not in this house.
DARCY: Oh, let her sing.
MORSE *(Continues)*:
> O fire of the devil, fire of love
> The truth is a lie and the pig's a dove.
SNELGRAVE: She doesn't sing like a Christian child.
MORSE *(Continues)*:
> The desert is cold and Hell is hot
> The mouth that kisses is sweet with rot.
DARCY: I don't think I've heard song in this house since—
MORSE: Can't you sing?
DARCY: I don't like to. But I like to hear it. Sometimes.
MORSE: Are you not hot in all that dress?

DARCY: No, child. I never wear anything but this sort of dress.

MORSE: Can I see your neck?

DARCY: What? Why, child?

MORSE: Because I think you must have a beautiful neck and it's the time of the plague and there's not much of beauty left in this city but you.

DARCY: Who taught you to lie so kindly?

MORSE: Learned it myself. Can I see?

DARCY: I will get you a looking glass and you can look at your own neck, which is lovely. Mine is not. I am old.

MORSE: Please.

SNELGRAVE: Leave my wife in peace.

MORSE: Let me see.

SNELGRAVE: Sit back down.

MORSE: I think you have the scar of the hangman about your neck.

SNELGRAVE: I said leave her be.

DARCY: She means no harm.

MORSE: Or perhaps the finger marks of someone who hates you.

DARCY *(Laughing)*: Perhaps the hole of a sword that went in here and came out there!

SNELGRAVE: Must you encourage such putrid imaginings? Enough. My head hurts from it.

(Snelgrave exits the room.)

DARCY: Stand here, child.

(Morse nears her.)

Closer. Let me feel your breath on my cheek.

(Morse moves closer.)

The breath of a child has passed through the lungs of an angel. That's what they say.

MORSE: My mother said to me that once a tiny piece of star broke off and fell from the sky while she slept in a field of wheat and it pierced her, here *(Motions to Darcy's heart but doesn't touch her)* and from that piece of star I was born.

DARCY: And your father. What did he say? That he molded you from a sliver of moon?

MORSE: My father is dead.

DARCY: I know. But what did he say about his little girl?

MORSE: My father was born dead. He stayed that way most of his life.

DARCY: I met your father, at the opera, once. He seemed a decent man.

MORSE: My father hit the maids. I saw him do it. Sometimes twice a day.

DARCY: Well, then, he kept order. A household must have order.

MORSE: He used a piece of leg from a chair. He kept it in the drawer of his writing desk.

DARCY: Sometimes servants misbehave. That's not your father's fault.

MORSE: Do you hit your servants?

DARCY: My servants are dead.

MORSE: Did you hit them?

DARCY: No, I didn't. But when they did not listen, I told my husband and he dealt with them as was necessary.

MORSE: Can I see your neck now?

DARCY: No, you cannot.

MORSE: Can I see your hands?

DARCY: My hands are private.

MORSE: I'm not afraid to die.

DARCY: You don't have to be; you won't die.

MORSE: I already know what it's like. To be dead. It's nothing fancy.

(Morse moves away from Darcy. She takes the hem of her dress in her hands.)

Just lots of nothing to see all around you and nothing to feel, only there's a sound that comes and goes. Comes and goes. Like this:

(She slowly tears a rip in her dress, up to her waist.)

Have you heard that sound before, Mrs. Snelgrave?

(Darcy does not answer. Morse speaks now to Bunce.)

And you, sitting there on your lily pad like a frog? Have you heard it?

BUNCE: In Northumberland. Yeah. A coal miner I was, when I was a kid. We heard all sorts of things down in the earth. And when our lanterns went out, our minds went to Hell.

MORSE: Did lots of you die down there?

DARCY: Morse.

BUNCE: Lost my baby brother in the mines. Well, he wasn't a baby, but he always was to us. Just thirteen, he was. We went deep for the coal. They kept pushing us. Pushing us deeper. The ceilings were half down most of the time. One fell in on top of us, six of us it were.

MORSE: Your brother was crushed?

BUNCE: Yes, he was. And the master, he kicked me 'cause I was cursing the mine. I jumped him and his men pulled me off. He kicked me again and I bit his ear in two. One of his guards popped a knife in my side. Never healed up right.

MORSE: What did he look like crushed up? Your brother.

DARCY: Stop it, Morse.

BUNCE: He looked like. Well. His face was the only part of him. Not crushed. His face looked. I don't know. What? Disappointed. I think.

DARCY: That's enough.

MORSE *(To Bunce)*: And his body?

BUNCE: His body. It was like. What? Like water. What was left of him. I couldn't take him up in my arms. He just. Spilled away.

(Morse nears Bunce, kneels down and simply looks at him. After some moments, Bunce looks away from her and at Darcy.)

SCENE FIVE

Outside of the Snelgraves' house. Just below the window. Kabe is guarding the house.

KABE *(Calls)*: Bills. The Bills. Stepney Parish, seven hundred and sixteen. White-Chapel, three hundred forty-six. The Bills. St. Giles's Cripplegate, two hundred seventy-seven. St. Leonard Shoreditch—

MORSE *(Pops her head out of the window above him)*: I got an uncle in St. Sepulchers. How's it there?

KABE: Two hundred and fourteen dead this week. How's the Snelgraves?

MORSE: We're all right.

KABE: You a relative?

MORSE: Mrs. Snelgrave says you're a thief.

KABE: Does she now? And how old are you, sweetheart?

MORSE: Twelve. Mr. Snelgrave says you're the worst sort of rabble.

KABE: We're always rabble, we are, when we come out from our alleys and lanes and rub shoulders with Snelgraves, hawk an innocent gob o' phlegm on their doorstep. They're not much company, how 'bout you?

MORSE: Mr. Snelgrave says you're not much above vermin.

KABE: Does he now? And have you ever seen a little mousie?

MORSE: I seen rats.

KABE: Ever had a sweetheart?

(Morse shakes her head no.)

Doctors say virgins ripe for marriage are ripe for the infection, their blood being hot and their seed pining for copulation.

MORSE: Mr. Snelgrave says you want us to die. Then you can come in and loot.

KABE: I could show you a jewel that'd change your life.

MORSE: Go ahead then.

KABE: Don't know if you're grown enough.

MORSE: I'm old on the inside. Show me.

KABE: Hold onto that window.

(Kabe stands directly under her and opens his pants. Morse looks. And looks.)

Well!

MORSE: You're a man, then?

KABE: Of course I'm a man. A bull of a man. A whale of a man.

MORSE: Sometimes people pretend.

KABE *(Closing his pants)*: What you just saw wasn't pretending.

MORSE: Don't like all the strawy hairs on it.

KABE: Have you no manners, you prince's whore? You should be beaten. Have you ever been beaten?

MORSE *(Laughing at him)*: Lots of times. Can you get me a Certificate of Health from the Lord Mayor so I can pass out of the city?

KABE *(Shrieks with laughter)*: You're a card, aren't you!

MORSE: I'm dead serious.

KABE: He's no longer in town.

MORSE: Yes he is. Lord Mayor of London. He's the only one who stayed.

KABE: Not counting the poor, child. The poor's all stayed. And what I hear tell, that's not the mayor in the mayor's house but a madman who broke in and jumps naked through the garden, cawing like a crow at night. The rest of the court's gone too. All that's got wealth has fled from the plague. And God's followed them.

MORSE: The Snelgraves haven't fled.

KABE: That's not for trying. They just got unlucky; their servants died before they could leave 'em behind to starve.

MORSE: Get me a Certificate so I can pass the blockades.

KABE: I got ahold of a few of those papers at the very start, but now. Well. They're as rare as . . . And what would you give me in return?

MORSE: Don't have much.

KABE: Let me have a feel of your leg. Go on.

MORSE: Why?

KABE: I've got an idea. Or two.

MORSE *(Hangs a leg out the window)*: There's my leg.

KABE *(Feeling her leg)*: A bit bony. I can't get you a Certificate even if I wanted, but—

(Morse starts to pull her leg back in, but he hangs on.)

Wait! I can get you some sugar knots. I know an old man who's got a bucketful.

MORSE: Got no money.

KABE: I'll make you a deal. You let me, ah, kiss your foot and for every kiss I'll get you a sugar knot.

MORSE: Deal.

(Kabe kisses her foot, twice. Then sucks on her big toe. Morse kicks him.)

You said kiss, not suck.

KABE: What's the difference?

MORSE: An apple. A suck is worth an apple.

KABE: Thief.

(He sucks on her toe. Then she pulls her leg up.)

That was a nibble, not a suck!

MORSE: Two sugar knots and an apple. And the worms in the apple better be alive!

KABE: You'll die by the plague, child. I feel it in me shins.

MORSE: Then I'll be good at being dead. My father and mother are already dead. Poor Daddy. Poor Mommy. Dead, dead, dead.

KABE: Stupid brat. What you lack is fear. This past week, I got the bodies piled so high in my cart I could hardly see over the tops of them. *(Beat)* Hey. I know an old woman who's got tangerines, still good, that she wears under her skirts. She says they stay fresh down there because she's hot as the tropics.

MORSE: Get me a tangerine too.

KABE: Bring me a jewel of Mrs. Snelgrave's. Anything. Just make sure the gem's hard.

MORSE: I'm not a Braithwaite anymore, you know.

KABE: And I am not a guard at your door. But if you crawl out of that window, I will kill you and sleep well this night.

MORSE: Perhaps I'll kill you first.

KABE *(Calling)*: The ninety-seven parishes within the walls: one thousand four hundred and ninety-three. Parishes on the Southwark Side: one thousand six hundred and thirty-six. *(Sings)*

We'll all meet in the grave
Then we'll all be saved.
You with your coins
Me with me scabs.
You with clean loins
Me with me crabs.

We'll all meet in the grave
Then we'll all get laid down
Oh, down, deep down.

SCENE SIX

Bunce washes the floor with vinegar. He uses a small rag and a bucket. Snelgrave watches him.

SNELGRAVE: I heard the crier this morning. The Bills have almost doubled this week. Mostly the Out-

Parishes of the poor. But it's moving this way. A couple of persons I know personally have died. Decent people. Good Christians on the surface. But there's the key. On the surface. When the poor die, the beggars, it's no riddle. Look down at their faces and you'll see their bitter hearts. When the rich die, it's harder to tell why God took them; they're clean, attend the Masses, give alms. But something rotten lurks. Mark my words, Bunce. A fine set of clothes does not always attest to a fine set of morals.

(Bunce, wiping the floors, nears Snelgrave's shoes.)

Are you afraid, Bunce?

BUNCE: Sir?

SNELGRAVE: Are you afraid of the plague?

BUNCE: Who isn't, sir?

SNELGRAVE: It is written in the Ninety-First Psalm of the Book: "Thou shalt not be afraid for the pestilence that walketh in darkness . . . A thousand shall fall at thy side, and ten thousand at thy right hand: but it shall not come nigh thee." That doesn't mean I don't ever doubt, Bunce. I use vinegar.

BUNCE: Those are fine shoes, sir. The finest I ever saw this close up.

SNELGRAVE: Cost me as much as a silk suit. A bit tight on my corns, but real gentlemen's leather. I would wager your life, Bunce, that you'll never wear such fine shoes as these.

BUNCE: I'd wager two of my lives, if I had them.

SNELGRAVE: A little learning, Bunce: patterns will have it that you, a poor sailor, will never wear such shoes as these. And yet, the movement of history, which is as inflexible as stone, can suddenly change. With a flick of a wrist. Or, I might say, an ankle. Watch while I demonstrate. *(Slips out of his shoes)* Put them on, Bunce.

BUNCE: Sir?

SNELGRAVE: Put my shoes on your feet.

BUNCE: My feet are dirty, sir.

SNELGRAVE: Then have my socks on first.

(Bunce holds up the fine socks and examines them.)

Go on, then.

(Bunce carefully slips on the socks, then the shoes. The two men stand side by side looking back and forth at their feet. Snelgrave wiggles his bare toes.)

Now, Bunce. What do you see?

BUNCE: I see the master is without shoes. And his new servant. He is wearing very fine shoes.

SNELGRAVE: And history? What does history tell you now?

BUNCE: Not sure how that works, sir.

SNELGRAVE: Historically speaking, the poor do not take to fine shoes. They never have and they never will.

BUNCE: I'm wearing fine shoes now.

SNELGRAVE: Yes, but only because I allow it. I have given history a wee slap on the buttocks and for a moment something terribly strange has happened: you in my shoes. However, what we see here is not real. It's an illusion because I can't change the fact that you'll never wear fine shoes.

BUNCE: But I'm wearing them now, sir.

SNELGRAVE: Only because I gave them to you. In a moment I am going to take them back, and then history will be on course again. As a matter of fact, it never strayed from course, because what we're doing here is just a little game.

BUNCE: What if I kept the shoes?

SNELGRAVE: Kept them? You can't keep them. They're mine.

BUNCE: I know they're yours, sir. I'm just asking what if I kept them?

SNELGRAVE: That's not a historical question.

BUNCE: No. It's a game question. You said this was a game, sir.

SNELGRAVE: So I did. Well, if you kept them I would go and get another pair before my feet got cold.

BUNCE: Then we'd both have a pair.

SNELGRAVE: You're not attacking the problem correctly. If we both have a pair, how will people tell our feet apart? They'll look the same. That's not history, Bunce, that's obfuscatory.

BUNCE: May I have your cane?

SNELGRAVE: You most certainly may not.

BUNCE: I just want to hold it, sir. It's finely carved. I'll never hold a cane like that in my life.

SNELGRAVE (*Reluctantly hands it to him*): I'm not a cruel man.

(*Bunce takes the cane, tucks it awkwardly under his arm.*)

Not like that. It's not a piece of firewood you're lugging for the stove.

(*Snelgrave snatches it back. He delicately tucks it under his arm and walks this way and that.*)

BUNCE: It doesn't look right on you without the shoes, sir.

(*Bunce holds out his hand and after a moment's hesitation, Snelgrave hands the cane to him. Bunce carries the cane almost properly this time.*)

SNELGRAVE: That's it. Elbow a bit higher. I always think of it as walking across the hands of children. You must do it lightly and carefully or you'll break their bones.

BUNCE: Is this it, sir? History?

SNELGRAVE: Certainly not. This is just practice.

BUNCE: Practice for what?

SNELGRAVE: Brrrrr. My feet are cold. The shoes, please.

(*Bunce walks once more to and fro, then stops face to face with Snelgrave, close. Silence for some moments. Bunce hands Snelgrave the cane and removes the shoes, slowly, then the socks. He sets the shoes carefully and neatly*) *between them, laying out the socks one by one. The two men look at the shoes between them. They watch each other some moments, then Bunce returns to his bucket and rag. He cleans. Snelgrave picks up his shoes and socks.)*

The Bills are up. Way up this week. We'll need to vinegar this room twice a day from now on. Starting tomorrow. One can't be too cautious. I'll send my wife in with some bread for you when you're done.

BUNCE: Yes, sir.

(Snelgrave begins to exit.)

Sir?

(Snelgrave turns to hear him.)

I'm not a cruel man, either, sir.

SNELGRAVE: I know that, Bunce. I wouldn't have taken you on as my servant if I had thought otherwise.

(Snelgrave exits. We hear the lock turn.)

SCENE SEVEN

Bunce adjusts his wrappings under his shirt. The door is no longer locked, and Darcy enters. She watches him for some moments. He's unaware and curses the wrappings that are beginning to fall to pieces in his hands. We hear Kabe singing offstage.

KABE *(Sings)*:
    Calico, silk, porcelain, tea
    It's all the same to the poor man and me.
BUNCE: Ah, fuck the Lord.
KABE *(Continues)*:
    Steal it in the Indies, haul it cross the sea
    And now it's nothing between the plague, you and me.
BUNCE: Ow! Fuck his Angels too.
DARCY: I brought you some clean linen.

BUNCE *(Backing into his corner)*: Beg your pardon, missus. I thought you three were asleep.

DARCY: They are. Does it hurt all the time?

BUNCE: Only when I sit a lot. On the sea I'm standing most of the time and I feel best.

DARCY: Here's a clean shirt. It belonged to our servant boy. I've soaked it in vinegar and cloves. It's safe.

BUNCE *(He takes the shirt)*: Thank you, missus.

DARCY: I brought some clean strips too. So you can rebind it.

BUNCE *(He takes them)*: You're kind.

DARCY: I don't want blood on my floors.

(They each wait for something from the other.)

BUNCE: Perhaps you should go back to the kitchen, missus.

DARCY: I will stay.

BUNCE: It's not pretty.

(Darcy doesn't leave. Bunce shrugs and painfully takes off his shirt. His old bandage is still in place. He begins to wrap the new one over it.)

DARCY: Take the old one off or it will do no good to put a clean one on.

BUNCE: It does no good anyhow but make it look better.

DARCY: I will do it.

BUNCE: No.

DARCY *(Taking the new bandage from him)*: Yes, I will.

BUNCE *(Angry, holding the old bandage in place)*: I said no, missus.

DARCY: All right then. Do it yourself.

(She tosses the bandage at his feet so that he must stoop to pick it up. He does so.)

BUNCE *(Wanting her to turn away)*: Please.

(She does so, annoyed. Turning his wound away from her, he rebinds it. We do not see the wound.)

DARCY: So you're a sailor. Merchant or Navy?

BUNCE: Merchant by choice. Navy by force.

DARCY: Then it's the sailor's life for you: drinking, thieving, whoring, killing, backbiting. And swearing.

BUNCE *(Playing into the cliché)*: Yeah. Swearing. And once or twice we took hold of our own fucked ship from some goddamned captain. We let our men vote if the bloody prick lived or died. Mostly our men voted he died, so first we whipped and pickled him, then threw the fat gutted chucklehead overboard. And because we couldn't piss on his grave we pissed on the bastard's back as he sank to the sharks below.

DARCY: A tongue that swears does not easily pray.

BUNCE: The times I was asked by my captain or his mate to beat a fellow tar? I can't count them. The times I refused? Maybe less than one.

(Some moments of silence.)

DARCY: I've never sailed on a ship. I married when I was fifteen. *(Beat)* Why did you come to our house?

BUNCE: The ships aren't sailing but the Navy's. I didn't want to get picked up again.

DARCY: Some would consider it an honor to serve the Navy.

BUNCE: Ay. Some would. Though I never met them.

DARCY: Do you have a wife?

BUNCE: I did for a little while, but I lost her. Was coming into port at Liverpool, merchant ship. Making short trips. Got picked up for the second time to serve His Majesty's ships. Didn't get back to port for eight months, and then my wife was gone. If she still lives, I don't know. The neighbors said she raved for months and went mad. Tick fever. But I don't believe it. She was a smart one. I think she just got tired of waiting and moved on.

DARCY: Did your wife have soft. Skin?

BUNCE: Soft skin? Well, no. It wasn't what you'd call soft. Her father was a ribband weaver and she worked by his side. Her hands were harder than mine.

DARCY: I'm sorry.

BUNCE: She used them well.

DARCY: Have you never touched a woman's skin that was soft?

BUNCE: Not a woman's, no. But I met a lad in the port of Bristol once, and he had skin so fine it was like running your fingers through water.

DARCY: You speak against God.

BUNCE: I'm speaking of God's pleasure.

DARCY (*Picking up the scraps of bandage that Bunce has discarded*): And his. Breast. Was it smooth as well?

BUNCE: His breast. It was. Darker. Like the skin of an apple it smelled, and as smooth.

DARCY: Did you love him?

BUNCE: For those few months I loved him better than I could love another in years. His name was Killigrew. We got picked up off the streets and pressed onto the same ship. Warred against the Hollanders. He died.

DARCY: I'm sorry.

BUNCE: The bastard. Always had the luck.

DARCY (*Taking off her earrings*): When this is over and we're allowed to leave here, you'll have these. You'll be able to eat a while and pay for shelter. They're real stones.

BUNCE (*Accepting the earrings; examining them*): Why am I to be paid like this?

DARCY: It's not payment. It's charity.

BUNCE: I'm poor, missus, but not stupid. If your husband catches me with these I might as well jump into the pits.

DARCY: He won't find them if you keep them well hid.

BUNCE: Hid where? You keep 'em. When we're all out and by our own legs, if you still feel moved to charity, you can give them to me once more.

(He hands them back. She puts them on again.)

DARCY: And this man you loved. Killigrew. Were his . . .
BUNCE: What.

(Darcy touches her own thighs. Not in a seductive manner, but as though she can't bring herself to say the word out loud.)

DARCY: Here. Was he smooth here?
BUNCE: What do you want, missus?
DARCY: For you to answer me.
BUNCE: And if I don't?
DARCY: We no longer lock you up. We trust you now.
BUNCE: All right. *(He nears her, close)* Close your eyes. I'll do you no harm.

(Darcy closes her eyes. Bunce softly blows air across her face. When he stops, she does not open her eyes.)

That's how it felt to touch him there.

(Some moments of silence.)

DARCY: I don't intend to die of the plague, Bunce. My husband has agreed to help me end my life if the tokens appear.
BUNCE: Not all that gets the plague dies.
DARCY: First the marks appear around the neck or groin. There's fever. Violent vomiting. The patient cannot control the body. The body fouls itself.
BUNCE: But if the swelling can be brought to break and run, sometimes a person can live. I saved a friend that way once. Cut the marks with a knife and bled them. He never could speak again, but he lived.
DARCY: No, no. The stench of the sores is unbearable. The body rots. And then the mind. Lunacy and madness is the end. I saw two of our servants die that way. Their screams are locked inside my head forever.
BUNCE: Would you like to know of any other parts of my lad Killigrew, missus?

DARCY: No. Thank you. I've heard enough. Just bless the Lord He's brought you into this house. Against our will, certainly, but I assume not against His. *(Beat)* I could have you hanged for speaking of such matters to a married woman of my position.

BUNCE *(Sings)*:
Lust in his limbs and rust in his skin
A bear without, and a worse beast within.

DARCY: I'm just an old woman. That's what you think. Well. Smile as you like. I once had a lover, and his arms were so strong that my skull was crushed in his grip. With his bare hands he plunged between my ribs and took hold of my heart. A wafer between his fingers, it dissolved. Sometimes I wake up in the dark and stand in the hall and I can feel the cold draft pass freely through my chest as though there were nothing there.

BUNCE: I'll have those earrings after all.

(Darcy is motionless, as though not hearing him. He gently slips the earrings from her ears.)

I'll find a place. I'm a pirate.

SCENE EIGHT

Darcy, Morse and Snelgrave in the room. Morse's wrists are bound with rope.

SNELGRAVE: The child's a thief, I tell you. What did I find in her pockets one morning last week? A set of my Spanish gold coins. "Just playing jacks with them," she says. She's got the manners of a servant and the tongue of a who—

DARCY: Don't you dare.

SNELGRAVE: That brooch belonged to my mother. Not you. The child will confess when I give her some of this.

(Snelgrave brandishes his cane.)

DARCY: I'll find the brooch. It's bound to have fallen when I was turning things out.

SNELGRAVE: The child will wear those ropes until we find it.

MORSE: I didn't steal your brooch.

SNELGRAVE: Hold your tongue.

MORSE: You belong in a cold, cold grave.

(Snelgrave raises his cane to hit Morse. She runs to hide behind Darcy.)

Help me, Mrs. Snelgrave.

DARCY: You did steal his coins.

(Snelgrave whacks and misses.)

MORSE: Yes, I did. But you gave Bunce some of his gin.

SNELGRAVE: She did what?

MORSE: I saw it with my own eyes, sir. Mrs. Snelgrave thought I was asleep. You were, but I wasn't, and she poured some of your gin into a bowl and she took it to him. She watched him drink it.

SNELGRAVE: Is this true?

MORSE *(Makes the sound)*: Slurp, slurp.

DARCY: He asked me the other day if we might spare some spirits. I said no. Later, I changed my mind.

SNELGRAVE: In the middle of the night?

DARCY: I didn't want to wake you.

SNELGRAVE *(To Morse)*: And what else did you see, Morse Braithwaite?

(Morse raises her roped hands to him. After a moment he understands the deal and takes off the ropes.)

MORSE: She asked him if the new bandage fit right. He said it felt a bit tight. He asked her to feel it.

SNELGRAVE: He asked her to feel what?

DARCY: This is ridiculous.

SNELGRAVE: You. Felt his bandage?

DARCY: I merely checked his bandage to make sure it wasn't pressing the wound.

SNELGRAVE: You did this. How?

MORSE: I can show you.

SNELGRAVE *(To Darcy)*: How did you check his bandage?

(Darcy doesn't answer, just shakes her head. Snelgrave calls Bunce.)

Bunce. Bunce!

(Bunce enters with the rag and pail.)

BUNCE: I haven't finished the kitchen walls yet, sir.

SNELGRAVE: Put down the vinegar. I want you to stand there. Right here. Yes. Nothing else. Just stand.

(Bunce stands with his back to the audience.)

Now, Mrs. Snelgrave. As my wife. As a Christian woman, show me how you checked that his bandage wasn't too tight. So that it wouldn't press the wound. *(Beat)* Do it, woman, or so help me what I do to him will not be worse than what I do to you.

(Darcy slowly nears Bunce.)

Just a minute, my dear. Surely, in the dark, his belly full of my gin, it would be difficult to feel the tension of his. Bandage. With your glove on. You must have taken off one of your gloves, didn't you? *(Whispers, with menace)* Didn't you?

MORSE: Yes, she did. Because her glove dropped on the floor as he was slurping the gin. Slurp, slu—

SNELGRAVE *(To Morse)*: You shut your mouth. *(To Darcy)* Take off your glove. Let our good servant Bunce see what's touched him in the dark.

DARCY: William.

SNELGRAVE: Darcy?

(Darcy stands before Bunce and removes her glove. We cannot see her bare hand because Bunce blocks our view.)

Have a look, Bunce.

(Bunce does not look down at Darcy's hand, he looks at Snelgrave.)

BUNCE: If Mrs. Snelgrave wishes to keep her hands private, sir, it's—

SNELGRAVE *(To Darcy)*: Tell him you want him to look. Because you do, don't you? That's the nature of secrets. They yearn to be exposed.

DARCY: You may. Look.

BUNCE: If it pleases you, missus.

DARCY: It does.

(Bunce looks down at her hand. He does not react. Then he looks at Snelgrave, who deflates. Morse slowly comes around Bunce to have a look. She's amazed rather than disgusted. She backs away and turns to Snelgrave.)

MORSE: You did this to her!

SNELGRAVE: It was an accident.

MORSE: You did this.

(Darcy puts her glove back on.)

SNELGRAVE *(Calm now)*: No, child. It was the fire did it to her. When she was seventeen. Just two years after we married. We lived outside the city then. There was a fire in the stables. She insisted on saving her horse. It was a wedding gift.

MORSE *(To Darcy)*: Did you save the horse?

DARCY: No.

SNELGRAVE: She burned. My beautiful wife, who only the night before I'd held in my arms. Naked, she was—

DARCY: Quiet, William.

SNELGRAVE: I used to kneel at your feet, by the bedside at night.

(Bunce steps back and stands beside Morse. They watch the Snelgraves.)

And you'd let your robe fall open. Your skin was like. Like. There wasn't a name for it on this earth.

(Darcy puts her gloved hand on his head, she comforts him almost automatically. He closes his eyes.)

For hours on end in the night. My God, how I loved you.

DARCY *(Moves away from Snelgrave; speaks with calm reserve)*: Some of the animals freed themselves. The dappled mare my father gave me broke out of her stall. Her mane was on fire. She kept leaping and rearing to shake it off but she couldn't shake it off. The mare ran in circles around the garden. Faster and faster she ran, the fire eating its way to her coat. Her coat was wet, running with sweat, but that didn't stop the fire from spreading out across her flanks. A horse on fire. In full gallop. It was almost. Beautiful. It would have been. Beautiful. But for the smell. I can still smell them. After thirty-six years. The horses. Burning.

(Morse puts her hand in Bunce's hand, and the two of them stand watching the Snelgraves. This action should be a subtle, almost unconscious gesture, on both their parts.)

SCENE NINE

Kabe outside on the street below the Snelgraves' window. He is half-naked and wears a pan of burning charcoal on his head. He is preaching.

KABE: A monster, last week, was born at Oxford in the house of an Earl. His name on fear of death I do withhold. One eye in its forehead, no nose, and its two ears in the nape of its neck. And outside in the garden of that very same house, a thorn which bore five different fruits. And, good people of this city, if we must read these phenomena as signs—

SNELGRAVE *(At the window)*: Kabe.

KABE: And we must. Listen not to the liars and hypocrites—

SNELGRAVE: Did you get the quicksilver?

KABE: —for they will tell you that it is the wrath of God against an entire people, corrupt in both spirit and in heart.

(Kabe stops preaching, steps back and speaks to Snelgrave.)

Got it. Babel, Babylon, Sodom and Gomorrah, cow shit I tell you.

SNELGRAVE: And the walnut shell?

KABE: Had a little trouble with the walnut shell. Hazelnut is all I could come by.

SNELGRAVE: A hazelnut shell? Have you gone mad? Dr. Brooks's pamphlet specifically states that the quicksilver must be hung about the neck in a walnut shell.

KABE: With the hazelnut, only five shillings.

SNELGRAVE: You said four yesterday.

KABE: That was before the Bills went up again. *(Turns back to preach)* And I say to you if it is God's wrath, then why has He chosen Oxford for the birth of this monster?

SNELGRAVE: What about the oil and frankincense?

KABE: Because Oxford is where the court has retired, the king and all his fancy, fawning courtiers. Because the plague— *(To Snelgrave)* Couldn't get any— *(Preaching)* is a Royalist phenomenon. Who dies? One simple question. *(To Snelgrave)* But I do have a toad. *(Preaching)* Who dies? *(To Snelgrave)* Not dead two hours. *(Preaching)* Is this not a poor man's plague? *(To Snelgrave)* Bore a hole through its head and hang it about your neck.

SNELGRAVE: What if my wife spies it?

KABE: Keep it under your shirts. Should dry out in a day or two.

SNELGRAVE: Two shillings.

KABE: Right. *(Preaching)* Go to the deepest pit near Three Nuns' Inn, if you dare, and you will see who it is that dies, their mouths open in want, the maggots moving inside their tongues, making their tongues wag as though they were about to speak. But they will never speak again in this world. The hungry. The dirty. The abandoned. That's who dies. Not the fancy and the wealthy, there's hardly a one, for they have fled, turned their back on the city. Clergymen, physicians and surgeons, all fled.

SNELGRAVE: Have you thought again about my little offer?

KABE *(To Snelgrave)*: Sorry.

SNELGRAVE: I could make you rich.

KABE: As well as dead if I let you escape. *(Preaching)* And here we perish on the streets in such vast number as much from lack of bread and wages as from the plague—

SNELGRAVE: Where are your clothes? And what's that you got on your head?

KABE: Pan of charcoal. Keeps the bad air from my head when I unplug my finger from God's arsehole.

SNELGRAVE: Blasphemer! Put on your clothes. You're a Snelgrave Guard.

KABE: Not on Tuesdays I'm not. *(Nods to offstage)* On Tuesdays old Stewart fills in for me.

SNELGRAVE: Why, you're behaving like one of those madmen. Those conjurers. Those dealers with the Devil.

KABE: Solomon Eagle, at your service.

SNELGRAVE: This is outrageous. I won't have a conjurer guarding our door! It's bad enough that I'm kept captive by you, Kabe, but that you summon more scum from their hellholes to stand below my windows. My house. My street. My city!

KABE *(Preaches again)*: —Is on the verge of the eternal storm of chaos. Orphan's money is on loan by the Lord Mayor to the king, and Parliament takes no action. They stir their soup with our bones. The grass grows up and down White Hall court and no boats move on the river but to war. Dead as dung upon the face of the earth we all shall be if we do not resist. I say to you: get off your knees. Rise up! Rise up! *(Beat)* But how do we begin? With this. With this, my friends. *(Takes out a small vial of liquid)* The road to the poor man's Heaven: only six shillings! Solomon Eagle's plague water.

SNELGRAVE: Six shillings! That's robbery.

KABE *(Preaching still)*: Is your dignity not worth six shillings? It's your duty to keep your body strong for this long and bloody struggle! Do not let the monsters of Oxford beat you down. Arise, arise into all your glory! You, the mob! The dissolute rabble! Six shillings! Six shillings, and the world is yours!

SNELGRAVE: I'll give you five.

(Snelgrave drops the coins to Kabe, who catches them in a small jar of vinegar.)

Do I drink it?

KABE: One thimbleful each night before retiring. Also anoint the nostrils, ear holes and anus twice a day. *(Beat)* Sir Braithwaite's girl. She died with her parents.

SNELGRAVE: How do you know?

KABE: Spoke to one of the maids that used to work there. Her husband did their garden. He found the family dead. They say there was something stuffed in the dead child's mouth. Some kind of animal.

SNELGRAVE: She can't be dead! She's alive and well and a pest in my house.

KABE: The maid used to bathe the Braithwaite girl. Maid said the girl had a scar the shape of a key 'cross her belly. Happened when she was a baby. Some kind of accident. *(Beat)* I've been thinking, sir. If one of you dies in there, can we pull the body out the window? We doubled up the boards on your door and it will be a hell of a work to open it up again.

SNELGRAVE: The dying is done in this house, I thank the Lord. And when the dying is done in this city, Kabe, you better run, because I smell a Leveller's blood in you, ringing loud and clear. I thought we buried the lot of you.

KABE: My father was a Leveller, sir. His son's just a poor man with a pan of charcoal on his head. And now the old man's dead.

SNELGRAVE: Plague?

KABE: One of my toads, sir. Had a dozen of them in a bucket at the bedside. One of them got out and, well, my father, he snored and down one went and got stuck and the old man choked to death.

SNELGRAVE: A proper death for a man of his station. Levellers. Diggers. I say cut them to pieces or they will cut us to pieces.

KABE: Do you want the toad as it is, or do you want me to bore the hole?

SNELGRAVE: You do it. And get me a piece of string to hang it on as well.

KABE: Wife's piss also works wonders.

SNELGRAVE (*Realizing he's being taken in*): Vermin.

KABE: Use your wife's urine to purify, before that sailor does.

SNELGRAVE: You'll be dead soon . . .

KABE: But will she let you have it?

SNELGRAVE: And I'll find you in your lime pit and piss in your mouth.

SCENE TEN

Snelgrave, Darcy, Morse and Bunce in the room. Boredom. Morse sits and ties figures out of cloth and sticks. Then she glances about the room. Her eyes rest on Darcy. She stands and goes to her.

MORSE: I can smell your heart.

DARCY: Can you?

MORSE: It's sweet. It's rotting in your chest.

(*Snelgrave snorts.*)

My mother didn't smell like you. She smelled like lemons.

DARCY: That's lovely.

MORSE: Because she was always afraid.

(Snelgrave snorts again.)

Last night I dreamed that an angel tried to land on our roof. But he had no feet so he couldn't stand. He crawled in through the window, to touch our faces, but he had no hands. He said to me, "Come to my arms." But he had none. This morning I woke up and there was a feather in my mouth. Look.

(Morse shows Darcy a small, white feather. She runs the feather gently over Darcy's face.)

SNELGRAVE: Must we listen to this senseless babble day in and day out. I'm sick of it. Bloody sick of it.

DARCY: Then pass your time in the kitchen.

SNELGRAVE: Kabe says Sir Braithwaite's daughter died in her own house. Says they found her naked. Naked and dead. Stripped.

DARCY: Kabe is a liar.

MORSE: He showed me his mouse.

SNELGRAVE: He says the daughter had a scar. Under her skirts.

DARCY: A scar?

SNELGRAVE: On her stomach.

MORSE *(To Darcy)*: Is the rest of your body burned?

DARCY: Yes

MORSE: What does it feel like?

SNELGRAVE: I think we should have a look.

DARCY: Feel like? Most of the places on my skin I can't feel.

(Morse runs her hand lightly down Darcy's arm, slowly.)

MORSE: Can you feel that?

DARCY: No. Yes. There. At the elbow.

(Morse caresses Darcy's neck through the cloth.)

SNELGRAVE: She's strong, but Bunce could manage.
DARCY: Yes. There. *(Beat)* Not there. No. Maybe. No.
SNELGRAVE: Bunce could do it.

(Morse runs her hands slowly over Darcy's breasts. Darcy does not stop her. This action is no different from how Morse touched Darcy's arms. Snelgrave stands over them.)

MORSE: Can you feel this?
SNELGRAVE: A scar the shape of a key.
DARCY *(Sincerely trying to answer Morse's questions)*: Not yet. Yes. There. Under your left hand. I can feel something there.
MORSE: What do you feel?
SNELGRAVE: We could all be in danger.
DARCY: I feel . . . I don't know. No one has touched me there. In years.
SNELGRAVE *(Grabbing Morse's arm)*: It's about time we found out just who you are, young lady. Bunce!
DARCY: Let go of her.
SNELGRAVE *(Shoving Morse into Bunce's arms)*: You're the strongest, Bunce. Strip her.
BUNCE: I don't think I should be the one, sir.
SNELGRAVE: You do as I tell you.
BUNCE: Will you show him your belly, Morse?

(Morse shakes her head no but does not physically resist. She is calm.)

(To Morse) I'm sorry, then.

(Bunce begins to unbutton Morse's shirt buttons.)

DARCY: Bunce. Don't you dare.

(Bunce looks from Snelgrave to Darcy.)

SNELGRAVE: You cross me?

DARCY: I sponged the child. Twice. She has the scar. But your idiot Kabe is mistaken. It's not a key. The scar is like a spoon.

> *(To Snelgrave)* After the fire. Not once. Not even to embrace me. I was. Even changed. I was still—

SNELGRAVE *(Interrupts)*: How could I have loved you? It was never about who you were but about what was left of you.

(Morse raises her skirts to reveal her stomach, which has no scar.)

MORSE: The angel took my scar.

(Snelgrave glares at his wife.)

In exchange for the feather.

BUNCE: I think I'll vinegar the kitchen walls again, sir.

(Snelgrave puts out his cane to stop Bunce.)

SNELGRAVE: Tell me something, Bunce. If you had a wife and she lied to you. Lied to you, in front of company. What would you do?

(Bunce is silent.)

You'll learn, Bunce.

(Snelgrave shoves Bunce toward Darcy, and accidentally touches Bunce's wound. Bunce winces. Snelgrave looks at his hand in disgust and then wipes it off.)

Get that thing to stop oozing! There she is. The liar. And perhaps a whore. Though she'd have to do all her whoring in the dark because. Well. As a young woman she was rather large up top. How would you sailors say it?

BUNCE: Well-rigged, sir.

SNELGRAVE: Yes. As a young woman she was well-rigged. Let's just say that half her sails have been burned away and leave it at that. *(Beat)* As you stand there,

Bunce, looking at your wife, you realize that she's not only a liar but unsound under all that linen. *(Beat)* Strike her. *(Beat)* I said strike her.

BUNCE *(To Darcy, as he prepares to hit her)*: I'm sorry, missus. *(He raises his arm to strike her)*

MORSE *(Sinking to her knees, quietly)*: Mother? *(Beat)* Hush, hush. Do not cry.

(The others look at her. Morse has wet herself. She is ill. The piss slowly makes a line across the floor between them.)

I am filled. With angels.

SCENE ELEVEN

Morse still sitting on the floor, alone, in dim light. In the cell or place of confinement, as in Scene One.

MORSE *(Whispers)*: I can't. I can't remember.

(Sound of a slap. This time Morse flinches at the slaps.)

She smelled. Of lemons.

(Another slap, harder.)

Maybe she was my age. No. She was. Lissa was. A year younger. She had brown hair as long as a horse's tail and like cakes her dresses were. Rimmed with yellows and blues. Lissa had a fat stick that she kept in her trunk of toys and she would sneak up behind me as I swept the floors and hit me across the back. When I cried, she'd let me hold the bird that her grandfather brought home with him from India. It was a green and black bird and it could sing a melody. When I held it I could feel its tiny heart beating inside its chest.

(Darcy enters and stands in the shadows of the cell.)

Sometimes when Lissa's father scolded her she would come running to me and fling herself into my arms and weep. Her tears soaked my dirty frock.

(After some moments she gets to her feet and feels her dress. It is wet.)

Ugh. I've wet myself. *(She takes the dress off and casts it in the corner. She is wearing long underwear, perhaps a boy's, underneath)* And then I got sick and Mr. Snelgrave shouted, "Plague! Plague!" but I had no tokens.

(Darcy takes up the dress and holds it, then exits with it.)

My teeth swelled. I vomited. I had the spotted fever. For three days, Mrs. Snelgrave held me in her arms. *(Beat)* That week Kabe said the pits were near overflowing. But Kabe said it wasn't only the dead that went to the pits. Some of the living went to the pits to die of grief. More than once, he said, when he tried to pull the grievers out of the pits he heard a sound like a stick snapping in their chests.

Lissa's father, Mr. Braithwaite, died first. Then the mother. They died quickly. In each other's arms. From inside out they rotted. Lissa died more slowly. We were alone in the house. She said, "Hold me." Her body was covered in tokens. *(Beat)* But it wasn't Lissa's blood that was on my sleeve. *(Beat)* Who was alive and who was dead? In the pits their faces looked the same. Dried out by grief. And their hearts snapping in two inside their chests. Such a sound, Kabe said. Such a small, small sound, like this: *(She makes a small sound)*

(Blackout.)

ACT II

SCENE ONE

Snelgrave and Bunce in the room.

SNELGRAVE: And what was the longest period you sailed without port?

BUNCE: Two years. Though we docked, we couldn't leave the ship, so afraid was our captain that we'd not come back.

SNELGRAVE: You're still a young man.

BUNCE: I was never a young man, sir.

SNELGRAVE: Well, in the name of God, what did you do with your natural instincts while so long at sea?

BUNCE: Stayed alive. As best we could.

SNELGRAVE: I mean with your baser instincts. Those instincts against God.

BUNCE: Aboard the vessels I sailed, we never murdered our captain. Though once we threw one overboard after he beat the cook with a pitch mop.

SNELGRAVE: Bunce. You are in my house. I come in contact with the court and Parliament. I attend Cabinet meetings. At this very moment the Dutch are nuzzling at our shores.

(Snelgrave gives Bunce an orange. Bunce takes it but does not eat. He lets out a whistle—oranges are a delicacy even in good times.)

On these long voyages, without the comforts of a wife, what did you do to satisfy your unseemly satisfactions?

BUNCE: Between the Devil and the deep blue sea, there's little satisfaction, sir.

SNELGRAVE *(Whacks his cane)*: At night, Bunce. Packed in there man to man, godforsaken flesh to godforsaken flesh. You're halfway to Madras and it's sweltering hot and you wake with the hunger of a shark. But not for food. The Devil is foaming at your lips. What do you do, man? You're frothing with desire. What do you do?

BUNCE: I don't know as I ever frothed with desire, sir.

SNELGRAVE: The Lord, may He be forgiven, Bunce, gave you a foul and fleshful instrument that resides in your loins. And though you may attempt to ignore this instrument of debasement, in the darkness of a ship, among the sweat of rats and tired men, this instrument certainly led you—

BUNCE *(Interrupts)*: You mean my prick, sir?

SNELGRAVE: Not in this house.

BUNCE: It goes where I go, sir.

SNELGRAVE: Exactly. And where does it go when your body is snarling and gnashing and snapping like a wild dog and it must be satisfied or you'll die!?

(Bunce is silent.)

God curse you! Speak!

(Bunce nears Snelgrave, close, too close. He takes Snelgrave's finger, examines it a moment, then forces it through the rind of the orange. Bunce turns the orange on Snelgrave's finger, slowly, sensually. Then he pulls the orange off of Snelgrave's finger. Involuntarily, Snelgrave looks at his wet finger. Bunce raises the orange over his head, squeezes it and drinks from the hole in the rind.)

I issue commissions to the Navy Board. *(Beat)* I draft resolutions to send to the king.

(They look at each other.)

SCENE TWO

Snelgrave, Darcy, Morse and Bunce in the room. Morse now sits on the mat in the corner with Bunce. She wears long johns. Darcy coughs once, twice.

BUNCE: Can I get you some water?

DARCY: No, thank you, Bunce.

SNELGRAVE *(Mocking)*: "Can I get you some water? Can I get you some water?" What's happened to your manners? It's Mrs. Snelgrave. Mrs. Snelgrave. "Can I get you some water, Mrs. Snelgrave." *(Beat)* Bunce.

BUNCE: Mrs. Snelgrave.

SNELGRAVE: That's right. That's right.

DARCY: William.

SNELGRAVE: I'm an old man, Bunce. I sleep sound. Do you sleep sound?

BUNCE: Usually, sir.

SNELGRAVE: They say a man who'd put to sea for pleasure would go to hell for pastime. *(Beat)* What's your pastime, Bunce? Heh?

(Snelgrave pokes at Bunce with his stick. Morse runs to Darcy.)

We'll be out of here one day. Never see each other's rotten faces again. But where will you go? What will you do? I have work. I have friends. Do you have work, Bunce? Do you have friends?

MORSE: I'm his friend.

SNELGRAVE *(To Morse)*: Ha. You're just a flea. *(Beat)* Tell us another story, Bunce. A real brute of a sea story.

We've got some time left. To kill. I'll give you two shillings if it's good

BUNCE: No, sir.

SNELGRAVE: No?

MORSE: He said no.

SNELGRAVE: What's the matter, Bunce? What's got under your skin? (*Poking him again with his stick, harder*) What's on your mind?

BUNCE: I got four things on my mind, sir.

SNELGRAVE (*Still poking him*): Go on. I'm intrigued. Four things.

BUNCE: First is that stick you keep poking me with. Second is when I get out of here, I won't sail for the Navy again. Ever. I'll kill somebody first, even if it's me. Third is your wife, Darcy Snelgrave. And fourth is your wife as well. I count her twice 'cause she's much on my mind—

SNELGRAVE: You filthy— How dare you think of my wife!

BUNCE: You don't, sir, so I thought I might.

SNELGRAVE: What? What? What do you think of my wife?

DARCY: Stop this, William.

SNELGRAVE: What do you think of my wife?

BUNCE: The way a tar thinks, sir, you don't want to know.

SNELGRAVE (*Still poking him*): No. I don't. You swine. Eat your words. Eat them. (*He forces the stick in Bunce's mouth*) Eat them.

(*Bunce firmly but calmly grabs the stick and walks Snelgrave backward until Snelgrave sits in his chair.*)

BUNCE: Move, sir, from this chair and I'll push this stick through your heart.

SNELGRAVE: Darcy?

DARCY (*Calmly*): Morse, bring me the rope.

SNELGRAVE: Darcy!

(*Morse gets rope and she and Darcy tie Snelgrave in the chair.*

Banging at the window.

Bunce pulls a knife and warns Snelgrave. Kabe pops his head in.)

KABE: A morning to all, good neighbors. Mr. Snelgrave, Mrs. Snelgrave. Rabble. Want the Bills this week? Not leveling out. God save the king I say. The Devil won't have him.

MORSE: We're playing: we're going to cook Mr. Snelgrave.

KABE: No harm done, heh? And here's something for your game, Morse.

(Kabe throws Morse an orange.)

Mrs. Snelgrave? Need anything?

(There is no reply. An awkward silence.)

Well. I'm off, as the scab said. Working the pits. Deaf Stewart'll take over for me tonight. Throw something at him when you want his attention.

MORSE: Can you get me some good linen from the pits? I want a new dress.

KABE: There's a king's ransom in them pits. And along the roads. Bodies just asking you to strip 'em. If the family ain't robbed them first. Probably before they died . . .

DARCY: Morse! Kabe! Have you no sympathy . . .

KABE: They don't need it anymore, do they, Mrs. Snelgrave. Mr. Snelgrave.

SNELGRAVE: Kabe . . .

KABE *(Ignoring Snelgrave's plea)*: What's terrible at the pits isn't the dead. What's terrible is that there are persons who aren't dead but are infected with the plague and they come freely to the pit, shouting, delirious with fever, half-naked, wrapped in blankets, and they throw themselves into the pits, on top of the dead, and expire there.

SNELGRAVE: Kabe!

KABE: Others are still dying. They leap about the pit, roaring, tearing the clothes from their bodies, taking up sticks and sharp stones and cutting open their sores to relieve the pain, some hacking away at their flesh until they fall down dead in their own blood. Ay, that's what's terrible. Not death, but life that has nothing left but still won't give itself up.

(Kabe waves and is gone.)

SNELGRAVE: Let me go.

(Bunce begins removing Snelgrave's shoes.)

What in God's name are you doing?

(Bunce puts on the shoes.)

BUNCE: I'm practicing.

(Morse puts the orange in Snelgrave's mouth.)

SCENE THREE

Night. Bunce sits on his mat in the corner, watching over Snelgrave, who sleeps, still tied to his chair. Darcy enters. They watch each other silently in the dark.

DARCY: He sleeps.
BUNCE: Yes.

(Some moments.)

What do you want, missus?
DARCY: I want. To see it.
BUNCE: Why?
DARCY: I think about it. All the time. What it must. Look like.
BUNCE: That's what you think about?
DARCY: Please. Lift your shirt.
BUNCE: You know what I think about, Mrs. Snelgrave?

DARCY: Maybe it's a joke. A lie. And when you leave here you'll go out in the streets and pretend you're Christ, with a wound that doesn't heal, and they'll give you alms.

BUNCE: Excuse me, but it's none of your damn business.

(Darcy turns to leave.)

Darcy.

DARCY: You're not to call me that. Ever.

BUNCE: I don't want you to see it. *(Beat)* But you can touch it. If you must.

DARCY: Yes.

BUNCE: Give me your hand.

(She does so.)

Close your eyes, missus.

(Darcy closes her eyes.)

Keep them closed.

(She nods. He guides her hands under his shirt.)

Feel it?

(Some moments.)

DARCY: There.

BUNCE: Yeah.

DARCY: It's a small. Hole. Does it hurt?

BUNCE: I don't know. Some of the skin, it has feeling left. Go on. Some of it doesn't.

DARCY: There.

(Bunce winces; almost imperceptibly:)

BUNCE: What?

DARCY: My finger. I've put my finger. Inside. It's warm. *(Beat)* It feels like I'm inside you.

BUNCE: You are.

(After some moments, Darcy takes her hand out from under his bandage. There is blood on her fingers. She looks at her hand as though it might have changed.)

DARCY: You should have died from a wound like that.

BUNCE: It was an accident.

DARCY: An accident?

BUNCE: That I lived.

DARCY: Do you know I've hardly given you a thought in these weeks, but every night I ravish you in my sleep. Why is that, Bunce? Can you tell me why that is?

BUNCE: It's nothing to worry over, Mrs. Snelgrave. You people always want to fuck your servants.

(Darcy raises her arm to hit him. Bunce stops her.)

You haven't an idea in hell who I am.

DARCY: You're a sailor. You steal. You kill.

(Bunce begins to run his hands along her arms, much as Morse did earlier, slowly, watching her face to see what she can feel.)

BUNCE: I worked the Royal Navy off and on for eleven years. Here?

DARCY: No.

BUNCE: Deserted when I could. In between I skulked the city. There?

(Darcy shakes her head no. Bunce moves on slowly to touch her shoulders and neck.)

I got picked up on the waters—here?

DARCY: Yes.

BUNCE: . . . By the Spaniards and served them against the French. There?

(Darcy shakes her head no.)

Then the Hollanders against the English.

(Bunce goes down on his knees. He puts his hands under her dress to touch her ankles. We cannot see his hands or her legs as her dress is long. She doesn't stop him, though she looks to see if Snelgrave is still sleeping. The rest of the scene should be very subtle. Darcy does her best to hide both her fear and pleasure and she hides them very well.)

Then I was taken up again by the English out of Dunkirker and served against the Hollanders. *(Beat)* There? *(Moving his hands higher up her legs)* There?

DARCY: I don't know. Yes. I think so.

BUNCE: Last I was taken by the Turks—

DARCY: The Turks.

BUNCE: Where I was forced to serve them against the English, French, Dutch and Spaniards and all Christendom. The last time I got picked up, I was in church.

DARCY: Church.

BUNCE: In Bristol. The press gangs had orders to pick up all men without property, above fifteen. They must have raided half a dozen churches to get the men they needed. *(Moving his hands up further)* And here? *(Beat)* Most of those lads didn't know the first thing about sailing, let alone war. In the first hours we sailed, two of them got tangled in the mizzen shrouds and swept overboard. Another fell from the jib boom.

DARCY: Jib boom?

BUNCE: There was one boy who took sick with the motion. His neck and face swelled with the retching. Then his tongue went black. He held out his arms to us. For mercy. Then he vomited his stomach up into his hands and died. *(Touching her)* This? Yeah. Here. *(Beat)* We sailed to battle the Dutch at Tescell.

DARCY: Tescell.

BUNCE: Over twenty ships went down on fire. And the gulls. Screaming above the cannons. They wouldn't fly from the ships. Here? *(Beat)* Some of them. Their wings caught fire, so close did they circle the sinking masts. When the battle was over, half of the men. Dead in the water. Floating face down in the waves, still in the Sunday suits they'd been picked up in. *(Beat)* I sailed ships for Navies most of my life. *(Touching her intimately)* And here? Yeah. Right here. *(Beat)* In all that time I didn't kill. *(Beat)* Mrs. Snelgrave?

DARCY *(Whispers)*: Yes.

BUNCE: I never killed. It was in me though. Do you want me to stop?

(Darcy does not answer him.)

SCENE FOUR

Snelgrave still tied in his chair. Bunce curled up and asleep on his mat. He doesn't stir through the entire scene. Morse sits and plays with two small cloth-and-stick dolls. She is wearing one of Darcy's dresses, which doesn't fit her at all, but she is happy to be dressed in it.

MORSE: And the two lovers were happy and the sky a blue grape and the birds sang. *(To Snelgrave)* Can you make the tweet of the birds?

SNELGRAVE: If you untie me.

MORSE *(Uses a doll to speak)*: I can't, Mr. Snelgrave. If I let you go, you will break me in half with your cane. *(To Snelgrave)* If you don't want to play, then shut up. *(Back to her game)* And the two lovers were happy and the sky a fat apple and the birds sang. And the world—

(Snelgrave begins to make bird sounds. Morse listens a moment. She approves.)

And the birds sang sweetly and the world was good and— *(She looks at Snelgrave's bare feet)* —even the rich had shoes. But one day the world changed. *(She strikes a tinderbox)* And it never changed back. *(She holds one of the dolls near the flame)*

SNELGRAVE: Don't do that. *(Beat)* Please.

MORSE: The young man said. But the fire angel would have her heart.

(She lights the stick doll on fire and sets it on the floor to burn. They watch it burn out.)

Even her voice was burned, but still he heard her say, "Hold me," and the young man came to her and—

SNELGRAVE: No. He didn't come to her. He was a coward, your man.

(Darcy almost enters the room but then stops and watches them. They are intent on the story and do not see her.)

MORSE: He knelt down beside her—

SNELGRAVE: He walked away.

MORSE: —and put his hand into the ashes that were her body.

SNELGRAVE: He turned his back.

MORSE: The young man sifted the ashes until he found what was left of her heart.

SNELGRAVE: Small and black and empty it was—

MORSE: But it was her heart.

SNELGRAVE: And the young man put the burnt organ—

MORSE: No bigger than a walnut shell—

SNELGRAVE: —into a glass of his own blood.

(While Morse speaks the following, Snelgrave softly makes bird sounds as before.)

MORSE: And there the heart drank and drank until it was plump once more. And though the prince could never hold her in his arms again, she being now only the size of his palm, he could caress her with his fingers, and when it was winter the heart lay against his cold breast and kept him warm.

(Darcy leaves. They do not notice.)

SNELGRAVE: I'm an ordinary man. I never meant to be cruel.

MORSE: Neither did Sir Braithwaite. And yet when my mother, a maid in his house for fourteen years, came to him one morning with the black tokens on her neck, he locked her in the root cellar. He was afraid they'd close up his house if they found out someone had taken sick. Neither food nor water he gave her. I lay outside the cellar door. With the door between us, we slept with our mouths to the crack so that we could feel each other's breath.

SNELGRAVE: We didn't lock up our maids. We called for a surgeon.

MORSE: She said, "Hold me," because she was cold, but the door was between us and I could not hold her.

SNELGRAVE: Enough of this. Get me some water, child.

MORSE: Did you bring them water when they were dying?

SNELGRAVE: Yes.

MORSE: You lie. You sent your boy to do it. You never looked on them once they were sick.

SNELGRAVE: I couldn't help them. It was God's wish.

MORSE: You locked them in the cellar.

SNELGRAVE: That's not true.

MORSE: And they died in the dirt and blood of their own bodies. And their last breath blew under the door and found your fat mouth and hid inside it and waited for the proper moment to fill your throat.

SNELGRAVE: You are an evil, evil girl. If your mother were alive—

MORSE: My mother lives in your mouth, and one day she will choke you.

SNELGRAVE: Who's your father, girl?

MORSE: I was born from a piece of broken star that pierced my mother's heart.

SNELGRAVE: More likely Sir Braithwaite. Masters make free with their maids. I'll be honest. I've done so myself. Perhaps this gentleman you despise and ridicule was your own father. Heh? How about that, little girl? Ever thought of that?

(Morse stands staring at him some moments. Then she quickly lifts the long dress and flashes him. This action is not seductive. For Morse it is as though she were pissing on him. After a moment, he turns his head away. She picks up the doll that played the prince. With a kick she scatters the remains of the burnt doll on the floor. She exits.)

SCENE FIVE

Darcy, Bunce, Morse and Snelgrave, still tied to his chair. Morse has taken off Darcy's dress and goes about in her long johns again. Snelgrave is dressed in Bunce's clothes, which fit poorly. Bunce is putting on Snelgrave's pants. The shirt doesn't fit him, so he throws it aside. There is laughter and an initial sense of merriment from all four of them.

SNELGRAVE: Ha! They're a poor fit. You see! Untie me, Darcy.

DARCY: Please stop asking me that. Tomorrow perhaps. Not today.

SNELGRAVE: Bunce. I'll pay you in gold if you let me go.

BUNCE: The child has already given me half your gold, sir.

SNELGRAVE: But I have more at the Navy Board. Much more.

MORSE *(Brings the vinegar bucket and begins to wash Snelgrave. He pays no attention)*: First we clean the meat. Then we cook it.

SNELGRAVE *(To Darcy)*: You do realize we can't go on after this as man and wife.

DARCY: We haven't gone on as man and wife—

SNELGRAVE: I'll put you out in the streets.

DARCY: —since I was seventeen.

SNELGRAVE: You'll be the shame of the city. Less than a whore. You'll live in the kennel, stink—

DARCY: La, la. And I will strip and walk naked to your Navy Board, and in the courtyard I will dance.

MORSE: Like a pinecone on fire she'll dance.

SNELGRAVE: There's no life for you outside of this marriage, outside of this house. Bunce can't take care of you.

MORSE: But Bunce can tie knots. I can tie a cat's-paw best. Mrs. Snelgrave can do a Flemish-eye faster than he can.

SNELGRAVE: Tying knots with Bunce now, are we? How sweet. How delicious. Tell me, Bunce, what's her cunny like?

(Bunce doesn't answer.)

Bread that's left too long in the oven?

DARCY *(To Bunce)*: Why don't you answer him?

(Silence some moments. Bunce shrugs, then takes a drink of water. He leans over Snelgrave as though to kiss him, and almost kisses him, but instead he lets the water trickle slowly out of his mouth across Snelgrave's mouth and face. Snelgrave is so shocked by the audacity and sensuality of this act that by the time he resists, Bunce is through.)

BUNCE: That's your wife, sir. Though I haven't yet had the pleasures you assume. Only with my left hand. My right hand aches with jealousy.

(Snelgrave closes his eyes and appears to be praying. Bunce looks at Darcy for approval. She blushes. Snelgrave opens one eye and sees her blush. He spits at her but misses.)

SNELGRAVE: If all you needed was a man as low as this to bring you 'round, I could have paid Kabe to do it.

MORSE: I saw Kabe's mousie once. Its tail was long and skinny.

DARCY: No one brought me 'round, William. I've lain beside you like a piece of old charcoal most of my life and, well, if that's what I am—

SNELGRAVE *(Interrupts)*: I wouldn't expect much pleasure in return, Bunce. She's an old woman. Her mouth stinks. Her—

MORSE *(Sticking her bare toe in his face)*: What will you pay me if I let you suck my toe?

SNELGRAVE: You foul child!

DARCY: It seems centuries ago, but you used to weep at the pleasure I gave you.

MORSE: Kabe paid me a sugar-knot for a kiss.

SNELGRAVE *(To Darcy)*: You lie. *(To Bunce)* I bet she hasn't pleased you, has she?

MORSE: Small fruits and berries for a suck on the little toes.

DARCY: Answer him, Bunce.

MORSE: Larger fruits for a suck on the big one.

BUNCE: No. She hasn't.

DARCY *(To Snelgrave)*: He's never asked me to.

SNELGRAVE: You think a man needs to ask?! *(To Bunce)* Listen to that! She says you've never asked her!

BUNCE: Well, sir. I just sort of expected she'd take what she wanted. It's always been that way between us kind, hasn't it?

SNELGRAVE: Ha!

MORSE: Ha!

BUNCE: What's changed?

MORSE: You're wearing new shoes.

BUNCE: That I am. And a man in these shoes should be able to ask . . .

SNELGRAVE: Go on.

MORSE: Yes?

BUNCE: Will you, Mrs. Snelgrave . . .

SNELGRAVE: Yes?

MORSE: Go on.

BUNCE: Bring. A poor sailor. And part-time servant. To his crisis?

(Snelgrave bursts out laughing, and Morse, copying Snelgrave, laughs too. Bunce blushes.)

DARCY: I don't think I could—

SNELGRAVE: See? It wasn't only me. She didn't like it after the fire either.

DARCY: I don't know a great deal about—

SNELGRAVE: It was a horror even to lie beside her.

DARCY: Other people. Their bodies.

SNELGRAVE: For years, the smoke rose out of her mouth as she slept.

MORSE: But she could learn. Couldn't she, Mr. Snelgrave?

SNELGRAVE: Learn? Her? Never, child.

MORSE: Of course she could. If Bunce stands here. And Mrs. Snelgrave right there.

SNELGRAVE: What?

MORSE: Come on. Don't be stupid.

(They follow her orders.)

Mrs. Snelgrave puts her hands on his chest. Go on.

SNELGRAVE: His chest?

BUNCE: Isn't that my bit?

MORSE: Not this time, it isn't.

SNELGRAVE: You're all mad.

MORSE: Then she gives him a little kiss on the cheek.

(Darcy does so.)

SNELGRAVE: Mad!

MORSE: Then she takes off her glove. Mrs. Snelgrave?

(Darcy takes off her glove.)

And she lets it drop to the floor. Like a leaf. Ha.

(Darcy lets the glove drop.)

Then Mrs. Snelgrave, she lets her hand slowly move down his chest, slowly, down. Yes. To there.

(Darcy's hand rests on Bunce's belt.)

SNELGRAVE *(To Morse)*: Where were you schooled, slut?

MORSE: Keyholes. *(Beat)* And now it's only polite to make sure Bunce is still with her, so she says, "May I?"

(Darcy doesn't speak.)

SNELGRAVE: She can't say it! Ha.

MORSE: "Do you want me to touch you?" she says.

(Bunce doesn't answer.)

SNELGRAVE: "Yes, I do," he says.

MORSE: And then we do this.

(Morse blindfolds Snelgrave.)

SNELGRAVE: Hey! Devil's spawn. Take that off.

MORSE: And I go to the kitchen.

SNELGRAVE: Take it off!

(Morse sighs, takes the rag from the bucket, and puts it in his mouth. She exits.)

DARCY *(Wanting Snelgrave to hear them)*: Shhh. I don't want my husband to hear us.

BUNCE: We'll be as quiet as the dead.

(Snelgrave screams through his stuffed rag.)

SCENE SIX

Early morning light. Snelgrave slumped in his chair. Morse enters in a nightdress—Snelgrave's shirt discarded by Bunce in the previous scene. Morse approaches him, closer, closer until their faces are almost touching.

MORSE: That wasn't a poor bird you did yesterday. It was quite good, really.

(She touches him, then shakes him. He is dead.)

Where did you go, Mr. Snelgrave?

(She unbuttons his shirt and checks his chest and neck.)

You haven't even got the tokens.

(She slowly begins to untie Snelgrave as she speaks the following.)

Sir Braithwaite's daughter had a bird. A green and black bird. Whack, whack went her stick on my back when I swept. Then she'd let me hold the bird so I'd stop my crying. The bird had a song like a long, long spoon, and we could sip at it like jam. And the song put a butterfly inside our mouths, and it opened its wings in there and made us laugh. *(She sits with the rope in her lap)* But everyone died in that house. And then Lissa was dying, too, and we were alone, and she lay on the floor with the tokens shining black on her neck. The tokens would not break and run, and Lissa wept from the pain. She said, "Hold me." *(Beat)* She could no longer see and was blind. *(Beat)* She said, "Hold me," and I said, "Give me your dress." She couldn't take it off, because she was too weak, so I undressed her. Lissa said, "Hold me now." She was small and thin without her dress. I said, "Give me your shoes," and she let me have them. I put on the dress and the shoes. I went to the looking glass. The silk of the dress lapped at my skin. The ruffles whispered hush hush as I walked. Lissa said, "Hold me, Morse. I'm so cold." I went to her then. *(Beat)* But then she was. Dead. I sat beside her, holding the bird. It sang for her. It sang for hours and hours until its heart stopped in my hands. *(Beat)* It was Lissa's bird. I could take her dress and shoes but I couldn't take the bird. Even dead, it was Lissa's bird. Not mine. *(Beat)* I opened her mouth and put the bird inside.

(She goes to Snelgrave.)

You are dead. I can hold you.

(She gently embraces his body.)

SCENE SEVEN

Below the window, outside, Kabe is singing.

KABE:

Tyburn tree, Tyburn tree
Hang anybody but the poor man and me.

(Bunce leans out of the window.)

BUNCE: Pssst.

KABE:

Hang the king, Hang the duke
If I survive you'll be the death of me.

BUNCE: I got gold.

KABE: Says the man in chains.

BUNCE: I'm going out through the cellar.

KABE *(Ignoring Bunce)*: The king's coming back.

BUNCE: I got gold to pay you.

KABE: Kabe and king don't see eye to eye. Hell'll break loose. No place for a man of ability.

BUNCE: I'll throw in a pair of shoes the likes you've not seen before. Gentlemen's leather.

KABE: Chaos. Destruction. Mammon's back. Swarms, Sodom and all. Maybe I'll off to Oxford. Pass the monster on the way. Bow and wave.

BUNCE: And a pair of earrings.

KABE: Living's a nasty business.

BUNCE: I think they're emerald.

KABE: How's Mr. Snelgrave this morning?

BUNCE: I'm not Snelgrave.

KABE: Yes, you are. *(Beat)* The gold and the silk suit. Put the earrings in the pocket. You keep the shoes. Dumb Samuel will be on some night this week. I

can't tell you when. Keep watch. He can't shout, but
be quick. They'll kill you.

BUNCE *(About to thank him)*: Kabe—

KABE *(Interrupts)*: I don't care enough about you to hate
you, Rabble. *(Beat)* Tell the girl she'll have to give me
a suck, on the mouth this time, or no deal. Said the
cock to the chicken.

BUNCE: I heard you.

KABE *(Recites)*:

I don't like sailors, they stink of tar
But my lass she smells of the falling star.

(Bunce disappears from the window. Kabe sings:)

Tyburn tree, Tyburn tree
Can't find work for any fee
The plague's got your tongue, worm's at your bone
You're as near to me as the West Indy.

Tyburn tree, Tyburn tree
Won't you, won't you make love to me!

SCENE EIGHT

*Bunce is putting a few spare items (a shirt, bread) onto a piece of
cloth that he will later tie up as a sack. Morse watches him. Snelgrave, dead in his chair, sits with a small cloth over his face.*

BUNCE: Don't know. Out of the city if I can. And find work.
Back up North maybe. Some quiet parish that's not
got too many poor. God willing.

MORSE: You don't believe in God.

BUNCE: If there's employment, I'll believe and more.

MORSE: You could stay.

BUNCE: Not now. I'd might as well rope myself and walk
to Tyburn. Save them and me trouble.

MORSE: But my word and Mrs. Snelgrave's . . .

BUNCE: Her word? Can't trust that the right story would stick in her mouth. Who's to say she wouldn't be front row just to see me rise up in me britches after I drop down and into hell.

MORSE: Rise up in your britches?

BUNCE: It's the rush of blood to your, to me . . . I can't stay.

MORSE (*Nodding toward Snelgrave*): They have to come and get him. (*Beat*) They'll throw him in the pits, though it wasn't plague, won't they?

BUNCE: He won't care.

MORSE: I don't mind him here. Now. He doesn't smell.

BUNCE: Not yet.

MORSE: And me?

BUNCE: Mrs. Snelgrave will care for you.

MORSE: She has no heart. That's what she told me.

BUNCE: Trust her; she's a liar.

MORSE: You didn't mind how she felt? Her skin.

BUNCE: You don't feel with your hands.

MORSE (*Holding out her arms*): Am I soft?

BUNCE (*Touches her arm*): You are. (*Beat*) You feel. Alive.

MORSE: Everyone leaves.

BUNCE: Ay.

MORSE: Even when they stay.

(*Morse takes the remaining stick doll out of her pocket and puts it on the small pile Bunce is about to wrap up.*)

It wants to go with you.

BUNCE (*Picking up the stick doll and looking at it*): Who is it?

MORSE: It's me.

(*Bunce puts the stick doll on his pile and ties it all into a bundle. Then he takes some rope from his pocket to show Morse one more knot. Darcy enters and stands watching them. They don't notice her.*)

BUNCE: I'll show you a last one, then I'm off. Thumb knot you use to tie the mouse and collar on the mast. You always go in here, not around. A good knot is like a dead man's heart; you can't break it.

(Bunce notices Darcy standing there. She is quietly watching them. Her face and hair are wet with sweat.)

MORSE *(Making the knot)*: You can't break my heart. It's made of water.

(She shows him her knot. She, too, sees Darcy.)

BUNCE: Your dress is wet.

DARCY: That's because my head is full. Of ocean. And the shells are sliding back and forth in my ears. *(Touching her head)* It's hot in here. Very hot.

BUNCE *(To Morse)*: Get a blanket.

(Morse stands transfixed on Darcy.)

A blanket! And some towels.

(Morse gets them.)

DARCY: You mustn't bother.

(Bunce nears her.)

Stay back.

BUNCE: The tokens. Are they on your neck or thighs?

DARCY: They're in my mind.

BUNCE: We've got to make a fire. Are the botches hard yet?

(Darcy doesn't answer. He approaches her again.)

Take off your dress. Let me look.

DARCY: Never. *(Beat)* You must get out. Take the child with you. *(She reveals a knife.)* I will not hesitate.

(Bunce moves close enough to her so she can cut him.)

BUNCE: Neither will I.

(Darcy lowers the knife. Weakened by fever, she sits. Bunce drops to his knees and raises her skirts.)

(To Morse) It's her thighs. Get some coals from the kitchen. And some wet cloth.

(Morse exits. Bunce puts his arms under Darcy's dress and begins to massage her thighs vigorously.)

We've got to soften the botches. With heat. Then we can lance them.

(Darcy sits in a daze. She stares at Snelgrave in his chair.)

DARCY: Take it off.

(Bunce starts to unbutton her dress. She stops him.)

The cloth.

(Darcy indicates Snelgrave. Bunce removes the small cloth covering Snelgrave's face. Morse returns with a bucket of coals and wet clothes.)

Is he laughing, Morse?

(Morse looks at Snelgrave's face.)

MORSE: No, Mrs. Snelgrave. He's weeping. But he's so far away we can't hear him.
DARCY: Is he cold?

(Morse touches Snelgrave's arm. Bunce rips up cloth.)

MORSE: Like snow, he is.
DARCY: I envy him.
MORSE: Does it hurt?
DARCY: Here. *(Indicating her stomach)* As though I had swallowed. Large pieces of glass.

(Bunce takes up a hot coal and wraps it in the wet cloth.)

BUNCE: You'll feel this, Mrs. Snelgrave.

(He puts the coal under Darcy's dress, against her skin. Darcy flinches.)

MORSE (*Attempting to distract her*): Did you care for him?

DARCY: Who?

MORSE: Mr. Snelgrave.

DARCY: I knew him only as a boy. After the fire, he bore the same name, but that was the only resemblance. Yes. As a boy. Perhaps I loved him. Look at him there. Can you believe it, Morse? We used to touch each other for hours. We thought we were remaking ourselves. Perhaps we were. For each morning we were someone new and the world was almost a surprise, like biting into a piece of fruit with your eyes closed. (*Beat*) No more, Bunce. Please. It does no good.

(*Bunce puts another wrapped piece of coal under her dress. Darcy stifles a scream.*)

MORSE (*Distracting Darcy*): Did William kiss you many, many times, Mrs. Snelgrave?

DARCY: Many, many times. And his tongue so cold. It covered my skin with frost.

(*Darcy screams. Bunce takes the knife from her hand and begins to bring it under her skirt to lance the tokens. Suddenly Darcy is completely lucid. She stops Bunce's hand.*)

No.

BUNCE: If I can make them run there's a chance.

DARCY: Goddamn you, Bunce. The life is pouring out of me. (*Shouts*) Help me! (*Quietly*) Help me.

BUNCE: I'm trying to save your life.

DARCY: That's not what I mean.

(*Bunce shakes his head no. Morse moves away and watches them.*)

Do you love me?

(*For a moment, Bunce laughs in a desperate manner.*)

I said, do you love me?

BUNCE: Not enough to kill you.

DARCY: Then. Let me.

BUNCE: Don't ask. Shhh. Please.

(Bunce lays his head in her lap. She takes the knife from his hand.)

I haven't the courage.

(There is silence for some moments.)

MORSE: I do.

DARCY: You're not afraid?

(Morse shakes her head no.)

Take my hand. Come then. Now squeeze it with all your might.

(Morse does so.)

MORSE: I'm strong. I am.

BUNCE: No.

DARCY: If you stop me, you'll regret it. And I'll curse you the moment I die. *(Beat)* You can leave the room, sailor. I'm not asking you to stay.

(Bunce stares at her for what seems a long time. Then he kisses her, gently, on the forehead. As he begins to move away, she pulls him back and forces him to kiss her, hard, on the mouth. Then Bunce goes to his mat and kneels there, his face to the wall. Darcy speaks to Morse.)

So you will help me.

MORSE: What will you give me?

DARCY: Well, I don't think I have anything left.

MORSE: Your gloves.

DARCY: All right, my gloves.

(Darcy removes her gloves. She puts Morse's hands on the knife and her own hands over Morse's.)

You must not waver, Morse. Not for one moment. Do you understand?

(Morse nods. Darcy places the blade point against her chest, over her heart. Darcy closes her eyes.)

MORSE: Don't close your eyes, Mrs. Snelgrave. All you'll see is blackness.

(Morse puts her face close to Darcy's face.)

Look at me. At my face.

(Darcy opens her eyes.)

DARCY: Yes.

MORSE: The breath of a child has passed through the lungs of an angel. You said that.

(Darcy nods.)

So the breath of an angel now covers your face. Can you feel it? *(She blows on Darcy's face.)*
And I will hold you, hush, hush. The angel's tongue is plump with blood and my mouth so cold it covers your skin with snow as the flames, like scissors, open your dress. And my kiss is a leaf. It falls from the sky and comes to rest on your breast. And my kiss is strong and pierces your heart—

(Morse helps Darcy drive the knife into her heart.)

Like a secret from God.

(Darcy is dead. Morse pulls out the knife. She holds it out to Bunce. Morse is completely still, perhaps in shock. Finally Bunce turns around.)

It is done. We are dead.

SCENE NINE

Semi-darkness. In the cell or place of confinement as in previous scenes. In the shadows we see the dead Snelgraves, still in their chairs. Nothing of Bunce or of Bunce's presence remains. Morse stands center stage, again in her dirty dress.

MORSE: Can I go now? *(Beat)* There's nothing more to tell of them.

Years it was. Or weeks and days, by the time the doors were opened. The city was empty. The air was sweet with sugar and piss. And it was quiet. So quiet. And I walked down to the quay side. The boats were still. There was no wind. The river was not moving. Everyone had gone. One way or another.

(Kabe enters in the shadows. He covers Snelgrave with a cloth.)

I stood by the banks and looked in the water. There were no fish. There was nothing but water. Water that didn't move. But then, I saw a child floating there. On her back. She rose so close to the surface I could have touched her. A girl of nine or ten. Pale and blond she was. And naked. She had no marks. In each hand she clutched a fist of black hair. Her mouth was open and filled with the river. As I reached in the water to touch her, a ship hoisted its sail. A door slammed in the street. One, two, three voices called out to one other. A bell rang. And the city came alive once more. *(Sings)*

Oranges and lemons
Sing the bells of St Clements.

(Kabe covers Darcy with a cloth.)

When I looked down in the water again for the body of the child, it was gone. And I was glad. I was glad it had gone.

(Kabe exits.)

Kabe once said to me, "Our lives are just a splash of water on a stone. Nothing more." *(She kneels, as though in prayer)* Then I am the stone on which they fell. And they have marked me.

So beware.

Because I loved them, and they have marked me.

(Morse sits. She takes the orange from her pocket. She holds it in her lap, looking at it, her head bowed. We hear Kabe singing, offstage, though his voice fills the entire cell.)

KABE:

Farewell said the scab to the itch
Farewell said the crab to its crotch
Farewell said the plague to death's ditch
Farewell said the dead to their watch.

(Morse tosses the orange high into the air. Just as she catches it, the lights go black.)

END OF PLAY

SELECT BIBLIOGRAPHY

Burg, Barry Richard. *Sodomy and the Pirate Tradition: English Sea Rovers in the Seventeenth Century Caribbean.* New York: New York University Press, 1995.

Defoe, Daniel. *A Journal of the Plague Year.* Oxford: Oxford University Press, 1999.

Latham, Robert. *The Illustrated Pepys: Extracts from the Diary.* Berkeley: University of California Press, 1983.

Morton, A. L. *A Peoples History of England.* London: Lawrence & Wishart, 1992.

Rediker, Marcus. *Between the Devil and the Deep Blue Sea: Merchant Seaman, Pirates and the Anglo-American Maritime World, 1700–1750.* Cambridge: Cambridge University Press, 1987.

Underdown, David. *Revel, Riot and Rebellion: Popular Politics and Culture in England 1603–1660.* Oxford: Oxford University Press, 1987.

IN THE HEART OF AMERICA

1994

**To my mother, Sonia de Vries,
who gave me a conscience.**

In the Heart of America had its world premiere on August 3, 1994, at the Bush Theatre in London. The director was Dominic Dromgoole. Scenic design was by Angela Davies, the lighting design was by Paul Russell and the sound design was by Alan Mason. The cast was as follows:

CRAVER PERRY	Richard Dormer
FAIROUZ SABOURA	Sasha Hails
LUE MING	Toshie Ogura
REMZI SABOURA	Zubin Varla
BOXLER	Robert Glenister

In November 1994, *In the Heart of America* was produced by Long Wharf Theatre, New Haven, CT, for their workshop series. The director was Tony Kushner. Set coordination and properties were by David Fletcher, costume coordination was by Patricia M. Risser, lighting was by Kirk Matson, sound was by Brenton Evans and script development was provided by Sari Bodi. The cast was as follows:

CRAVER PERRY	David Van Pelt
FAIROUZ SABOURA	Irene Glezos
LUE MING	Wai Ching Ho
REMZI SABOURA	Firdous Bamji
BOXLER	Lanny Flaherty

CHARACTERS

CRAVER PERRY, a white male, early twenties
FAIROUZ SABOURA, a Palestinian-American, mid-twenties
LUE MING, a ghost, but more solid
REMZI SABOURA, Fairouz's brother, early twenties
BOXLER, the soul of Lieutenant Calley

TIME

All scenes are in the present time of the story, except for the scenes between Remzi and Craver, and Remzi and Fairouz, which take place in the past. In some scenes the past and present collide.

PLACE

A motel room, a military camp in Saudi Arabia, another room, the Iraqi desert.

SETTING

Minimal and not "realistic."

And I await those who return,
who come knowing my times of death.
I love you when I love you not.
The walls of Babylon are close
in the daylight, and your eyes
are big, and your face looms
large in the light.

It is as if you have not been born yet,
we have not separated, and you
have not felled me, as if above
the storm tops every speech is
beautiful, every reunion,
a farewell.

—Mahmoud Darwish

ACT I

SCENE ONE

Lights up on Craver doing a headstand in a cheap motel room. Fairouz is standing in the shadows, watching.

FAIROUZ: He sent me a horn in a box. It was a ram's horn.

CRAVER: He is a funny guy.

FAIROUZ: Do you laugh at him?

CRAVER *(Gets to his feet)*: What did you say your name was?

FAIROUZ: I don't laugh at him.

CRAVER: What's your background? He's never clear where he's from.

FAIROUZ: Can you tell me how he's doing?

CRAVER: I told you over the phone I haven't heard from him in months.

FAIROUZ: You are his best friend.

CRAVER: I'm sorry to hear that.

FAIROUZ: Where is he? *(Beat)* Mr. Craver.

CRAVER: Perry. Mr. Perry. Craver's my first name. C-R-A-V-E-R. How did you get my address?

FAIROUZ: Remzi wrote in a letter . . .

CRAVER: I hardly know him.

FAIROUZ: He wrote: "Craver and I are never separate."

CRAVER: People get lost. Call the army.

FAIROUZ: I did.

(Craver does another headstand.)

CRAVER: This kid over in Saudi taught me how to do this. It's not keeping your legs in the air; it's how you breathe. See? You got to push the air up through your lungs and into your feet. Then your feet will stay up, float like balloons.

FAIROUZ: Can Remzi do that? Stand on his head like you?

CRAVER *(Back on his feet)*: Remzi has no balance.

FAIROUZ: He wrote me that he loved you.

CRAVER: And who do you love?

FAIROUZ: I threw it out. The ram's horn.

CRAVER: We must have bought a dozen horns while we were over there, but not one of them was good enough to send his sister. He wrote her name on the inside of it. F-A-I-R-O-U-Z. Fairouz. That was the name he wrote.

FAIROUZ: It had a bad smell.

CRAVER: Fairouz isn't anything like you.

FAIROUZ: Horns make noise.

CRAVER: He said she was like a flower.

FAIROUZ: I don't like noise. Remzi knows that.

CRAVER: No, he said she was like milk, sweet, fresh milk.

FAIROUZ: He likes to race. Did he race with you? He's not fast but he won't believe it.

CRAVER: Fairouz would have appreciated his gift.

FAIROUZ: Do you expect me to beg you?

CRAVER: Know what we call Arabs over there?

FAIROUZ: I'm not afraid of you, Mr. Perry. When I find out, I'll be back. *(She exits)*

CRAVER *(Calls after her)*: Fairouz! *(Beat)* He was my friend.

SCENE TWO

Craver asleep, worn out. A figure of a woman—an apparition or perhaps something more real—enters. Craver wakes.

CRAVER: Are you looking for him too?

LUE MING: I might be. Who?

CRAVER: Remzi. Remzi Saboura.

LUE MING: Are you Mr. Calley?

CRAVER: No. I'm not.

LUE MING: Oh my. I'm in the wrong house.

CRAVER: How did you get in?

LUE MING: I was homing in on a small jewelry store in Columbus, Georgia. Is this Georgia?

CRAVER: Kentucky. Motel 6.

LUE MING: And you're not Calley?

CRAVER: Are you Chinese?

LUE MING: Oh no. I was born in Hanoi.

CRAVER: What are you doing here?

LUE MING: I've never left my country. I'm a real home-body.

CRAVER: You speak good English.

LUE MING: Haven't tried it before, but it's going nicely, isn't it?

CRAVER: What do you want?

LUE MING: He's about five-foot-ten, red in the face, and likes colorful fish. He should be in his fifties by now.

CRAVER: I'm not Calley. I can't help you.

LUE MING *(Sniffs)*: A trace. Yes. You smell of him. He's your buddy. Who are you?

CRAVER: Craver Perry.

LUE MING: What do you do?

CRAVER: Not much right now. I'm . . . on leave.

LUE MING: Ah. An army fellow. Where were you stationed in Vietnam?

CRAVER: Vietnam? I wasn't in Vietnam. I was in the Gulf. In Saudi. In Iraq?

LUE MING: How can they fight in Vietnam and the Gulf at the same time?

CRAVER: We're not fighting in Vietnam.

LUE MING: Of course you are. Why, just yesterday my grandfather was out in the fields trying to pull a calf out of the mud. The rains. So much rain. You flew

over with your plane and bang, bang, bang, one
dead cow and one dead grandfather.

CRAVER: I've never even been to Vietnam.

LUE MING: Of course you have.

CRAVER: The Vietnam War ended over fifteen years ago,
lady.

LUE MING: Are you sure?

CRAVER: Positive.

LUE MING: Who won? My God, who won?

CRAVER: You did.

LUE MING: Oh I wish I could have told Grandpa that this
morning. *(Beat)* So I missed the house and the year.
But not the profession. How many gooks have you
killed?

CRAVER: I don't kill gooks; I kill Arabs.

LUE MING: Really? Arabs?

CRAVER: Not just any Arabs. Iraqi Arabs. Saddam Arabs.
But that war is over now too.

LUE MING: Who won?

CRAVER: We had a kill ratio of a thousand to one.

LUE MING: Oh my! *(Beat)* What's it like to kill a woman?

CRAVER: I never killed anyone.

LUE MING: Such modesty! In my village alone you killed
sixteen people, seven pigs, three cows and a chicken.

CRAVER: I never killed anyone in my life. I never got that
close.

LUE MING: Does it feel the same to shoot a cow in the
back as it does to shoot a man in the back?

CRAVER: Get the fuck out of my room.

LUE MING *(Caresses his face)*: I can't leave now! I think
we're falling in love.

SCENE THREE

*A year earlier in the Saudi desert. Craver and Remzi in positions
to sprint.*

REMZI: I get more traction running on this sand.

CRAVER: Get on your marks.

REMZI: Like a streak of light I'll pass you by, Craver. Just watch.

CRAVER: Get set!

REMZI: You just watch me.

CRAVER: Go!

REMZI: Wait! Wait! Cramp. Shit.

CRAVER: Bad luck to get beat before we start.

REMZI: I'm going to visit the village where my parents were born. When I get my first leave. Want to come with me?

CRAVER: Nope.

REMZI: Don't like to be seen with Arabs. Look. I've got more money than you. You're broke and I'm Arab. That about evens it out, doesn't it?

CRAVER: The CBU-75 carries eighteen hundred bomblets, called Sad Eyes. Sad Eyes.

REMZI: What do you think it's like . . .

CRAVER: One type of Sad Eyes can explode before hitting the ground.

REMZI: . . . to kill someone?

CRAVER: Each bomblet contains six hundred razor-sharp steel fragments.

REMZI: I wonder what I'll feel like after I do it?

CRAVER: It's nothing personal: we're not just here to get them out of Kuwait, but to protect a way of life.

REMZI AND CRAVER: Flawed it may be, but damn well worth protecting!

CRAVER: Those poor bastards are so brainwashed by Saddam, they need to kill like we need oxygen.

REMZI: When I went in for the interview, the recruiter asked me was I against taking another person's life.

CRAVER: If you are, you could fuck up an entire war.

REMZI: I just went in for the interview to piss my mother and sister off. The recruiter said: "What you need, son, is all right here." He looked at me, and I looked back. Then he said something that changed my life: "The army will give you a quiet sense of pride."

CRAVER: "A quiet sense of pride." *(Beat)* I'm not going to die.

REMZI *(Casually)*: I am.

CRAVER: It's hot here. Why does it have to be so hot here? Can't we just turn the sun up a few degrees and roast those motherfuckers! All these weeks with our ass frying in the sun, crawling through the sand like mutts, and the drills, drills, drills. Tomorrow might be the real thing. *(Beat)* We've got eight types of guided bombs.

REMZI: I wonder if you'll see it.

CRAVER: There's the GM-130, an electro-optically or infrared, two-thousand-pound, powered bomb.—See what?

REMZI: How I die.

CRAVER: Then there's the GBU-10 Paveway II, a two-thousand-pound, laser-guided bomb based on an MK-84.

REMZI: Let's say I'm lying over there, dead as can be, and then you see it's me, from a distance. But you still have to walk over to my body to check it out. So, how would you walk?

CRAVER: We've got Harm missiles, Walleyes, Clusters, and guided anti-tanks.

REMZI: Craver. This is something important I'm talking about. Let's say I'm you and I see me lying up ahead, dead. I stop in my tracks. I'm upset. We were friends, and I've got to cross the thirty or so feet between us. *(Does a "walk" over to the imaginary dead body)* No. That feels too confident.

CRAVER: And you wouldn't feel confident because . . .

REMZI: Because I'd be thinking: that could just as easily be me lying there as him.

CRAVER: Right. So maybe you'd do it like this. Kind of . . . *(Does his "walk" up to the imaginary body)*

REMZI: That's too careful.

CRAVER: Yeah. And too scared. I mean, I might be feeling in a pretty nice way, thinking about being alive and not quite as dead as you.

REMZI: You've got a point there. You might be feeling pretty OK.

CRAVER: And fucking lucky too, 'cause the blood's still rolling through my veins.

REMZI: Something like this maybe. *(Does another "walk," a sort of combination of the others)*

CRAVER: Yes! That's it! That's it! Let me try. OK. I see you up ahead of me, twenty feet, maybe thirty, and I want to get closer to you . . . Why do I want to get closer if you're dead and I know it's you? I mean, there's nothing else to figure out then, is there?

REMZI: Because . . . I'm your friend, and you'd rather be the one to report my death than some jerk who doesn't know I exist.

CRAVER: Right. So here I go.

REMZI: Get on your mark.

CRAVER: Get set.

REMZI: Go!

CRAVER *(Copies Remzi's walk, but not quite as well)*: That didn't feel right.

REMZI: Your shoulders are too tight. Loosen up. See it before you, my body up ahead.

CRAVER: How did you die?

REMZI: This Iraqi we shot dead isn't dead. He's almost dead, but he's got just enough strength to fire one more time. When I turn my back—bang!—he shoots me.

CRAVER: Where?

REMZI: In the neck.

CRAVER: Got it.

REMZI: So there I am in the sand, a bullet in my neck.

CRAVER: And it's hot. A fucking hot day, and the sun is pissing a hole through my fucking hot head.

REMZI: Exactly. And I'm dead.

CRAVER: But I'm alive.

REMZI: And glad to be that way.

CRAVER: But you were my buddy. We were friends . . . just friends or good friends?

REMZI: Pretty good friends.

CRAVER: Pretty good friends.

REMZI: Right. And now you have to cross the distance between us.

CRAVER: About thirty-five feet.

REMZI: And then you do it. The walk. The shortest and most important walk of your life. And you have to believe you can do it, with dignity in your stride, power and, above all, a quiet sense of pride.

CRAVER: I'm ready.

REMZI: So am I.

(They link arms and walk in unison.)

SCENE FOUR

Fairouz is also practicing a walk, in a similar, but different, motel room.

FAIROUZ: Keep your chin in the air at all times. As though your chin has a string attached to it that is pulling it up.

(Lue Ming appears and walks in unison behind her. Fairouz doesn't notice her.)

No, a hook is better, a hook in your chin like a fish. Beauty lesson number seven: walking with grace.

LUE MING: It's all a matter of balance.

FAIROUZ *(Seeing Lue Ming)*: Not you again. I told you I don't know Calley.

LUE MING: Your friend Craver said you might know.

FAIROUZ: He's not my friend.

LUE MING: Are we still in Kentucky?

FAIROUZ: Yes.

LUE MING: American boys are so interesting! Full of secrets. All roads lead through him. My road. Your road. Dominoes in the dark.

FAIROUZ: Have you tried the other motel, across the street?

LUE MING: Calley's a soldier. A lieutenant. Of Charlie Company. A unit of the Americal Division's 11th Light Infantry Brigade. Very light. So light some thought he was an angel when he came home.

FAIROUZ: How do the women walk in your country?

LUE MING: Not as upright as we'd like. Hunched over a bit most of the time.

FAIROUZ: Show me.

LUE MING (*Shows her*): The lower a body is to the ground, the less of a target.

FAIROUZ: I can't move without making noise. Clump, clump, clump. My mother always wanted me to walk with what she calls "presence." When I was in the fourth grade I had to walk home from school.

LUE MING: Show me. How you walked home from school.

FAIROUZ: It was only three blocks. (*She walks again*)

LUE MING: Yes. I think I remember it now.

(*Now they both practice their walks.*)

FAIROUZ: There were some older children in the seventh grade. Two boys and a girl. They stopped me on the sidewalk. They wanted me to take off my shoes.

LUE MING: You should meet my mother; she has one foot.

FAIROUZ: To see the toes.

LUE MING: She stepped on a mine on her way for a piss.

FAIROUZ: Not the toes, but the hooves. They said I had hooves for toes. Devil's feet.

LUE MING: It was March 16, 1968.

FAIROUZ: Devil's feet.

LUE MING: Why, you weren't even born then, were you?

FAIROUZ (*Chants*): Devil's feet. Devil's feet.

LUE MING: Devil's feet?

FAIROUZ: Yes. *(Chants)* Fairouz has devil's feet.

LUE MING *(Chants)*: Dirty Arab devil, you go home.

FAIROUZ *(Chants)*: Dirty Arab devil, you go home

LUE MING: Get her shoe. Pull off her shoe.

FAIROUZ: Hold her down and pull off her shoe!

FAIROUZ AND LUE MING *(Chant)*: Dirty Arab, dirty Arab, you go home!

FAIROUZ: Remzi! *(Beat)* Remzi.

LUE MING: Arab! Slope! Dink!

FAIROUZ: No. They didn't call me that: slope.

LUE MING: Thought I'd throw it in. Slope. Dink. Gook.

FAIROUZ: "Gook" I've heard of.

LUE MING: The Philippines war. It was used again for Korea, and then recycled for Vietnam. How did they get your shoe off?

FAIROUZ: I can't remember. I can figure the distance from right here, where we're standing, to the center of the earth, but I can't remember just how the shoe came off.

LUE MING: But it did come off? And when they saw you didn't have devil's feet did they let you be their friend?

FAIROUZ: A happy ending? It was for them. I think they were scared of me. Afterwards, they weren't.

LUE MING: And now you have a devil's foot?

FAIROUZ: It does look a bit like a hoof now. The bone's curved wrong. Do you know what's happened to my brother?

LUE MING: I think we met each other once, but we were headed in different directions.

FAIROUZ: My God, where? Where did you see him?

LUE MING: I don't know anymore. We passed each other in a rather bad storm, and he reached out and touched my sleeve. Then he was gone.

FAIROUZ: Thank God. He's alive.

LUE MING: I didn't say that, my dear.

FAIROUZ *(Not listening)*: He's alive!

SCENE FIVE

The past. Remzi and Fairouz are talking. Fairouz is polishing his combat boots.

FAIROUZ: You're becoming a stranger.

REMZI: Look. I'm sorry about the occupation and that you don't feel you have a homeland, but I do. And it's here. Not over there in some never-never land.

FAIROUZ: I hardly recognize you.

REMZI: Iraq invaded a sovereign country. That's against international law.

FAIROUZ: International law? Ha! Your own land is over-run, occupied, slowly eaten up . . .

REMZI *(Mocks)*: Village by village, orchard by orchard. Decades and decades of UN resolutions . . .

FAIROUZ: And no one's ever smacked a Desert Shield on those bastards!

REMZI: There's just no parallel.

FAIROUZ: There's always a parallel. Did Mother ever tell you how she broke her hip before she came to America?

REMZI: She fell down when she was running away from the soldiers . . .

FAIROUZ: No. She was running toward the soldiers.

REMZI: I've heard this so many times it's a sweet little lull-aby that could rock me to sleep. So Mother saved Father and they broke her hip with a rifle butt. Crack, crack. Bone broke. Hobble, hobble for the rest of her life. What do you expect me to do, hobble around for the rest of my life? You're so serious. Open your mouth and laugh for a change. You used to do that, remember? Get out of the house. Throw a party. Go to the Burger King on the corner and order some fries. *(Beat)* You're an American girl. Enjoy it.

FAIROUZ: I'm an Arab woman.

REMZI: You've never even been there.

FAIROUZ: Neither have you!

REMZI: If you walked into our village today, they'd tar and feather you.

FAIROUZ: Fuck you. I'd put on a veil.

REMZI: The veil's not the problem. You haven't been a virgin since you were thirteen.

FAIROUZ: How dare you!

REMZI: I'm sorry.

FAIROUZ: I was at least fourteen!

(They laugh.)

Mother still says to me: "The honor of a girl is like a piece of glass. If it's broken, you can never glue it together again."

REMZI: Why don't you tell her the truth?

FAIROUZ: It's my truth. Not hers. You hardly know her, and she lives five minutes away!

REMZI: I can't talk to her.

FAIROUZ: Learn Arabic.

REMZI: No. She should learn English. She's been here over twenty years.

FAIROUZ: She speaks English. She just won't.

REMZI: You're still doing the shopping for her, aren't you?

(Fairouz doesn't answer.)

You should move out.

FAIROUZ: In the stores, for years, she'd lift me in her arms, and whisper in my ear: "Chubbes."

REMZI: "Chubbes."

FAIROUZ: And I would say: "Bread." "Halib," and I would say: "Milk."

REMZI: "Halib."

FAIROUZ: She's our mother.

REMZI: You were going to be a nurse, a doctor or something. Get your degree. Get a job. I want a quiet life. As an American citizen. That's good enough for me. Beats living in the past.

FAIROUZ: An American citizen. What is that? This government pays for the guns that force us off our land.

REMZI *(Interrupts)*: Allah, spare me! Jesus Christ! It's not my land. I'm not into redrawing maps or being trapped in the minds of crusty grandparents.

FAIROUZ: We're your family.

REMZI: Some family. More like a selection of Mesopotamian ruins.

FAIROUZ: Why don't you learn a little something about—

REMZI: About ruins?

FAIROUZ: The Intifada?

REMZI: What? They're finally letting the women out of their houses to throw stones?

FAIROUZ: We throw stones. We run unions. We go to prison. We get shot.

REMZI: Oh, martyrdom! Why don't you get out of the house and throw a few stones around here! You've got a big mouth, Fairouz, but your world is this small. I'm sick of being a hyphen: the Palestinian, the gap between Arab-American. There's room for me here. Where I have my friends.

FAIROUZ: Ah, yes. Your friends. You tell your friends I was born that way.

REMZI: You're going to blame me that no one wants to marry a girl with a gimpy foot.

FAIROUZ: My foot is deformed, but my cunt works just fine!

REMZI: You have a mouth full of dirt, Sister. What is it you want from me?

FAIROUZ: What I want? *(She speaks some angry lines to him in Arabic)*

REMZI: Gibberish, Fairouz. Save it for the relatives.

(Fairouz speaks another line of Arabic to him.)

I'm not a refugee. It's always somewhere else with you, always once removed. I am not scattered.

FAIROUZ: If I could go to war with you, I'd shoot my enemies first, then I'd shoot the ones who made them my enemies.

REMZI: Enemies. Always the enemies.

FAIROUZ: There are three kinds of people. Those who kill. Those who die. And those who watch. Which one are you, Remzi? Which one are you? I know. I know which one you are, don't I?

REMZI: Go to hell. I was a kid. A child. You'll never let it go, will you?

FAIROUZ: I just don't want you to join up without knowing that sometimes I still hate you.

SCENE SIX

The Saudi desert in the past. Remzi and Craver are doing jumping jacks. Boxler enters.

BOXLER: That's enough. Take a rest.

REMZI AND CRAVER: Yes, Lieutenant.

BOXLER: At ease.

CRAVER: Thank you, sir.

BOXLER: No "sirs" and "thank yous." We're equal when I say at ease. Where are you girls from? Haven't seen you around.

CRAVER: Echo Company A-2-3, sir.

REMZI: Those fatigues you have on. I don't think I've seen those kind before.

BOXLER: Special Forces.

CRAVER: I can smell the mothballs.

BOXLER: I like a sense of humor. *(To Remzi)* Where are you from, babe?

REMZI: The States.

BOXLER: I mean, where are your parents from?

REMZI: My father died when I was just a kid. My mother never told me where she was from.

BOXLER: Now that's not nice . . . Parents owe the knowledge of their roots to their sons. A root must know its origins. You, my son, are a root living in the dark without a compass, and you have no idea what kind of tree is going to sprout forth from your skull. I'd say, American Indian, maybe. No. Could be your mommy is from Pakistan. Then again, could be South of the Border. It's hard to tell these days.

REMZI: Yes. It is.

BOXLER: But never mind. We're all family here, aren't we?

CRAVER: Do you know about the Sad Eyes, sir?

BOXLER: Boxler's my name. And of course I know about the Sad Eyes. I've seen them on the faces of many a soldier who comes back without his buddy at his side.

CRAVER: The weapon. Sad Eyes is a weapon.

BOXLER: That's what I love about war. The creativity of it. *(Beat)* Shall we?

CRAVER AND REMZI: Ready, sir.

(As Boxler speaks, he takes out a blindfold and puts it on. He gets to his knees.)

BOXLER: Now, let's say you have a situation. A delicate situation. You've taken an Iraqi prisoner. He has a secret, and you need to get this secret without breaking international law, the Geneva Constrictions, etc. Prisoners must be treated humanely. Please tie my hands behind my back.

(No response.)

Do as I tell you. Use your handkerchief.

(Remzi ties Boxler's wrists.)

All right. Interrogate me.

(Neither Craver nor Remzi responds.)

Bang, crash! Rat-tat-tat-tat! Howl! There are bullets flying all around you. This camel jockey knows where the reserve forces are located, and if they aren't destroyed you and your buddies are minced meat. *(Beat)* Interrogate me!

REMZI: What's your name? I said: what's your name? He won't talk, Craver. What do we do?

BOXLER: Be firm.

CRAVER: Tell us your name, shit bag, and we'll go easy on you.

(No response from Boxler.)

Give him a push.

BOXLER: That's an idea. Go on.

(Remzi pushes him, but not hard.)

That's a start.

(Craver does so, but harder.)

You two Barbies, you think just because you push me around a little I'm going to spill my guts? You're nothing but piss-ants with one hand tied behind your back.

(Craver shoves him, and he falls over.)

REMZI: One hand tied behind our backs?

(He strikes Boxler. Craver strikes him, too.)

BOXLER: You two dandelions aren't getting anywhere. Hey, baby doll, yeah you, the one with the dark skin, are you a half-breed?

REMZI: No. But you are. *(He kicks Boxler in the stomach)* You fucking sandnigger.

BOXLER: From what I can see of your face, you're a sand-nigger yourself.

(Remzi kicks Boxler again.)

What a farce: a sandnigger killing sandniggers.

(Remzi keeps kicking until Boxler lies still. Some moments of silence.)

REMZI: Sir? Did I hurt you, sir?

(Boxler doesn't move.)

CRAVER: Oh shit.

(Remzi and Craver free Boxler's wrists and uncover his eyes. Boxler springs to his feet, unharmed.)

BOXLER *(To Remzi)*: That was good. For a first time.

(Suddenly he punches Remzi in the stomach. He collapses.)

Pity is what you leave behind you, son, back home, tucked under your pillow with your teddy bear and girlie magazine. Now get to your feet, you stinking Arab.

(Remzi starts to get up, but Boxler pushes him over with his foot. Remzi attacks Boxler; Boxler restrains him.)

That's it. That's it. Now hold on to it! Hold on to that anger. Stoke it. Cuddle it, and when the right moment comes take aim and let it fly. A soldier without anger is a dead soldier.

CRAVER: What about me, sir?

BOXLER: What about you?

CRAVER: How do I get that anger when I need it?

BOXLER: Where are you from?

CRAVER: Town of Hazard. Kentucky. Sir.

BOXLER: Let me see your teeth? Hmmm. Trash, are you?

CRAVER: Yes, sir.

BOXLER: Joined up because you couldn't get a job.

CRAVER: Yes, sir.

BOXLER: Father dead?

CRAVER: Yes, sir. The mines, sir.

BOXLER: Burned to a crisp in an explosion?

CRAVER: Suffocated. His lungs, sir.

BOXLER: A pity you weren't with him when he died.

CRAVER: It was like something sawing through wood. His breathing, sir. I couldn't stand to hear it. But the Company wouldn't let him retire. He kept working. For the money, sir. We had to tie him into his chair to keep him at home.

BOXLER: Shat right there in his chair, did he? And you let your mother clean up his mess. Never offered her a hand. Tsk, tsk. Went out with your friends and got drunk on Pabst Blue Ribbon. But one night you came home early, and he was still sitting there, tied to his chair. Your mother was passed out on the couch.

REMZI: Sir, this is ridicu—

BOXLER (*Interrupts*): Yes, it is, isn't it? Because Craver then leaned over and said into his father's ear: "I'm sorry, Dad. I am so sorry." And do you know, Remzi, just what his father did to show his acceptance and respect for his prodigal son? He pissed. Right then and there. Pissed where he sat, and Craver didn't even know it until he looked down and saw he was standing in it. The piss soaked through his shoes, right into his socks.

CRAVER: When he went into the mines he was my father. When he came back out, he was something else. I couldn't love something else.

BOXLER: And you were out fucking some pretty little box in the back of his Ford pickup truck the night he drew his last, painful breath. You shot your come the moment his heart stopped.

REMZI (*To Craver*): Don't listen to him, Craver.

CRAVER: That's where you're wrong. I didn't come. I never came.

BOXLER: And why not? (*Beat*) What was the problem? Are you a funny little boy, one of those ha-ha little boys?

CRAVER: What are you going to do about it? Report me? I'll break your fucking neck.

REMZI: Let's get out of here, Crave.

(Craver shoves Remzi away.)

BOXLER *(To Craver)*: My, my. I can call your father a bro-
ken-down, coal-shitting, piss-poor excuse for the
American dream and you don't bat an eye, but when
I detect that you're a bit on the queer side . . .

REMZI: Craver?

*(Craver suddenly turns on Remzi. They push each other.
Craver knocks Remzi down and begins to choke Remzi.)*

Craver! Fuck! Craver!

BOXLER *(Whispers)*: Faggot. Shit-fucker.

REMZI: Stop it! Get off of me.

BOXLER: Sodomite. Fairy. *(Beat)* Feel it? Feel it inside you,
Mr. Perry? Now grab hold of it.

(Boxler finally pulls Craver off of Remzi.)

Catch it. Hold it like a bullet between your teeth.
And when the right moment comes, when you've
spotted your enemy, let it rip, my son. Let it rip. But
remember, aim is everything and unbridled anger is
of no use to you, it's like crude oil: worthless without
refinement. But you've got to know where to direct
it. Out there, my friend. Out there, in Indian territory,
beyond the sand dunes where the camels lie in wait.
Think of them as culprits in the death of your father.
If the ragheads hadn't shot our buffalo, we could
have swapped them for their camels, and then we
wouldn't have needed the coal mines to begin with,
and your father would have worked in an auto factory,
and he'd still be alive today.

CRAVER: That's not how it happened. *(Beat)* Sir.

BOXLER: You can give his death any reason you want.
Facts are not infallible. They are there to be inter-
preted in a way that's useful to you. Why, your presi-

dent does it, and he is no smarter than you. President Johnson says—

REMZI: President Bush.

BOXLER: Whatever the hell his name is, he said: "Our troops . . . will not be asked to fight with one hand tied behind their back." As you did in Vietnam. *(Begins to laugh)* Do you know how many tons of bombs were dropping on Vietnam? Four million six hundred thousand. It's awesome, isn't it?

REMZI: This is a different war, sir.

BOXLER: The tonnage dropped by the Allies in World War II was only three million. Now, my hands won't be tied behind my back when we go into Panama City. Operation Just Because, it will be called.

CRAVER: It was called Operation Just Cause. Just Cause.

REMZI: That was in '89. In December.

BOXLER: I'll be driving a tank there. They promised me I could drive a tank this time. The only nuisance is that crunching sound under my treads. A crunching sound, like this. *(Makes the sound)* Civilians have so little consideration.

CRAVER: You were never in Panama, sir.

REMZI: There were no civilian deaths to speak of.

BOXLER: But not to speak of, I'd say about three thousand. Now, when we went into the barrios of Grenada . . .

REMZI: Just where haven't you been, sir?

CRAVER: To hell. He hasn't been to hell, but he's on his way there.

BOXLER: Oh, there you're wrong. I stood outside the gates for a very long time. In rain and snow, fire and brimstone, but they wouldn't let me in. I don't know why they won't let me in.

(We hear Lue Ming's voice offstage calling:)

LUE MING: Fairouz! Fairouz!

BOXLER: Now we're ready for lesson two. How to handle women in combat.

(*Lue Ming calls: "Where are you?" in Vietnamese.*)

Hear it?

(*Remzi and Craver do not hear Lue Ming's voice. Boxler begins to slink away.*)

Can't you hear it? Poor hound. She's still after me. Still sniffing at my tracks.

FAIROUZ (*Offstage, calling*): Remzi! Remzi!

SCENE SEVEN

Fairouz is blindfolded. She moves about the dark motel room carrying small paper lanterns. Throughout the scene Lue Ming moves about, taking up different positions in relation to Fairouz—here, now there—sometimes surprising Fairouz with her voice. Just prior to Fairouz speaking, Lue Ming begins to sing a Vietnamese lullaby.

FAIROUZ: I can see through it anyway.

LUE MING: This is how we must operate: able to pinpoint the enemy even though we are almost blind. Night vision. Strategy where there should be none.

FAIROUZ: Like a bat?

LUE MING: If you like. Now. Think past the obstacles, that which hides your objective. Map out the lie of the land as you remember it and have never seen it.

FAIROUZ: And forget the motel carpet?

LUE MING: Hands up! Don't you know there's a war on? Keep your head. Look for what is not there.

FAIROUZ: Imagine the land I can't see.

LUE MING: Once, an American soldier called himself my brother.

FAIROUZ: Sounds like a friendly war.

LUE MING: In the first years the soldiers gave us toffee and boiled sweets.

FAIROUZ: By the rice paddies? In Saigon?

LUE MING: Tu Cung, actually. By the coast. *(Beat)* Rush always gave me gum, Juicy Fruit gum. He called me his little sis. Once he gave me a ribbon to put in my hair. I had very long hair, beautiful thick hair that I wore in a braid down my back. *(Beat)* But one day Rush didn't bring any gum and he took out his knife and cut off my braid.

FAIROUZ: Was it a slow knife? Serrated are slow.

LUE MING: Oh no, it was a quick knife, a Rush knife, and he strapped my hair to the back of his helmet. His friends laughed and laughed. Rush looked so very silly with his camouflage helmet on and this long, black braid hanging down his back.

FAIROUZ: It was only hair.

LUE MING: I'd be careful if I were blindfolded.

FAIROUZ: I like it. I could go anywhere in the world right now, and to do it I wouldn't have to lift a finger.

LUE MING: Or a foot.

FAIROUZ: I'm four hundred and thirty miles from home. This is the first time I've been outside of Atlanta. The first time I've flown in a plane.

LUE MING: I despise flying. It puts my hair in a tangle.

FAIROUZ: Could you get a message to Remzi?

LUE MING: Your brother's not accepting messages these days.

FAIROUZ: I'm sorry, but I don't have time for your lost braid. What's done is done. My brother is alive, and we must think about the living and wait for my brother to send word. *(Beat)* I'm sick of waiting. And I can't stop waiting.

LUE MING: Those who wait, burn.

SCENE EIGHT

Fairouz and Remzi. The past.

FAIROUZ: Did you get the vaccines you needed?

REMZI: Yesterday.

FAIROUZ: Then everything's in order?

REMZI: All set to leave. The big adventure awaits me. Little brother goes to war.

FAIROUZ: When we were small, the children from our school would come to our house to have a look at my funny foot. You made them pay a dime each time they had a look.

REMZI: I split the profit with you, fifty-fifty.

FAIROUZ: It was my foot.

REMZI: It was my idea.

FAIROUZ: I used to lie awake at night, for years, dreaming of ways to kill you. I thought: if I kill him, there will be no one to hate. I was investing my hatred in you. It was a long-term investment. Really, I think you owe me some thanks.

REMZI: For hating me?

FAIROUZ: Yes. Then you wouldn't be surprised by the hate of the world.

CRAVER *(Offstage)*: Remzi! Remzi!

(Craver, offstage and "somewhere else," calls Remzi's name, and Remzi exits. Lue Ming enters.)

FAIROUZ: Listen to me. You don't have the right balance. I do. You see, I love you, but I hate you too. I have to. Tightly, tightly. As though at any moment either of us could slip off this earth. Are you listening to me?

LUE MING *(Answering as Remzi)*: Yes, I am, Fairouz. I'm listening.

FAIROUZ: Go say good-bye to Mother. She's in her room, and she won't come out. She says they'll kill you. Just like they killed Father.

LUE MING (*As Remzi*): That was an accident, and you know it. He fell onto the lily pads and into the pond and drowned.

FAIROUZ: His face was messed up. As though he'd been hit many times.

LUE MING (*As Remzi*): Water can do that to a face.

FAIROUZ: I've told Mother that, Remzi. Over and over I've told her that it's the Iraqis you're going off to fight, but she keeps saying (*Speaks in Arabic and then translates*) "They'll kill him. The Yankees will kill him." Silly old woman. She's all mixed up.

SCENE NINE

A military camp in Saudi Arabia, in the past. Remzi is sitting alone and reciting.

REMZI: Tabun. Mawid. Zbib, trab ahmar, dibs.

(*Craver enters. He listens to Remzi a while.*)

Maya, zir, foron.

CRAVER: Sounds like you had a good leave.

REMZI: Zbib, trab ahmar, dibs. Raisins. Red soil. Molasses.

CRAVER: Really? How amazing . . .

REMZI: I went to visit my father's village. On the western side of the Hebron Mountains. Al-Dawayima. According to my mother, there were five hundred and fifty-nine houses there.

CRAVER: I didn't know you were back.

REMZI: Tall grasses, wildflowers, scrubs. That's all that's there now. Dozers have flattened the houses.

CRAVER: When did you get back?

REMZI: I went to the refugee camp nearby, but I couldn't speak the language. I could point, though.

CRAVER: We went on alert a couple of times. Lucky we didn't start without you.

REMZI: A Palestinian farmer explained to me that there are three varieties of fig suitable for preserving—asmar, ashqar, abiyad. The black fig, the blond and the white. Craver. I was a tourist there. An outsider.

CRAVER: You're a Palestinian.

REMZI: One old woman took me in for coffee, because I didn't know anyone and had nowhere to go. She called me "Yankee Palestina." These people lose their homes. They live in poverty, and they're the enemies of the world. *(Throws Craver a bag of figs)* I brought that for you.

CRAVER: Nice you remembered I existed. I think of the three, I'm the white fig variety. How do you say it?

REMZI: Abiyad.

CRAVER: Yeah. Abiyad. *(Tastes a fig)* These are nasty.

REMZI: You're not eating them right. You don't just plug them in your mouth like a wad of chewing tobacco. You've got to eat them with a sense of purpose. *(Eats one)* With a sense of grace.

(Craver picks out another one.)

CRAVER: With a quiet sense of pride?

REMZI: Exactly.

(Craver eats it.)

CRAVER: Nastier than the first one.

REMZI: No. Look. You're gobbling.

CRAVER: Why didn't you buy me a souvenir, like a nice little prayer rug?

REMZI: Eating is like walking. My sister taught me that. There's a balance involved. You have to eat the fig gently. As though it were made of the finest paper. *(Puts a fig in his own hand)* Look. I'll put the fig in my hand, and, without touching my hand, you pick it up. Gently.

(Craver starts to use his fingers, Remzi stops his hand.)

With your mouth. *(Beat)* Go on. See if you can do it.

(Craver leans down to Remzi's open hand and very carefully and very slowly lifts the fig from Remzi's hand. Craver holds the fig between his lips.)

Now take it into your mouth. Slowly.

(Remzi helps the fig inside Craver's mouth.)

Slowly. There . . . Well. How does it taste now?

CRAVER *(After some moments of silence)*: Did you take a lot of pictures?

REMZI: On the streets of Atlanta I've been called every name you can think of: pimp, terrorist, half-nigger, mongrel, spic, wop, even Jew-bastard. And to these people in this camp it didn't matter a damn that I was some kind of a mix. Some kind of a something else, born someplace in a somewhere else than my face said. Or something like that. Do you know what I mean?

CRAVER: Haven't any idea.

REMZI: So. What's on for tomorrow?

CRAVER: Drills. Red Alert. Stop. Go. Stop. Go.

REMZI: Every day it's any day now.

CRAVER: I just want it to start.

SCENE TEN

Lue Ming and Fairouz rehearsing for Fairouz's travels. Lue Ming is wearing Remzi's boots.

LUE MING: Your shoulders are too tight. That's what they look for. Tight shoulders, pinched faces.

FAIROUZ: My face isn't pinched.

LUE MING: If you're going to find your brother, you have to cross borders. But not with sweat on your upper lip. Try it again. Not a care in the world. Right at home. *(Assumes the posture of an immigration officer)* Passport? Hmmm. North American?

FAIROUZ: Yes, sir.

LUE MING: Tourist?

FAIROUZ: Yes.

LUE MING: How long? How long have you been a tourist?

FAIROUZ: Most of my life, sir.

LUE MING *(Speaks as herself)*: Don't be perverse. *(Speaks as officer)* First time out of the United States?

FAIROUZ: Yes.

LUE MING: Relatives here?

FAIROUZ: Yes. I mean, no. I mean I do, but they—

LUE MING *(Interrupts)*: Just what do you mean, Miss . . . Saboura?

FAIROUZ: My parents were born here.

LUE MING: Here? Born here?

FAIROUZ: Yes.

LUE MING: You mean right where I'm standing? *(She lifts her feet and looks under them)*

FAIROUZ *(Looks at Lue Ming's boots)*: Yes. *(Beat)* Where did you get those?

LUE MING: Do you think they're stuck to my shoes?

FAIROUZ: I know those boots. What?

LUE MING: Your parents. Do you think they're stuck to my shoes?

FAIROUZ: I don't understand.

LUE MING: I assure you it was an accident. One minute they're alive, and, well, the next minute they're under my shoes.

FAIROUZ: My brother is lost.

LUE MING: Lucky man.

FAIROUZ: I'm Palestin—

LUE MING: Don't say it! Don't say it! It's like a bee that flies into my ear and fornicates there.

FAIROUZ: Don't you think you're overdoing it?

LUE MING: You must be prepared for them to throw anything at you. *(Beat)* Purpose of your visit?

FAIROUZ: Your ruins.

LUE MING: Yes. Lots of ruins. I like ruins. Your voice reminds me of one. Are you sad? Are you missing someone close to your heart? Pull up your shirt. I don't have all day.

(Fairouz raises her shirt.)

Education?

FAIROUZ: Doctor. I haven't finished the degree.

LUE MING: Ah, a person who quits?

FAIROUZ: I plan to go back.

LUE MING: You can't go back to Al-Dawayima. There's no place to go back to. *(Beat)* So you're Arab?

FAIROUZ: American.

LUE MING: American?

FAIROUZ: Arab.

LUE MING: Make up your mind!

FAIROUZ: I'm a Palestinian-Arab-American. From Atlanta. Sir.

SCENE ELEVEN

Fairouz enters Craver's motel room.

FAIROUZ: Did he talk to you about his visit to the Territories?

CRAVER: Not a word.

FAIROUZ: He never likes to learn anything new.

CRAVER: Ever heard of the Beehive? It's the ultimate concept in improved fragmentation. It spins at high velocity, spitting out eighty-eight hundred fléchettes.

FAIROUZ: Fléchettes?

CRAVER: Tiny darts with razor-sharp edges capable of causing deep wounds.

FAIROUZ: What is a deep wound? How deep exactly?

CRAVER: To the bone. You should leave now.

FAIROUZ: I got a letter from the army.

CRAVER: Know the DU penetrator? Cigar-shaped, armor-piercing bullets. The core of the bullet is made from radioactive nuclear waste.

FAIROUZ: They say he's missing.

CRAVER: When fired, the DU's uranium core bursts into flame. Ever had forty tons of depleted uranium dumped in your backyard?

FAIROUZ: Not in action, just missing.

CRAVER: Things get lost. People—

FAIROUZ: Get lost. But why not you? Why didn't you get lost?

CRAVER: Because I fell in love. In our bunkers at night, Remzi used to read the names out loud to us, and it calmed us down. He must have read that weapons manual a hundred times. All those ways to kill the human body. Lullabies. It was like . . . they were always the same and always there, and when we said them to ourselves there was nothing else like it: Fishbeds, Floggers and Fulcrums. Stingers, Frogs, Silkworms, Vulcans, Beehives and Bouncing Bettys.

FAIROUZ: Did you love my brother?

CRAVER: I can't remember.

FAIROUZ: But you can. You will. Remember!

CRAVER: I remember . . . what my first . . . favorite was: the B-52, the Buff. B-U-F-F. The Big Ugly Fat Fellow, it can carry up to sixty thousand pounds of bombs and cruise missiles.

FAIROUZ: All right. Let's try something more simple.

CRAVER: It has survived in front-line service for three generations.

FAIROUZ: Not about numbers, but about flesh.

CRAVER: It has an engine thrust of thirteen thousand seven hundred and fifty pounds and a maximum speed of five hundred and ninety-five miles per hour. It's slow but it's bad.

FAIROUZ: If you could give his flesh a velocity?

CRAVER: The Buffs, the B-52s, won the Gulf War. Not the smarts. Not the smarts.

FAIROUZ: Or a number, what would it be?

CRAVER: Ninety-three percent of the bombs dropped were free-falls from the bellies of Fat Fellows.

FAIROUZ: If you could give his flesh a number?

CRAVER: Only seven percent were guided, and, of these half-wits, forty percent missed their targets.

FAIROUZ: A number that's short of infinity? Was that your desire for him?

CRAVER: Forty . . . forty-five percent of the smarts . . . they missed . . .

FAIROUZ: Something short of infinity?

CRAVER: They missed their targets.

FAIROUZ: Did you or did you not fuck him?

CRAVER: That *(Beat)* is a lot of missed targets.

FAIROUZ: OK: Mr. White Trash likes Arab ass, yes? Is it good? Is it sweet like white ass? Do you find it exotic?

CRAVER: I'm not that kind of a soldier.

FAIROUZ: He could be a bastard, my brother. But if you fucked him and then hurt him in any way, I'll tear your heart out.

CRAVER: Remzi never said he had a sister with a limp. His sister, he said she walked like a princess.

FAIROUZ: Was he gentle with you? Sometimes when we were children he would soak my foot in a bowl of warm water, with lemon and orange rinds. He would blow on my toes to dry them. He thought if he cared for my foot, day by day, and loved it, that somehow it would get better. *(Beat)* What was it like to kiss him?

CRAVER: After the Buffs it was the GR. MK-1 Jaguar with two Rolls-Royce Adour MK-102 turbofans. A fuselage pylon and four wing pylons can carry up to ten thousand pounds of armaments . . .

(Remzi now "appears." Fairouz moves away and watches, as though watching Craver's memory.)

REMZI: The Jag can carry a mix of cannons, smarts and gravity bombs. And get this: maximum speed: Mach 1.1.

CRAVER: Then there's the brain of the electronic warfare central nervous system: the E-3 Sentry, Boeing.

REMZI: If there ever was an indispensable weapon, it is the E-3 AWACS, capable of directing UN forces with tremendous accuracy. Improvements include:

CRAVER: A better Have Quick radar jamming system and an upgraded JTIDS. Able to manage hundreds of warplanes airborne at any given moment.

REMZI: At any given moment?

CRAVER: Any given moment.

REMZI: How about now?

CRAVER: We could go to jail. It's illegal in the army.

REMZI: So are white phosphorous howitzer shells. So are fuel-air explosives.

CRAVER: We don't decide what gets dropped.

REMZI: Would you kiss me if I were dead?

CRAVER: Why would I kiss you if you were dead?

REMZI: Would you kiss me if I were alive?

CRAVER: I had a thing for the Sentry jet, but how long can love last, after the first kiss, after the second, still around after the third? I dumped the Sentry jet and went on to the Wild Weasel, F-4G. Like a loyal old firehorse, the Weasel was back in action.

REMZI: Have you ever touched the underbelly of a recon plane? Two General Electric J79-15 turbojets.

CRAVER: If you run your hand along its flank, just over the hip, to the rear end, it will go wet. Not damp but I mean wet.

REMZI: Have you ever run your face over the wing of an A-6 Intruder, or opened your mouth onto the tail of a AV-8B Harrier II? It's not steel you taste. It's not metal.

CRAVER: Ever had a Phoenix missile at the tip of your tongue? Nine hundred and eighty-five pounds of power, at launch.

(Craver moves to kiss Remzi, but at the last moment Remzi moves away.)

FAIROUZ: Is that how you kissed him?

CRAVER: I kissed a girl for the first time when I was twelve. She had a mouth full of peanut butter and jelly and that's what I got. Have you ever seen an airplane take off vertically? That's what I was when I kissed Remzi, like the AV-8B Harrier II, straight up into the air, no runway, no horizontal run, but VTO, vertical takeoff.

FAIROUZ: Why don't you say it?

CRAVER: One Rolls-Royce turbojet going up, engine thrust twenty-one thousand five hundred pounds maximum speed.

FAIROUZ: Please. Just say it.

CRAVER: Forever. Remzi said to me the first time he kissed me: "What are you now, Craver Perry? A White Trash River Boy who kisses Arabs and likes it?" I said, "I'm a White Trash, River Boy, Arab-kissing Faggot." And the rest, as they say, is history. *(Beat)* Remzi was, as they say, history too.

FAIROUZ: Remzi is dead, isn't he?

CRAVER: I said he was history. That's something else.

FAIROUZ: How can this be funny to you?

CRAVER: If you saw your brother lying dead in the sand, just what would you say to him? Imagine it. There he is. Dead on the sand. A bullet in his neck.

FAIROUZ: Bled to death?

CRAVER: Maybe. What would you do?

(Fairouz touches his face.)

Like that? Would you touch Remzi like that? What if he didn't have a face? What if his face were gone too?

(She kisses Craver on the cheek.)

That would take a lot of guts if he didn't have a face.

FAIROUZ: What was it for? You're of no use to me. Just a dead brother now. Zero. No more Remzi to hate. No more Remzi . . .

CRAVER: . . . to love. That's right. Do you think we're doing it too, falling in love?

(Fairouz moves away from Craver.)

FAIROUZ: Would Remzi like that? *(Beat)* Do you like to watch or do you like to kill? You haven't tried dying yet, have you? Perhaps you should.

CRAVER: There's nothing wrong with your foot.

FAIROUZ: You're kind. I see why Remzi was so attached to you.

(Remzi enters, unobserved by either of them.)

My brother was the kind that watched. Is he the other kind now, Mr. Perry? *(Beat)* I think I'm going to scream.

(Craver now sees Remzi and backs away, watching the two of them, as though he is seeing them both in the past. Remzi holds her foot.)

REMZI *(Talking to her gently)*: Just once more.

FAIROUZ: I can't. I can't

REMZI: You've got to do it or you'll never walk right. Just once more.

FAIROUZ: Just once more. Only once more. Will it be better then?

REMZI: Soon. It will be better soon.

(Remzi twists her foot, and she lets out a sound of pain that is part scream and part the low, deep sound of a horn.)

ACT II

SCENE ONE

Lue Ming appears, out of place and time. She summons up the Gulf War: the deafening sound of jets, bombs, guns. The war sounds continue through the following invocation.

LUE MING: My sweet. My love. Come out from your hiding. Oh, my little angel, my tropical fish. Swim to me through the corridors of air. I am waiting for you. Come home. Come home.

(The war sounds stop.)

Yes. Yes. It's you.

(Boxler appears.)

It is always, only you, could ever be you.

BOXLER: Boxler.

LUE MING: Is that it now, "Boxler"?

BOXLER: I have nothing to say to you.

LUE MING: You're looking so well. So robust. So alive. And happy?

BOXLER: When I'm training my girls.

LUE MING: And what do you teach them?

BOXLER: Are you enjoying your visit?

LUE MING: Some of your cities make me feel right at home. Burned out, bodies in the street, the troops restoring order. They're so much like Vietnam.

BOXLER: You're Vietcong, aren't you?

LUE MING: I hear your record sold over two hundred thousand copies. You're a pop star.

BOXLER: That was thirty . . . twenty-five . . .

LUE MING: Twenty-one years ago. Just how much time did you get?

BOXLER: I got labor for life, but three days later I was out of the stockade, courtesy of President Nick. Then I got thirty-five months in my bachelor pad at Fort Benning with my dog, my mynah bird and my tank full of tropical fish.

LUE MING: Could you sing it for me? That song? *(Sings the following to the tune of "The Battle Hymn of the Republic":)*

My name is Rusty Calley
I'm a soldier of this land!

BOXLER: I'm a hero, you know. I'm a hero, and you're a dead gook.

LUE MING: Don't try to sweet-talk me. It won't work.

BOXLER: They took care of me. Friends in high places. I have a jewelry store and a Mercedes. I have a lot to be grateful for.

LUE MING: Have you missed me terribly?

BOXLER: I'm sorry, but I can't place you.

LUE MING: Take a look at my face, closely.

BOXLER: Nope.

LUE MING: You'll remember the walk. There is no one in the world who walks like Lue Ming. *(She walks)*

BOXLER: Sorry.

LUE MING: How is it I can remember you and you can't remember me?

BOXLER: What's done is done.

LUE MING: And what's done is often done again and done again.

SCENE TWO

Remzi and Craver are watching the bombs dropping over Baghdad from a long distance. We hear the muffled thuds of the bombs and see beautiful awe-inspiring flashes of light far off.

REMZI: One, two. And there. Three. Look at it. Cotton candy. Carnival. Dancing. Craver. You're missing it. That one! *(Beat)* "And all the king's horses and all the king's men . . ."

CRAVER: "Couldn't put Humpty together again."

(An even bigger flash of lights. Craver joins him. They both watch.)

REMZI: Do you think he really wanted to be whole again?

CRAVER: Who?

REMZI: The egg.

CRAVER: What?

REMZI: Do you think he wanted to be put back together?

CRAVER: How the hell should I know what an egg wants?

REMZI: I should be dead but I'm not.

(They see a tremendous explosion.)

CRAVER *(Sings)*: Happy birthday, Baghdad.

REMZI: I think he was tired of being a good egg.

CRAVER: Make a wish.

REMZI: Yeah. A birthday.

CRAVER: If you sit out in the dark, they light up all around you. Like that. Back in Hazard. Just like that. All over the sky. Fireflies. There—

REMZI: That first time.

CRAVER: And then gone. There—

REMZI: Like. It was like—

CRAVER: And then gone.

REMZI: I was a window, and you put your hand through me.

SCENE THREE

Boxler and Lue Ming.

BOXLER: You're not bad-looking.

LUE MING: I know.

BOXLER: But I could never touch you. I mean, really touch you. I mean I know you are human, but. Well. *(Beat)* I was a child once. Hard to believe, isn't it? I had blocks and crayons, and when it snowed I'd open my mouth to catch the flakes on my tongue. I had a favorite blanket. I liked most to roll the corner of it into a little point and stick it in my ear. Then I'd fall asleep. All the sounds around me were muffled and soft.

LUE MING: My three-year-old daughter had a blanket, made from two scarves my mother sewed together.

BOXLER: I had a father I loved and a mother I loved, and then I went to school.

LUE MING: Show me what you teach the boys. Show me.

BOXLER: My teacher made us sit in a formation, with the whitest faces up front in the first row, then the second and third rows for the olive skins and half-breeds, and the fourth and fifth rows for the dark ones.

LUE MING: Remember: you have a situation. *(Puts on a blindfold)* You've captured a Vietcong, and you need to know the whereabouts of the others. Now be polite. You're an American soldier, and that means something.

BOXLER: Did you know they made bumper stickers with my name on it?

LUE MING: You know who I am.

BOXLER: Shut your squawking, bitch.

　　　(Calls) Hey, you two troopers. Over here on the double.

(Remzi and Craver enter. It seems we're in the desert again.)

Remzi, what's the best way to make a woman talk?

CRAVER: The dozers are clearing the area, sir.

BOXLER: Get on with it. What dozers?

REMZI: We're mopping up.

BOXLER: I said make her talk!

CRAVER: Can you tell us where Saddam's minefields are?

BOXLER: This is Vietnam, son.

REMZI: We're in Iraq, sir.

BOXLER: This is Panama City!

CRAVER: We have the Dragon M-47 assault missile, sir. Couldn't we use that instead?

BOXLER: Duty is face-to-face confession, son. Between two people. You and this prisoner. Well, go on. Take down your pants.

CRAVER: Sir?

BOXLER: Take down your pants. *(To Lue Ming)* Suck him.

LUE MING *(To Craver)*: Haven't we met before?

BOXLER: Suck him, or I'll cut your head off.

(Craver unzips his pants. Lue Ming begins to sing a Vietnamese lullaby.)

Jesus. Can't you even give her something to suck?

CRAVER: It's the singing, sir.

BOXLER: Remzi. Go get her kid. It's in the hut.

REMZI: What hut, sir? We're in the middle of a desert.

BOXLER: Get her fucking kid and bring it here, or I'll cut his dick off.

REMZI: What kid, sir?

BOXLER: What kid? There's always a kid.

LUE MING: The child is right here. In my arms.

(They all look at Lue Ming.)

REMZI: We're moving out. Now, sir.

CRAVER: Remzi.

REMZI: Let's go.

(They exit. Silence.)

LUE MING: I so much prefer it like this. The two of us. Alone.

SCENE FOUR

A U.S. military camp somewhere in the Iraqi desert. Remzi and Craver are stunned and worn out.

REMZI: Ancient Mesopotamia.

> *(Craver begins to whistle to the tune of "Armour Hot Dogs." Then Remzi joins him. They sing in a deadpan voice.)*

CRAVER *(Sings)*: "Hot dogs. Armour hot dogs. What kind of kids eat Armour hot dogs?"

REMZI *(Sings)*: "Fat kids, skinny kids, kids that climb on rocks."

CRAVER *(Sings)*: "Tough kids, sissy kids, even kids with—"

REMZI AND CRAVER *(Sing)*: ". . . chicken pox! Love hot dogs. Armour hot dogs. The dogs kids love to bite."

CRAVER: I always loved that song when I was a kid.

REMZI: It made me feel included.

CRAVER: Yeah.

REMZI: Which kid were you, the fat kid?

CRAVER: The tough kid.

REMZI: Of course.

CRAVER: Some of those fuckers were still moving.

REMZI: Right here, where we're sitting, long ago they gave us the zero and the wheel.

CRAVER: Civilians.

REMZI: Irrigation and organized religion and large-scale trade.

CRAVER: But there are no civilians in Iraq.

REMZI: Laws and cities and schools. *(Beat)* That was in 2000 B.C.

CRAVER: Bad fucking luck.

REMZI: The first poet known in history.

CRAVER: Those pilots took whatever bombs they could get their hands on, even the clusters and five-hundred-pounders.

REMZI: A woman called Enheduanna.

CRAVER: Imagine dropping a five-hundred-pound bomb on a Volkswagen! Every moving thing. Terminated. Thirty fucking miles of scrap metal, scrap meat. All scrapped. *(Lets out a howl that is half celebration and half terror)* And I've never seen guys dig that fast. Forty-nine holes the dozers dug.

REMZI: They were going home. We shot them in the back. There are laws regarding warfare.

CRAVER: You're going to get out of the truck this time.

REMZI: I can't.

CRAVER: Yes you can, and I'll make you.

REMZI: Don't ask me to do it, Craver. I'm warning you.

CRAVER: But I have to. Get out of the truck this time and walk along the road with me. Get out of the truck this time and help me. Help me.

REMZI: No.

CRAVER: Someone has to do it.

REMZI: But not you!

CRAVER: Fuck off.

REMZI: What was it like, you son of a bitch? To carry a man's leg?

CRAVER: We were ordered to pick up—

REMZI *(Interrupts)*: To carry a man's leg when the man is no longer attached?

CRAVER: To pick up the pieces and put them in the holes. The dozers covered the pieces we found with sand.

REMZI: Is that what you think we're doing, burying them?

CRAVER: We buried them.

REMZI: We're covering them up. So no one will ever know. I saw you, Craver. I saw you.

CRAVER: It was like a limb of a tree. No. It was like the branch of a tree. That's how heavy it was. I said to myself: Craver, you're not carrying what you think you're carrying. It's just a piece of tree. For the fire. And you're out in your backyard in Hazard, Kentucky, and he's still alive, my father, and my mother still laughs, and we're having a barbecue. And I can smell the coals.

REMZI: One of the bodies I saw . . . it was very . . . burned. In one of the vans. For a minute I thought. Well. He looked like . . . Maybe it was the sun on my head. I don't know. I put my finger inside his mouth. I wanted to touch him someplace where he wasn't *(Beat)* burned.

CRAVER: Touch me.

REMZI: Every fucking time it tastes different with you. No.

CRAVER: You didn't try and stop it, did you? *(Shouts)* Did you?

(Some moments of silence.)

REMZI: Why are we here *(Beat)* killing Arabs?

CRAVER: For love? Say it's for love. Don't say for oil. Don't say for freedom. Don't say for world power. I'm sick of that. I'm so fucking sick of that. It's true, isn't it? We're here for love. Say it just once. For me.

REMZI: We're here for love.

(They kiss.)

SCENE FIVE

Boxler appears with a black box. Lue Ming stands watching him in the shadows. Boxler speaks to the audience.

BOXLER: Trust me. I'm the man with the box. The Amnesty box. And this time I'm in . . . Iraq. Is that right? *(Beat)* This box you see before you is a very special box. It's a common device we use here within the military, a receptacle in which soldiers can relieve themselves of contraband, no questions asked. Would you like to drop something in it? You can't take those bits and pieces home with you. No, no, no. I've already made the rounds with the other troops. You're not alone. *(Lifts the lid just a bit but then slams it shut)* What distinguishes this particular box is its stench. Now some soldiers are more attached to their souvenirs than others; in one instance, a severed arm was discovered on a military flight leaving the base for Chicago. One might assume that someone somewhere would be disciplined for anatomical trophy-hunting, but no, not this time. Lucky, lucky. Are you listening? I'm ready for hell, but they won't have me and that's where they're wrong. *(Beat)* All that nasty shit, it took place all the time, before I even killed my first one. But they weren't interested then. And then when they were, bingo, there I was. *(Beat)* Yes, I did it. I never denied it.

(Lue Ming steps forward.)

LUE MING: March 16, 1968. Charlie Company . . .

BOXLER: A unit of the Americal Division's 11th Light Infantry Brigade entered—

LUE MING: Attacked.

BOXLER: Attacked an undefended village on the coast of Central Vietnam and took the lives—

LUE MING: Murdered.

BOXLER: And murdered approximately five hundred old men, women and children. The killing took place over four hours. Sexual violations . . .

LUE MING: Rape, sodomy.

BOXLER: Anatomical infractions.

LUE MING: Unimaginable mutilations.

BOXLER: Unimaginable. Yes. By the time I went to trial, public opinion was in my favor. T-shirts, buttons, mugs. One company wanted to put my face on a new cereal.

LUE MING: And my daughter?

BOXLER: It's over now. They say it's over.

LUE MING: The past is never over.

BOXLER: The war is over.

LUE MING: Which one?

BOXLER: Do you have anything you want to put in the box?

LUE MING: Can I take something out?

BOXLER: It's supposed to be a one-way thing.

LUE MING: Give the box to me. Give the box—

BOXLER *(Interrupts)*: I can't do that.

LUE MING: Give the box to me, or I'll hunt you across this desecrated world forever. *(Beat)* You owe me a favor.

(He hands it over to her. She opens the lid and feels about inside. She pulls out her braid.)

It's my braid. My braid!

BOXLER: Can we call it quits?

(Lue Ming looks at him but doesn't respond.)

SCENE SIX

Remzi and Fairouz the night before he leaves for the Mideast. Fairouz is tickling him.

FAIROUZ: I'm going to tickle you until you pee in your pants.

REMZI: Stop it. Get off of me! Stop it!

FAIROUZ: What will the other soldiers say?

(Remzi wrestles her off and now tickles her.)

REMZI: You're so jealous. You can't stand me leaving.

FAIROUZ: Let's meet up in the Territories.

REMZI: You'll have to come out of the house!

FAIROUZ: We could look for the village where we might have been born. We could go exploring, find relatives, take photos and—

REMZI *(Interrupts)*: If I get a leave, I'm going to go somewhere . . . fun. With my buddies. *(Beat)* Hey. But I'll

tell you what. I am going to send you back something very special.

FAIROUZ: Send something for Mother, too.

REMZI: Maybe I'll even fall in love over there and bring
somebody home with me. They do that in wars.
Come back with lovers and wives.

FAIROUZ: If you fall in love, will you let me meet him?

(Some moments of silence.)

REMZI: Now you're going to be punished for your foul
and lecherous tongue!

(He grabs her foot and begins to tickle it.)

FAIROUZ: Not that one, you fool! I can't feel it.

REMZI *(Playfully)*: Oops. Sorry! *(Grabs her other foot and tickles it)*

FAIROUZ: Stop it. Stop it! Now go on or you'll miss your
bus. *(Kisses him on the cheek to shut him up)* Nothing
more. Just go. Go on.

(Remzi exits.)

Get out of here!

*(Lue Ming appears. Fairouz talks to her as though she were
Remzi.)*

No. Wait a minute . . . It doesn't matter now . . . We
were children then. Are you listening to me, Remzi?
I'm thinking of leaving too, you know. Perhaps I'll
make a trip, all on my own. Yes. I might even start a
clinic out there, at the edge of the world. You don't
believe me? Well, you just wait. When I—

LUE MING *(Interrupts)*: Fairouz. I get leave in a few months.
Don't do anything rash. Just wait till I get back.

FAIROUZ: Those who wait, burn. *(Knowing now that it is
Lue Ming)* They won't send home the body.

SCENE SEVEN

Fairouz and Craver are in his motel room.

FAIROUZ: The army won't send home the body.

CRAVER: What's it matter? It's just a body. It's not him.

> *(Split scene: Remzi and Boxler elsewhere on stage. Boxler ties Remzi's hands and blindfolds him. Lue Ming stands watching.)*

FAIROUZ: I want to see his body. It belongs to us.

CRAVER: It. It. Just what the fuck are you talking about? He's gone. I don't want anything to do with the it.

> *(Fairouz's foot hurts her.)*

FAIROUZ: I think I twisted it again.

CRAVER: You should see a doctor. *(Beat)* Let me see.

FAIROUZ: I don't usually show men my foot unless I take my pants off first.

> *(Craver takes a look at her foot.)*

It doesn't smell very good, does it? Remzi used to crush grass, and dandelions, sweet clover, sometimes even the wings of insects, all together in a bowl. He was quite a medic.

LUE MING *(To Remzi)*: Devil's feet, devil's feet, devil's feet.

CRAVER: May I?

FAIROUZ: You want to kiss my foot?

CRAVER: Yes.

REMZI *(Chants with a deadpan voice)*: Fairouz Saboura has devil's feet.

FAIROUZ: Because you want to make it better?

LUE MING *(Chants)*: Dirty Arab devil, you go home!

FAIROUZ: Or because I told you he used to do that?

REMZI *(Chants)*: Dirty Arab devil, you go home!

LUE MING *(Chants)*: Get her shoe. Pull off her shoe.

CRAVER: Both.

REMZI *(Chants)*: Hold her down and pull off her shoe.

CRAVER: For both reasons.

FAIROUZ: All right.

(Craver leans to kiss her foot.)

REMZI: No!

(Fairouz pulls her foot away from Craver.)

FAIROUZ: Don't.

(Remzi cannot get loose. He is again "seeing" his sister being beaten.)

REMZI: Get the fuck off her, you motherfuckers!

FAIROUZ: Remzi!

BOXLER *(To Remzi)*: We had an Iraqi prisoner. I stuck the knife in, just below the sternum.

CRAVER: I won't hurt you.

BOXLER: And I slit him all the way down.

REMZI: All of you! Back off!

BOXLER: I pulled his rib cage wide open . . .

REMZI: Leave her alone!

BOXLER: . . . and stood inside his body. I said:

REMZI: Fairouz!

BOXLER: Hey, boys, now I'm really standing in Iraq.

CRAVER: I promise you, I won't hurt you.

(Fairouz lets Craver kiss her foot, then she kicks him. She takes a hammer from her skirt.)

Bitch.

REMZI: Get away from her!

CRAVER: Fucking . . . Arab whore.

REMZI: Get away from her. I'm warning you!

FAIROUZ: Take a look, Craver. This isn't a B-52. This isn't a Buff. This is a hammer. I could do to your face what they did to my foot.

CRAVER: Go on then. You fucking gimp. Go on. Do it! Hit me! Hit me, you fucking cunt! Please. *(Drops to his knees)* Please. Hit me.

(She raises the hammer as if to strike him, but instead she runs the hammer over his cheeks.)

FAIROUZ: How do you remember him now? *(Presses the face of the hammer to his mouth and moves it sexually)* Like this?

REMZI: No!

CRAVER *(Pushes the hammer away)*: No.

(Remzi goes "unconscious." Fairouz and Craver are alone.)

A plague. A flood. An ice age. That's what I expected when it was over and I got back here. An earthquake. Something that would rip this country wide open. Eighty-eight thousand tons of explosives dropped. That country is like a body with every bone inside it broken.

FAIROUZ: How did he die?

CRAVER: Every single bone. We tried. Day after day, but there were too many pieces. We couldn't get them all. Do you know how many pieces make up the human body? Two, three hundred thousand. *(Beat)* Dead. Maybe half of them civilians. We bombed the sewers, the electricity, the water. They'll die in the thousands because of bad water. Just bad water.

FAIROUZ: Give me an answer.

CRAVER: They came for us. Both of us.

FAIROUZ: But you're still alive.

CRAVER: The question here isn't how many feet were between Remzi and I. It could have been thirty feet. Or twenty-five. I think it was more like twenty.

FAIROUZ: Tell me.

CRAVER: I had practiced it with him. I got it down just right. Do you want to see how I walked?

(Craver does his "walk" for her as she watches him.)

Are you watching me? *(Continues his "walk")*

SCENE EIGHT

Boxler and Lue Ming alone.

BOXLER: I remember you. I think I do. Is that what you want? An apology? Why didn't you just say so? Hey. Really. I'm sincerely sorry. I've always been sorry. Besides, I wasn't completely heartless. You didn't know I shot your kid, because I shot you first.

LUE MING: You said you'd let her live if I did what you wanted. You couldn't get it up. That's why you killed us both.

BOXLER: I had a war on my mind.

LUE MING: What is it like to kill a child?

BOXLER: You're sick.

LUE MING: I have to know.

BOXLER: It's simple: a bit of . . . a clump of . . . a piece of . . . *(Beat)* . . . a piece of the future is alive, and then it isn't.

LUE MING: Were you ever in love?

BOXLER: Oh, yes. Long ago. I was born a human being, you know. But one can't stay that way forever. One has to mature. *(Beat)* Maybe it was you I fell in love with. I mean, it could have happened, couldn't it?

(He kisses her. She does not respond.)

LUE MING: Why wasn't one time enough?

BOXLER: Because I wanted to kiss you again. Naturally.

LUE MING: Why did you have to shoot her twice? Three times? Just to make sure?

BOXLER: Just to make sure, I did it four times. And shooting a child, if you must know, is rather exceptional. It's like shooting an angel. There's something religious about it.

LUE MING: I woke up after you and your troops were gone. I woke up with my child in my arms. A dead child weighs so much more than a live one. I carried her back to the village. When I was well again, I continued my work with the Vietcong. I was one of their top commanders. I searched for you everywhere. Everywhere. With more passion than one would a lost lover. But I never found you.

BOXLER: Just how did you die?

LUE MING: I can't remember. How long have you been dead?

BOXLER: Calley is still alive and well in Georgia, only I've run out on him. I'm his soul. Calley's dead soul.

LUE MING: His soul?

BOXLER: Yes, his soul and I'm homeless.

LUE MING: I don't believe in souls.

BOXLER: Neither do I, but here I am. I go from war to war. It's the only place that feels like home. I didn't kill your daughter. Calley did. I was inside him, looking out, but I didn't do it. I didn't pull the trigger.

LUE MING: You watched.

BOXLER: What else can a soul do but watch? We're not magicians.

LUE MING: Are you suffering?

BOXLER: I can't suffer. I can't, and it hurts me.

LUE MING: Is it terrible?

BOXLER: It tears me apart.

LUE MING: How long will this go on?

BOXLER: World without end.

LUE MING: Delightful. More than I'd hoped. *(Beat)* But I want you to make a sound for me.

(Split scene: Fairouz is watching Remzi and Craver, who do not "see" her watching them.)

BOXLER: No.

LUE MING: You owe it to me.

FAIROUZ *(Calls)*: Remzi.

BOXLER: I don't know what you're talking about.

FAIROUZ AND LUE MING: The sound—

FAIROUZ: . . . you made inside you. Not the second time.

LUE MING: Not the third or fourth. But the first time you died.

BOXLER: The first time I died.

LUE MING: Yes.

BOXLER: That would be sometime in November 1967. There was an old man. He was wounded. He wouldn't have made it anyway. I threw him down a well.

REMZI *(To Craver)*: I couldn't say it any louder. I whispered her name. *(Whispers)* Fairouz.

CRAVER *(Whispers)*: Fairouz.

REMZI: There were five of them.

FAIROUZ: Go on.

BOXLER: I threw him down a well. An old man. I heard his head go crack against the stone wall and then splash.

REMZI: One of the boys had just come out of woodshop. He'd been making an end table for his mother for Christmas. He had a hammer.

CRAVER: You were a kid, Remzi.

BOXLER: I was a child once. Did you know that? I liked to run naked and jump up and down on the bed. I had a bath toy. A blue bath toy. I can't remember what it was.

REMZI: They got one of her shoes off. Then the sock. I stood behind the bushes and watched.

CRAVER: You looked out for yourself. That was right.

REMZI: I was afraid that if I tried to stop them they'd do the same to me.

CRAVER: Shhhhhhhhh.

BOXLER: I threw him down the well. I heard a crack. I heard a splash. I heard a crack and a splash, and I died.

CRAVER: You were just a kid.

(Craver and Remzi kiss, and Craver removes Remzi's shirt.)

FAIROUZ: You were just a child.

BOXLER: When I killed him, I died, though I didn't make a sound when I died. My body just turned and walked back into the village to finish the rest of the job.

LUE MING: But I heard it. I heard the splash. And I heard you die.

FAIROUZ: Do you want to know what it sounds like?

LUE MING: What it sounds like to go on living and the child in your arms is so heavy and she is dead and you are dead and I am dead but—

LUE MING AND FAIROUZ: We just keep living.

BOXLER: Forever and ever.

LUE MING: It sounded like this:

(Lue Ming, Fairouz and Boxler all scream: "No." Their screams are deafening and mixed with the sound of thundering jets. Remzi and Craver look up at the awe-inspiring jets above them.)

SCENE NINE

Craver and Fairouz in his motel room. Craver is still holding Remzi's shirt.

CRAVER: That's beautiful. Sad Eyes. The CBUs were prohibited weapons, like the napalm, cluster and fragmentation. But Sad Eyes. Who would have had the heart to try and stop a weapon named Sad Eyes? Eyes like his. Not sad, really. But confused. Or furious. Or scared.

(Remzi appears as a vision. Craver speaks to him.)

The first time we made love, we were so scared and I started to cry. It was a first time for both of us, and it hurt. You leaned over me and kissed the back of my neck and you said over and over:

REMZI: You are my white trash, and I love you.

(Craver mouths the words along with Remzi.)

CRAVER AND REMZI: You are my white trash, and I love you.

CRAVER: They caught us together, out behind the barracks. They were lower ranks. Just kids. Like me. Kids who grew up with garbage in their backyards. Kids who never got the summer jobs, who didn't own CD players. They knocked us around. After a while, they took us to a room. Handed us over to an upper rank. There was a British officer and an Iraqi prisoner in there too, and they were laughing and saying: "Sandnigger. Indian. Gook." *(Beat)* Remzi. Well. He went wild. He jumped one of those officers. I was standing there. I couldn't move. I couldn't . . . Then somebody hit me over the head, and I went out. *(Beat)* The first time I came to, the prisoner was down and he kept waving his arms like he was swimming, doing the backstroke, and Remzi was there and I could hear his voice, but it was like trying to see through a sheet of ice. *(Beat)* My head was spinning, and it was snowing stars. In that room. In the middle of the biggest bunch of hottest nowhere in the world and it was snowing stars and Remzi in the center of it and this one officer or maybe it was two and there was a knife and the Iraqi had stopped moving—I think he was dead—and they were all over him and having a good time at it. Like kids in the snow. *(Beat)* Do you want to know how you died, Remzi?

REMZI: Friendly fire.

CRAVER: One of them had his arm around my neck, choking me, while another one held you down. I shouted for you to stay down but you wouldn't stay down. Each time he knocked you down you stood up. He hit you in the mouth so many times I couldn't tell anymore what was your nose and what was your mouth. *(Beat)* What did you call the other soldiers when you first joined up?

REMZI: Family.

CRAVER: When I woke up, I took him in my arms. The blood had stopped coming out. *(Beat)* Five foot . . . eleven inches. That's how tall you were. I used to run my hand up and down your spine like I was reading the bones.

REMZI: I wanted to travel everyplace on your body. Even the places you'd never been. Love can make you feel so changed you think the world is changed. Up till then, we'd survived the war.

(To Craver) What are you?

FAIROUZ *(To Craver)*: What are you?

REMZI *(Louder)*: What are you, Craver?

CRAVER *(Whispers)*: What are you? What are you? *(Shouts)* What are you, Craver?

(Remzi says the following words with Craver, beginning with "Indian." Remzi's words are spoken just a fraction sooner than Craver's.)

I am a White Trash,

CRAVER AND REMZI: Indian, Sandnigger, Brown Trash, Arab, Gook Boy, Faggot—

CRAVER *(To Fairouz)*: From the banks of the Kentucky River.

SCENE TEN

Remzi as a vision, as a child, making a "mix" for Fairouz's foot. Fairouz watches him, as though from a long distance. Craver listens from the shadows.

FAIROUZ: He and I. We were never children. We were pieces of children. After that. But what is a piece of a child?

REMZI: Grass. Black pepper. Gold. From a gold crayon.

FAIROUZ: Sweetness doesn't last. Bitter lasts. Bile lasts. I am looking. Yes. I am looking for him.

REMZI: Pancake syrup. Lots of that.

FAIROUZ: And I don't want to find him. Not now. Not tomorrow. But I'm looking.

(Craver exits.)

I don't want him to come back to me as him, but as a boy wearing my face. *(Beat)* Where you ended, I began.

REMZI: Ready, Fairouz? *(Calls)* Are you ready? *(To himself)* This one's just right. Won't sting.

FAIROUZ: And the sand. I can't sleep because of it. Everywhere. Inside my pillow. Inside my sleep. I'm walking. Walking and calling for you. But the sand slides below my feet, stopping me, keeping me in place. And the wind throwing handfuls. But then in the distance. I see. Something. Dark. Moving. Moving towards me.

REMZI: Eggshells. Mint.

FAIROUZ: And it seems hours, years, until I can see. What. Yes. That it's a child. Five or six. A boy. The wind has torn small pieces from your body. With each step you take towards me you are less whole. When we reach each other, you are almost transparent.

REMZI: It's too dry. *(Calls)* Bring me some water.

FAIROUZ: Almost nothing left. I know I must say your name. Now. But I can't. There's no sand in my mouth. No wind. But I can't say it.

REMZI *(Calls)*: Are you coming?

FAIROUZ: I can't. Say it. And then you're moving away from me, moving back. I open my mouth. To say it. I say: Fairouz.

REMZI *(Calls)*: Fairouz.

FAIROUZ: My own name. Not yours. And, in that moment, the sun drills brilliant through your chest. And then you are. Gone.

SCENE ELEVEN

Craver and Fairouz in his motel room.

FAIROUZ: The ram's horn. Why did he send me the ram's horn?

CRAVER: He carved your name on the inside. It took him three hours to do it. His sister would have appreciated it. You should have given it to her.

FAIROUZ: I am his sister.

CRAVER: Yes. You are.

(Craver does a headstand.)

FAIROUZ: Why do you do that?

CRAVER: I'm training my balance.

FAIROUZ: Remzi had no balance.

(Craver comes out of the headstand.)

CRAVER: No?

FAIROUZ: He said balance could be a bad thing, a trick to keep you in the middle, where things add up, where you can do no harm.

CRAVER: Remzi said that?

FAIROUZ: No. But he might have. *(Beat)* I'll go wherever I need to go. I won't leave them in peace.

CRAVER: Remzi said you were the best sister any brother—

FAIROUZ *(Interrupts)*: Don't. Please. *(Beat)* It's terrible, isn't it? To be freed like this. Are you going to talk?

CRAVER: I'm going to try.

FAIROUZ: But what is it for?

CRAVER: It might keep me alive. Talking about it might keep me alive.

FAIROUZ: I mean the ram's horn. What is it for?

CRAVER: He said.

(Remzi appears and gets in position to race.)

REMZI: I want to race.

CRAVER: He said if you blow on it, it will make a noise.

REMZI: I haven't had a good race in almost . . .

CRAVER: You're on! *(Joins Remzi. Gets down in a starting position to run with him)* Motherfucker. Ready?

(Craver is in two realities now and speaks to both Remzi and Fairouz with ease.)

FAIROUZ: A noise.

REMZI: I'm going to beat you this time!

FAIROUZ: All right.

CRAVER: On your mark.

FAIROUZ: Will it be loud?

REMZI: I'm going to pass you by so fast, I'm going to, bang, disappear right in front of you!

CRAVER *(To Fairouz)*: Fucking loud. *(To Remzi)* Get set?

REMZI: You just watch me.

FAIROUZ: Fucking loud. I like that.

REMZI: Just watch me!

FAIROUZ: Goddamn, fucking loud!

CRAVER AND REMZI: Go!

(The two men move to run. Lights go to black.)

END OF PLAY

SELECT BIBLIOGRAPHY

Augustin, Ebba, ed. *Palestinian Women: Identity and Experience.* New York: St. Martin's Press, 1993.

Bennis, Phyllis and Michel Moushabeck, eds. *Beyond the Storm: A Gulf Crisis Reader.* Ithaca, NY: Olive Branch Press, 1991.

Bilton, Michael and Kevin Sim. *Four Hours in My Lai.* New York: Viking Penguin, 1992.

Boyne, Col. Walter. *Weapons of Desert Storm.* Illinois: Signet Special, 1991.

Chomsky, Noam. *The Fateful Triangle: The United States, Israel and the Palestinians.* Cambridge, MA: South End Press, 1983.

Chomsky, Noam and Edward S. Herman. *Manufacturing Consent: The Political Economy of the Mass Media.* New York: Pantheon Books, 1988.

Clark, Ramsey and others. *War Crimes: A Report on United States War Crimes Against Iraq.* Washington, D.C.: Maisonneuve Press, 1992.

Cleaver, Richard and Patricia Myers, eds. *A Certain Terror: Heterosexism, Militarism, Violence and Change.* Chicago: American Friends Service Committee, 1993.

Darwish, Mahmoud. *Music of the Human Flesh: Poems of the Palestinian Struggle.* London: Heinemann, 1980.

Edelman, Bernard. *Dear America: Letters Home from Vietnam.* New York: Simon & Schuster, 1991.

Giannou, Christopher. *Besieged: A Doctor's Story of Life and Death in Beirut.* Interlink Publishing Group, 1991.

Gittings, John, ed. *Beyond the Gulf War.* London: CIIR, 1991.

Janz, Wes and Vickie Abrahamson, eds. *War of the Words: The Gulf War Quote by Quote.* Minnesota: Bobbleheads Press, 1991.

Khalidi, Walid and Muhammad A. Khalidi, eds. *All That Remains: The Palestinian Villages Occupied and Depopulated by Israel in 1948.* Washington, D.C.: Institute for Palestinian Studies, 1992.

Murphy, Jay. *For Palestine.* New York: Writers and Readers Publishing, Inc., 1992.

Peters, Cynthia, ed. *Collateral Damage: The "New World Order" at Home and Abroad.* Cambridge, MA: South End Press, 1992.

Said, Edward W. *After the Last Sky: Palestinian Lives.* New York: Columbia University Press, 1998.

Said, Edward W. *Covering Islam: How the Media and the Experts Determine How We See the Rest of the World.* New York: Random House, 1996.

Shaheen, Jack G. *The TV Arab.* Bowling Green, OH: Bowling Green State University Popular Press, 1984.

Shilts, Randy. *Conduct Unbecoming: Gays and Lesbians in the U.S. Military.* New York: St. Martin's Press, 1993.

Tucker, Judith E., ed. *Arab Women: Old Boundaries, New Frontiers.* Bloomington, IN: Indiana University Press, 1993.

Young, Elise G. *Keepers of History: Women and the Israeli-Palestinian Conflict.* New York: Teachers College Press, 1991.

PUBLICATIONS

The Guardian (U.K.)
The Independent (U.K.)
Lies of Our Times
M.E.R.I.P.
The Nation

The New Statesman and Society
The New York Times
Out Now
Z Magazine

THE WAR BOYS

1993

PRODUCTION HISTORY

The War Boys had its first performance on February 10, 1993, at the Finborough Theatre in London. The director was Kate Valentine, the design was by Fay Saxty and music was by Alex Valentine. The cast was as follows:

GREG	Bradley Lavelle
DAVID	Ethan Flower
GEORGE	Mathew Sharp

CHARACTERS

GREG, working-class Mexican-American, early twenties
DAVID, college-educated, white, privileged, early twenties
GEORGE, "home boy," white, early twenties

TIME

Now.

PLACE

A place that could be the Mexico/Texas border.

SETTING

Should be minimal and not "realistic." There is a raised
area on the stage that functions as a car or car area.

Part of a barbed wire fence to suggest a "border" is visible. Three men enter the stage one at a time. Each one is carrying a heavy-duty spotlight. One of them carries a small CB. Another carries a concealed weapon. With a look of mutual consent they take up their positions. They're now going to "play" the War Boys game. They play this game for real. The three of them crouch on a raised area, the "car area," of the stage in silence, scanning the border, until David points at something he "sees" moving out there.

DAVID: Put the brights on. Now! Now!

(They turn their spotlights on their "public.")

GEORGE: Fuckin' beaner. Look at him run!

DAVID: Sweet Christ, he's wearing my Adidas.

GEORGE: Call him down, Greg. He's slipping away.

GREG: This is car six of the War Boys. We got a slowrider sighted making for the crossing at fence line nine.

GEORGE *(Grabs "mike" from Greg)*: Should we go after him? Over. *(Listens)* Says he'll send a car over after he makes a stop at the ditch line.

DAVID: Dim them again.

(Lights are dimmed.)

I think we lost him. When he starts up the hill. Oh, yes, yes, look at him sprint.

GEORGE: Ninja, ninja, ninja.

DAVID: Think I wasted four years at Stanford for nothing?

GREG: Shit. Shit. He's in reverse.

DAVID: Come back, Marlboro Man. Come back to the Marlboro Land!

GEORGE: Damn. We lost him.

GREG: He'll be back.

DAVID (*To Greg*): How come you were late tonight? I like to start on time.

GREG: Sorry. Had to finish up at the library.

DAVID: Oh? Beating off on Chaucer again, hey, Greggie.

GEORGE: Who's she?

DAVID: The Wife of Bath, yeah, baby.

GEORGE (*Hears something*): Hey, did you hear that?

GREG: Sure. Swabbin' floors I get a lot of time to read. (*Beat*) I saw the other guys. They're at five tonight.

DAVID: Well, we're stuck right here until ten, then line seventeen till midnight.

GEORGE: Hey, want to see a trick?

GREG: By the way, David, it's a known fact that rich boys beat off three point seven times more than poor boys. Know why? (*Holds up his hands to David's face*)

GEORGE: I can hold a cigarette with my dick.

GREG: Because guys like me haven't got, excuse me, I mean "ain't got," all that free, leisure, wack-wack time.

GEORGE: Can we make it an early night tonight? Little bro is sick again.

DAVID: He's always sick. Take the kid to the doctor for a change why don't you.

GEORGE: Nothing I can't cure.

DAVID: With TLC, huh, Georgia?

GEORGE: Why not? Think I haven't got it in me?

DAVID (*Sniffs*): Smell that aroma? It's the feminine scent. I'm going to pick up its trail.

(*David snorts, then throws himself to the ground and begins to belly-crawl about the stage, searching for something across the border. George and Greg ignore him.*)

GEORGE: It's your go.

GREG: I'm not in the mood.

GEORGE: It's your go.

GREG: No thanks.

GEORGE: Come on. You promised. You played it with David last time.

(George rolls up his sleeve and after some moments, Greg does so wearily. Then Greg slaps George, though not hard, across the face. As they converse, George returns the slap, somewhat harder. Each slaps the other harder until one of them loses their balance. Meanwhile, David is still crawling about sniffing.)

GREG: So who's our contact tonight? *(Slaps George)*

GEORGE: Officer Sharons.

GREG: Shit. Sharons is a drunk-ass. Always too slow on the call-up.

GEORGE *(Slaps Greg)*: He says there's a hole they're getting through somewhere from three through seven.

GREG *(Slaps George)*: There's always a hole.

GEORGE: You ever notice something funny about my smile, Greg? *(Slaps Greg)*

GREG: Ask me about your breath.

GEORGE *(Slaps George)*: No, boy. The smile.

(George grins hugely and holds it. Greg slaps him hard.)

GREG: Food. In the corner of your mouth.
     Hear that? Listen.

GEORGE: What?

GREG: Listen.

GEORGE: I don't hear anything. *(Beat)* For a mop-boy you sure are stupid.

(George slaps Greg hard. He is knocked off his seat.)

It never lasts more than ten hits with you. You're a wimp.

DAVID *(Still crawling about)*: Psst. Here sissy, sissy, sissy.

GEORGE: I mean it. What kind of animal do I smile like?

GREG: A worm. How about a worm?

GEORGE: Hey, David, what was that fancy-ass word for "chewing" you used the other night?

DAVID: I see you. I see you.

GREG: Masticate.

GEORGE: Yeah. What animal do I masticate like? *(Chews loudly)*

DAVID *(Whispers)*: Come here. I won't hurt you.

GREG: A groundhog?

GEORGE: It's dead zone here.

(David circles back to their area, grabs Greg's leg and clings to him, exaggerating.)

DAVID: Oh, Father, who art in heaven, help me to step down from this stifling perch. Help me to respect manual labor, so I can wear filthy overalls, so I can make money with my own bare hands and get out of those oppressive neighborhood recycling programs.

GEORGE: Let's move.

GREG: We've got to wait till ten. *(Shakes David off)* Sorry, Buddy. Once an MC-er, always an MC-er.

GEORGE: What's an MC-er?

DAVID: Moose-Cuticle, you idiot.

GREG: Short for Middle Class.

DAVID: Go easy on him, Greg. He can only take a bit of learning at a time.

GEORGE *(Baring his rear to David)*: Have a bite from my left cheek, Mr. Diploma. *(Beat)* Hey, I've got a game we can play.

DAVID *(Standing and composing himself; to George)*: Nope. We're going to play mine. *(To Greg)* I would like to bet you five dollars you can't, excuse my coarseness, jerk off while I'm saying the Pledge of Allegiance.

GEORGE: I bet I could.

DAVID *(Still to Greg)*: Five bucks you can't.

(Greg ignores him.)

GEORGE *(Moves a good distance from them)*: I'll do it over here.

DAVID *(To George)*: Nope, I'll need to see the evidence.

GREG: You two are kindergarten.

GEORGE *(Moves closer)*: OK, but no peeking.

DAVID: On your marks.

GREG: This is the last time I'm out with you two.

DAVID: Get set.

GREG: I just want to make that clear.

GEORGE: Go.

DAVID: "I pledge allegiance to the flag, of the United States of America— *(Mimics a quarterback while he recites, both fast and slow)* and to the Republic for which it stands, one nation, under God, indivisible, with liberty and justice for all."

GEORGE: Start over.

DAVID: Five bucks. Now.

GEORGE: Fuck off. I already owe you two hundred and thirty.

DAVID: Now you owe me two hundred and thirty-five.

GEORGE: Yeah, well, I almost had you, bud. But when you got to the "and to the Republic" bit that brought me down.

DAVID: Your credit with me is going to drop, sir, if you can't improve your performance.

GREG: You two. Shit. *(Beat)* Listen, we stay in the car tonight or I'm quits with you guys.

GEORGE *(To Greg)*: Will you quit worrying?

GREG: I mean it.

GEORGE: We're friends, Greg. A promise is a promise.

DAVID: What about last Friday night? Standing on the sidelines observing it all. I could see it was tickling your palate.

GREG *(Interrupts)*: I was fucked-up that night. I'm not like you dogs.

(David meows.)

DAVID: But I polished my hood tonight especially.

GREG: Tonight we stay in the car and let the officers handle the rest.

DAVID *(Pushing Greg with his finger)*: Since when do you call the shots for this brigade? Hey? Who gives you a ride here in the evenings?

GREG: You do.

DAVID: Who pays for the gas?

GREG: You do.

DAVID: Who buys you your six-pack?

GREG: I just don't want things to get messy tonight.

GEORGE: Don't spoil the evening, Greg.

DAVID: Hey. I never swore I wasn't a sick individual now did I?

GEORGE: We'll be good. My bro's sick. I want to be home early. *(Gets on his knees and shouts toward the border, which is now the public)* Mama Mia. Come on, come on! Let's light this birthday cake!

DAVID: Hurry, hurry. Step right up. *(Kneels next to George, extends his arms to the public)* See the greatest show on earth.

(Greg now joins in. The tune for this song should give the sense of a chain-gang-type ballad. All three sing the "Border Song.")

ALL:

On the border, we can see the pretty sights,
some in the day, but the best ones at night.
Bring a six-pack of Bud and a bag of chips,
bring some soda pop and some tamale dip.

We can spot them running, we can watch them crawl,
we can tie them up, we can have a ball.
We can make ten dollars if we catch one alive,
the feds will pay us money and they'll give us no jive.

(David jumps up, toppling Greg.)

DAVID: Shhhh. Did you hear that?

GEORGE: What?

GREG: Where?

DAVID: Shhhhh.

(David sings again, but alone, as others tap out music.)

Barbaric? A clear case of missing morality?
You're wrong, this fun's a duty from the highest
    authority.
These beaners don't value life as we boys do,
we heard it from the top, they want to mix a racial
    stew.

GREG *(Sings)*:

Now we got dead-end jobs or the army option,
we can travel to kill or we can sell the MacLuncheon.

GEORGE *(Sings)*:

But why take orders or clean up someone's shit,
when we can light up the border, ten dollars a hit.

DAVID: You know what I heard today? They say some of
our own kind have crossed over there.

(All three are on guard and nervous.)

GEORGE: Over there?

DAVID: Forming a so-called "protect the Mex" band.
(Beat) Could be they're carrying knives.

GREG: I don't think so.

DAVID: Could be they're carrying guns.

GEORGE: Guns?

GREG: Don't listen to him, George.

DAVID: Scared, Greg?

GEORGE: Hey, I heard something.

DAVID: Shhhh. What was that?

GREG: George's gut.

DAVID: There it is again. Hear it?

(They all huddle.)

GEORGE: I heard it.

GREG: Shhhhh.

DAVID: Sounds like . . .

GEORGE: Like—

GREG: Like—

DAVID: Like a knife sharpening on a stone.

GEORGE *(Whispers)*: Let's get out of here.

GREG *(Whispers)*: Just some stones rolling down the hill, George.

DAVID *(Sees something)*: What's that?

GEORGE: Where?

GREG: Where?

DAVID: Something shining. Two. Three things shining.

GEORGE *(Whispers)*: Let's go.

GREG: I don't see anything shining.

DAVID *(Whispers)*: Blades. Knife blades. *(Shouts)* Blades!
(Throws a knife in front of them)

(Greg and George both scare and duck. David laughs at them.)

GEORGE: That's not very funny, David.

DAVID: With you two I can't resist.

GREG *(Clutching his stomach)*: Hold it.

DAVID: Must you repeat this performance every time there's a little excitement down here? I say "boo" and you puke.

(Greg moves upstage and begins to vomit.)

Couldn't you get some pills to keep it down? You're pitiful, sweetheart.

GEORGE *(Hands over ears)*: That noise gets to me.

DAVID: Five bucks says I can make it worse for you, Greg.

(Greg is oblivious to them; he's still sick. George stands over him with his arm raised like the Statue of Liberty. David sings:)

America, America
God shed his grace on thee
And crown thy good
With brotherhood
From sea to shining sea.

(As David sings, Greg recovers. Lights change slightly as he moves downstage right, near their public, wiping his mouth on his sleeve.)

You, my man, don't have the belly to take a joke.
GEORGE: Take it easy, Greg. He didn't see anything.
GREG: Yeah? Well, maybe I did.

(During Greg's monologue, George and David carry on in and around the car area. They are not unaware of Greg's performance, but they are not really interested in it. At times, however, they intervene. Greg addresses the border.)

(To border) Hey! Hey! *Dame dos cuchillos.* Throw me a couple of knives. *(Turns back to his friends a moment)* Think I haven't got it in me? Maybe I'll just step over there and find out if they're carrying knives. *(Spits on his palms, smooths back his hair, addresses border again)* Think I haven't got it in me? Scared, are you? *(Beat)* Hey. I bet you never belonged to the Boy Scouts. I did. The church choir? *(Holds a note)* I could hold the longest note. Then I went on to join the Sunday Dixie Band. And then the Blueshell Campaign to save the farmers. Then I joined the Border Brigade. *(Lifts his shirt and draws an imaginary line down the center of his body)* This half of me is *Mejicano.* This other half of me is WASP. *Como sabes* which side is which? My mother was Mexican. She used to tell me: "*Este lado es Mejicano.* This side is Mexican— *(Slaps left breast)* the side with the heart."
GEORGE *(Spots something)*: Look.
DAVID: Another one!

GEORGE: A beaner chick. In heat.

GREG: My father *me dijo* it was my lower half that was WASP, that I had his *cojones*— *(Grabs crotch)* but the brains of a beaner. *(Beat)* When I was a little *niño* I was two separate pieces, just below the surface, held together by skin.

DAVID: Here she comes.

GEORGE: Throw the brights on her.

DAVID: Not yet, not yet. Wait.

GREG: Didn't do sports. Didn't run during recess. Never got on a bike. *Nada ni mierda.* If I'd made the wrong move I'd split, right down the center.

DAVID: You're missing the spectacle, Greggie.

GEORGE: Open the sun roof. Hey, baby. Slip under the wire.

DAVID: We're the Holiday Inn.

GEORGE: The Light Up the Border Brigade.

GREG: *Mi padre*, he was a Senior *Agente* of the Border. He used to take a lot of slack for having married a Wet. But he always said it was strategy, that he knew them better, inside and out, on account of her.

DAVID: Come and get your red-hot, one-hundred-percent American hard-on.

GEORGE *(Sings)*: It's the real thing . . .

GREG: They say he was a good cop.

DAVID *(Sings)*: That's the way it should be . . .

GREG: He made OK *dinero*, helped me get a loan so I could buy my first car. Then I met my first girl. She was Chicana. *(Beat)* I figured, like father like son. And this *chica* was legal, nice trailer, two-parent family. She wasn't real pretty, but she gave me a feeling *(Beat)* like eatin' a bowl of frosted flakes with tequila. We were planning on living together, so I brought her home to meet my father.

DAVID: Look at that.

GEORGE: She's stuck.

DAVID: Her shirt's tangled up in the wire.

GREG: He called us into his office. I told him I was thinking about marrying her. He took a hold of Evalina's
long braid and tipped her head back. *(Beat)* Then he
stuck his fingers in her mouth and tested her molars.
He found the hole where she'd just had a tooth
pulled. He jammed his nail in it, and she yelled.
Then he just shook his head. He was disappointed.

GEORGE: She can't get loose.

GREG: Then he took out his wallet. "You can't marry a
woman with a bad set of teeth," he said. "It spoils the
breath." He counted it out: *veinte, quarenta, sesenta,
cien.* Two hundred bucks.

DAVID: Come on, Godiva. A few more shakes, and I'll let
you polish the hood of my new Mustang.

GREG: My Evalina was wearing an orange blouse that day,
with a blue ribbon braided into her hair.

DAVID: But she doesn't even look Mexican.

GEORGE: Maybe she's Arab.

GREG: He unbuttoned her blouse and tucked the money
in her bra. *(Beat)* Then he kissed us both on the forehead.

DAVID *(Shoving him)*: Go on, George. Talk to her.

GEORGE: But I can't speak Spanish.

DAVID: Shit Spanish. She's a bitch. Give her poetry.

GREG: Over breakfast the next morning he asked me if
I'd made the appointment with the dentist.

GEORGE: *Chica, chica.*

GREG: I said yes. I told him me and Evalina, we both
appreciated his advice.

DAVID: Not that. Marvell, stupid. Watch this: "When as in
silks my . . . beaner goes, then, then, methinks how
sweetly flows the greasafaction of her clothes. Next
when I cast mine . . ."

GEORGE: It worked. She's grinnin' like a raccoon. Hey,
hamburguesa!

GREG: I suppose Evalina went and got her teeth fixed. I
don't know. She wouldn't see me after that.

DAVID: This is America. Over ninety billion served.

GREG: I mean, *mi padre*, he was a strict man sometimes, but he looked out for me.

GEORGE: Move over. Let me out of the car.

GREG *(To George and David, who have begun to encroach too far on his story)*: Stay in the fuckin' car, George.

GEORGE: The lady needs to be rescued. *(To David)* Just watch this. You watching?

GREG: Asshole. We've got a deal with the feds. We spot them. That's all. If we fuck up again . . .

GEORGE: Fuck you, Greg. Hey, *muchacha*!!

DAVID: Look at old Georgie. He's combing back his hair.

GREG: You two baboon asses are fuckin' up my thing. *(Pushes George back)* Can't you shut up just a few more seconds until I'm done?

(George and David mock-freeze. For some seconds Greg doesn't know where to pick up again.)

I suppose Evalina got her teeth fixed. I don't know. She wouldn't see me after that . . .

DAVID *(Interrupts)*: No, no. You left off at *(Mocks Greg's voice)*, "He was a strict man, but he looked out for me."

GREG: Yeah. Thanks. *(Beat)* But he looked out for me. It was about a year later, and I came home to visit my mother. I told her about me and Evalina being over, about how Father had offered to pay to fix her teeth. I watched her pour a whole bottle of detergent into the washer. Then she said, like she might have been saying "hand me a towel," "And you let him do that?" *(Beat)* Then she smacked me across the face. Not hard. But it was the first time she ever hit me. Then she just kept saying it, over and over: *"Y lo dejaste hacerlo?"* And you let him do that?

DAVID *(Louder)*: And you let him do that?

GEORGE *(Louder)*: And you let him do that?

GREG: I almost said, "She was just a fuckin' beaner, Ma." *(Begins to laugh)* Wouldn't have been the appropriate thing to say. When my father walked through the door that night, "bang," she hit him over the head with a dinner plate. *(Raises arms slowly as though holding a gun and fires)* Bang . . . bang . . . bang . . . A few years later, my father *se murio.* Dead. I dragged around the half of me *que fue muerte,* his dead half. Sometimes I'd wake up in the middle of the night and I'd smell its deadness, like rotten cantaloupe. *(Beat)* So that's why I joined up. Because, even though my mother died shortly after, the beaner half of me wouldn't die.

DAVID: Hold it!

(He hurries over and lifts up Greg's foot.)

Look at this. You're standing on a sapling. How many times do I have to tell you to watch where the hell you're standing. Lucky you didn't break the poor little fellow's back. Go stand somewhere else.

(Greg moves a few feet away.)

GREG: Here?

(David motions with his hand for Greg to move a little farther.)

Here?

(David nods OK and returns to the car area. Greg continues.)

As a matter of fact, the beaner half of me began to move in on the other half. In no time at all I was seventy-percent beaner, and it keeps spreading. Before I know it, *uno, dos, tres,* I'll be a hundred-percent pure beef wetback. I'm feeling it in my bones. And my feet, they want to dance that cockroach song. *(Does a mild tap dance of sorts)* But every time we catch one of those *Mejicanos* crossing the border, the pressure eases up. *Y puedo descansar.*

DAVID: Look, George. She's still there. Waiting.

GEORGE (*Approaching public as though it were the girl*): Hey, Snow White. Want a bite of my apple?

GREG (*Continues*): The creeping flow of her blood in me backs up a bit, and I can rest for a while—

DAVID: That a boy, Georgie. Show her your intellect.

GREG: —and stop fighting it. (*Beat*) So I hunt. It's harmless, really. (*Strums barbed wire and sings, to the tune of "Oh, Susannah":*)

Oh, Evalina, no llores mas por mi

(*Greg stops, then starts again in English.*)

Oh Evalina, don't you cry for me
for I'm going on down to the border
with a six-pack 'cross my knee.

(*Greg laughs self-consciously, then speaks nervously to David as he nears the car area.*)

Make him get back in the car. She could pull a knife on him. (*To public again*) I try not to hurt them, though, especially the women.

DAVID: It's just like watching your VHS.

GREG: It's nothing personal. I mean, I loved my mother and she was one of them. (*To his friends*) Shit, come on, you guys. This isn't part of the deal. Can't you wait until I'm done?

(*George gazes across the public then begins to crawl closer as he "sees" the woman nearing the border.*)

DAVID: What's the matter, Greggie? Not getting the attention you need?

GREG (*Tries to get back to his story*): *Especialmente las mujeres*, the women. Just want to *espantarlos un poco*, scare them up a bit, let them know they don't belong here. And we get ten bucks for each one we catch. In a good week I can make seventy, eighty bucks. Helps on the bills.

DAVID: Get lucky, baby. Heads or tails.

GREG: But, hey, let's lighten up now. *Vengan. Vengan.* Loosen up. We'll pick up a bottle of rotgut tequila, cruise on down to Dairy Mart road and shine the brights on the wire, light 'em up, catch us some fish, some *peces* for supper, huh?

(Huge groan from David. Greg is disconcerted a moment.)

(To David) Fuck off. *(Beat)* I mean, we're all a mix, aren't we? *(Whispers)* But which half has got the heart, huh? Huh?

DAVID: Hey, Greg, how do you spell relief?

GREG *(Oblivious to David's interference)*: Come on. You can get some relief. Take your mind off of a long day's work.

DAVID: Well?

GREG *(To public)*: So how do you spell relief?

(George begins to caress the stage floor as he stares out at the woman. He does this sensually, carefully.)

DAVID *(To George)*: I spell it B-E-A-N-E-R-S.

GREG: Beaners.

(Greg jumps into the car.)

DAVID: George will teach her the lesson she needs. She'll run back home now, tell her compadres: "You're playin' with fire, and you can be burned by fire . . ." *(To George)* What's the rest of the pledge, George? I'll knock ten dollars off your tab if you can remember it.

GEORGE *(Remembering)*: It goes . . . It goes . . . ". . . can be burned by fire . . . and the . . . the . . . white man will rub two Mexicans together to make his fire."

GREG *(Interrupts)*: That's it. I'm walking. Get out of my fuckin' way.

DAVID *(Grabs Greg by collar)*: But old Ronald McDonald is going to score ninety billion and one tonight.

GREG: I'm calling Sharons.

DAVID: Can you smell the meat cooking, Greggie? Or are you going to spoil your appetite again? *(Beat)* Hey, give me that radio, you—

GREG: Calling for Officer Sharons. Calling for Officer—

DAVID: You idiot!

GREG: Emergency. A dozen beaners just broke the line at fence number—

(David hits Greg across the face with his gun.)

Fuck! You busted my goddamn nose.

DAVID: What has gotten into you?

GREG: I don't want things getting out of hand.

DAVID: You didn't mind things getting out of hand the other night, though, did you?

GREG: That was different. This one's a kid.

DAVID: Sure, sure. Old Greggie coaching on the sidelines. Grunt, grunt, grunt.

GREG *(Motioning to gun)*: OK. But you said you'd leave that at home tonight. Give it to me.

DAVID *(Calmly)*: But it's my toy, Greg. And this is my car. As a matter of fact, this is my brigade. I got us the deal with the feds, didn't I? Ten dollars a tag, remember?

GREG: Get back in the fuckin' car, George.

DAVID: You're not very appreciative, Greg. I don't like that in a man.

GREG: George!

DAVID: This is disappointing me, Greg.

GREG: We made a deal with the feds we wouldn't touch them anymore.

DAVID: George!

GEORGE: What? What? OK. Everything's cool. Don't get upset, Greg. *(Turns)* Look, she's fine. There she goes. I didn't touch her.

DAVID: Runnin' on back to Disneyland.

GEORGE: See? We can keep things in hand. It's cool.

GREG: Let's get out of here. This night is cracked.

GEORGE: Sure. Anything you say, Greg. We're all friends here, right?

GREG: Look. I want to have a good time too. Why do you two always have to fuck up my show?

DAVID: We'll be good little gentlemen from now on. Trust us, Greg.

GEORGE: Yeah. Trust us.

DAVID *(Sneering)*: And I apologize for slapping you. Really.

(Suddenly, David throws himself on George's shoulder and pretends to weep. Greg and George watch with concern. George is fooled; Greg is not.)

GEORGE: He's choked up.

DAVID *(Through his gasping)*: "This side is Mexican . . . the side with the heart . . ." Such a touching story, Greg.

GREG: Not bad, eh?

DAVID: There were times I thought I heard angels singing between the lines. *(Beat)* I mean, you're OK, Greg. *(Beat)* So, if it came down to it, down to the nitty-gritty, which would you choose, Birdseye's or Stouffer's?

GREG: I'm a canned foods man myself.

GEORGE: What's with the canned foods?

GREG: Shut up, George.

GEORGE: No.

DAVID *(To George)*: Take his advice, son, or you'll get your feelings hurt. *(To Greg)* Well?

GREG: Well?

GEORGE: Hey, I can make a balloon with my spit. *(He blows spit bubbles)*

DAVID: Did they go for it?

GREG: I'm not sure.

DAVID: You're not sure? Every soldier must be sure.

GREG: That's right. No uncertainty. No doubts.

GEORGE: Come on, Greg. Is that true, the bit about your dad and her molars?

GREG: Yep. But I threw in the part about him unbuttoning her shirt.

NAOMI WALLACE

DAVID: So you fabricated?

GREG: Only in a minor way.

GEORGE: And your dad, beaned to death with a dinner plate?

GREG: Nope. Cholesterol got him.

DAVID: He should have borrowed my rowing machine. *(Beat)* Shhh. Hear that, George?

(George shakes his head no while he listens.)

Sounded like a howl.

GREG: No, David. You're a howl.

DAVID: That's the border wolf. It howls like that just before it kills.

GEORGE: I didn't hear a howl.

GREG *(Joining in to get George)*: I did. It sounded like this. *(Springs up on car and howls. This should be more frightening than funny)* Well, how did I do?

DAVID: One minor criticism: your prose is a tad flat, somewhat backwards, too . . . working class. You've got to flex it up a bit.

GREG: You think so?

GEORGE: Can we quit early tonight? I need to call little bro.

DAVID: I'm sorry about Evalina.

GREG: Thanks.

DAVID: She was always nice to me when I came by your place for dinner. Once, she wiped the corners of my mouth with her apron. I think she appreciated my appetite. I always had a third helping.

GREG: You never met Evalina.

DAVID: You see how you restrict your imagination?

GEORGE: He's probably waiting up for me.

GREG: My imagination?

GEORGE: It's a nice thing to have someone waiting up for you.

GREG *(Poking David with his finger)*: All you're good at is giving points, Mr. Critic. Why don't you go stand out over there and see how many knives you can catch with your teeth. I caught three myself.

DAVID: Tsk, tsk. Do I detect a challenge? How infantile. But all right. *(Takes a dramatic breath, steps away from the car and faces the public)* All right. *(Calls)* Hello? Anyone at home? I know you're out there. And I'm calling especially to you sweet Yankee blue-bloods who belong on this side, not that one . . . Look, I am going to give you a target, right inside here. *(Opens his mouth wide and hisses for some moments)* Throw them right in here. Right in the bull's-eye. Or how about this? *(Turns his back to the public, spreads his arms and legs)* Aim for the spine. Go ahead. Give me a tickle. *(Beat)* They're not interested in me, Greg. It's you they're lusting for. See? They won't tickle with me. *(Beat)* All right then. *(Spins around)* Then I'll tickle with you. *(Beat)* Want to see me do an imitation of a baby radish with its roots growing?

GREG: A radish *is* a root.

DAVID: But the root has got roots as well and they crawl deep in the dark, like this.

(David squirms about. He is serious about doing a good imitation. He begins to make hissing sounds. Greg and George remain in or around the car area.)

Listen! Listen! You can hear them growing . . . radish roots. They make a sound when they grow— *(Makes a sound)* radiating out minute bits of heat into the wet dirt, making the wet dirt hiss. *(Makes hissing noises)* Hot in the mouth! The tongue burning. My sister and I. We'd fill up our mouths, see who could chew up the most before we spit them out like confetti, all over our shoes. *(Beat)* When my mother tried to leave, I said to her: "Mother, you're an insect, and, like the child you brought me up to be, I'll pluck out your wings." *(Beat)* After Sis passed away, I couldn't apologize about the radishes. I had wanted to send

Sis a nice card, some chocolates, maybe a balloon. She was an intelligent girl. When she left home, she said to me: "I'm root-bound here. And now I've got to crack my pot." *(Laughs nervously)* Telephone pole cracked her pot, too, you could say. *(Pretends to write a letter in the air)*

GREG *("Sees" a child in the distance)*: Check this out: a toddler.

GEORGE *(Yells)*: Hey, kiddo, *(Whistles)* want to play Master of the Universe?

DAVID: Dear Sis: Sorry about the radishes. Love, Bro. *(Takes off his shoe, polishes it on his thigh, and places it down carefully)*

GREG: Nope. Headin' his fanny back to them hills.

GEORGE *(Motioning toward David)*: He's strippin' again.

GREG: This is getting to be a yawn, David.

DAVID *(Ignoring them)*: Now, my mother was what you might call a . . . call a . . . *(Snaps his fingers until his friends give him his line)*

GREG: . . . a dignified type.

DAVID *(Continues)*: . . . call a . . . dignified type of insect, like the mantis. Her wings. Just wouldn't give, no matter how hard you tugged. One day my mother is making me PBJs three stacks high. The next day she's taking off her apron, balling it up, shoving it down the compactor, walking out. When I tackled her on the lawn, asked her why, she said I was old enough to take care of myself, that she was growing weary of the sight of me. She gave me a look then, the way a hole looks back at you if you're looking down in it. And then I knew she knew about Sis. *(Takes off other shoe, polishes it, and lines it up carefully next to the other one)* My daddy had a saying: Never . . . Never . . . *(He can't remember his lines)* Fuck!

GREG: Never shut your eyes.

DAVID: Never shut your eyes to a woman . . . because if you do, before you know it, she'll stick you full like a pin cushion, sew your scrotum to your ass, use you for a foot stool. *(Takes off one sock, lays it gently beside a shoe)* Radishes. A shame they ever existed. *(Beat)* I could have plucked out their wings like insects. But they wouldn't. Stand still. They squirm. They wiggle. They wreak havoc in your garden. *(Removes other sock. Notices bare feet and wiggles them in fascination)* Hey. You got to keep fit. If the body is a drag . . . *(Snaps fingers. No response. Snaps them again)*

GREG: Learn the shit, will you, David.

DAVID: Show some consideration, please?

GREG *(Wearily)*: If the body is a drag, the spirit's gonna— *(Sticks his finger in his mouth and gags)*

DAVID: —the spirit will gag. *(Sits down and begins to row)*

Row, row, row your boat
gently down the stream,
merrily, merrily, merrily, merrily
life is but a . . .

(He draws out last note.)

Radish!

(David quits rowing. Gets up and unbuttons his shirt.)

GEORGE *(To Greg)*: How much you think they're paying for this peep show?

DAVID: I mean, when you grow up you've got choices to make in life. So you choose: Johnny Carson or *Hee-Haw*, Seven-Up or Sprite, CBS or NBC, Beechnut or Juicy Fruit, Trident or Dentine. *(Beat)* I had a fiancée once. But every time I desired her and leaned to deliver the first real kiss of my life, this music began in my ear. *(Sings:)*

Wrigley Spearmint gum, gum, gum,
Wrigley Spearmint gum, gum, gum . . .

(As he repeats these lines, Greg and George sing the accompaniment to the song "Carry it with you . . . that great fresh

flavor" until David silences them with his arms, as a conductor of an orchestra would.)

Excuse me, gentlemen, but I like to do it solo. *(Beat)* Somehow the melody put me off kissing her. Or I'd reach in her shirt to fondle her breast and whisper bits of sassafras into her ear, but instead I'd start— *(Sings:)*

Gettin' that barefoot feelin',
drinkin' Mountain Dew . . .

(David laughs wildly as though tickled. Then speaks seriously.)

When things get hot,
cool is all you got.

(Beat) I couldn't get that music out of my brain. *(Beat)* I work for a law firm. *(Lays his shirt out on floor and kneels to button it up again)* My partner says he likes girls in their adolescence. My father liked them young, too, but he swore sheep had the greater dignity. He brought a girl home for me once when I made an A in Mathematics. And the three of us got drunk. *(Laughs)* All I remember are three white hooves and one black one. *(Stands and sings in opera style)*

Baa-baa black sheep,
can I tickle your wool?

I've only been arrested once. After Sis's funeral. I went out hacking up neighbors' gardens, hunting for radishes. This officer picked me up, along with this Chicano teen from downtown. At the jail he thought I'd passed out. She was fighting like a whirlwind, so he put a gag on her in the cell adjacent to mine and pulled off her trousers. I could see the girl's face. She was trying to scream, but the gag wouldn't let her. The officer was so busy with her he didn't see me reach my arm through the bars and touch her face. She had hair that curled like Sis's. Come on, I whispered to her, scream, scream, damn you. And her whole face was screaming, only no sound was coming out, and I felt like someone pulled my plug, because I started to scream instead: *(Whispers)* No! No! and I kept on screaming until the officer put out my lights.

GREG: There! George! There's two of them!

GEORGE: Where? I can't see anything.

GREG: Right there! Look . . . Nope. Lost them. Damn.

DAVID: Then I dreamt about Sis, both of us up to our wrists in the dirt, fishing for radishes in the garden. Like a pearl in an oyster, she'd say, when she pulled one up out of the dirt. *(Beat)* . . . She was my . . . my . . . *(Snaps fingers. No response)* Hey!

GEORGE AND GREG: Fuck you!

DAVID: She was my . . . friend.

(David takes off his britches, lays them out. He stands in his underwear. The shape of a person is now laid out on the floor.)

GREG: Not the all-cotton Armani trousers.

DAVID *(Playfully)*: Now, which one is me? This one? *(To self)* or that one? *(To suit on floor)* Or is that old Sis lying there? *(Beat)* Sis and I were from an aspiring middle-class neighborhood. Even as kids we were smart enough to keep our eyes on the next rung of the ladder.

(While David tells the following, George crawls into David's space, climbs onto the clothes and does push-ups over them.)

Naturally, we hung around the top of the cream neighborhood parks so we could mingle with the best. I mean, in our town we were the "betters," but we aspired to be the best. Well, some of the kids we met there started calling me a pussy for hanging out with my sister. I was twelve and she was ten. They said I could join their club but that I'd have to choose, them or her. Of course I said I'd choose them, because I knew I could make it up to Sis later when we got home.

(Now George flips over on his back and is motionless. David stands over him.)

But then they gave me a dare in order to join. And they held her down.

(David kneels over George's body. George is lifeless.)

They pulled up her skirt. They dared me. If you say no to a dare, you're a pussy. I could not be a pussy. But everything was getting sort of out of focus. I took the radishes out of my pocket. I had three of them, big as chestnuts that she and I dug that morning. I put them inside her.

(David kicks George hard in the side; he does this with no apparent emotion.)

I put them inside her. She just kept whispering my name. She wouldn't scream. Just saying: *(Whispers)* "David, no. David, no. David, no. David, no."

(George moves out of David's "show.")

She never looked me in the face again, for eleven years, until her Toyota hit that telephone post. Then she had to look at me. Lying in that coffin, she had no choice but to look up at me. *(Speaks to clothes on floor)* "I'm sorry, Sis," I said. *(Speaks each word in isolation)* I am sorry.

(After a moment, David spits on the face of the clothes figure. This action is almost tender.)

Insects. Insects we were. And they plucked out our wings. *(Beat)* I'm not pulling your leg like Greg was. See, when you break a human being in half, right over your knee, crack, like a stick, there is no fixing him. Like there was no fixing her, my little sis.

(David covers his face with hands as in a moment of agony, but then he starts laughing. Greg walks into David's space.)

GREG: Come on, come on. *Rapido, rapido.* "Bingo," goes *la cabeza*: David, you knock off wets for a kick, because you feel guilty about the . . . let's call it the vegetable rape of your *pobre hermana*. Go ahead, put yourself in the frame. Frame the pig.

DAVID: It was misplaced anger, transfer of violence, all due to a dysfunctional home.

GREG: It feels better, doesn't it, once you get a handle on the *problema*?

DAVID: I appreciate the kindness, Greg, but get the sweet Jesus out of my gig.

GREG *(Returning to car)*: You're not living up to your degree, David.

DAVID: Certainly I am *(Beat)* regretful about Sis. *(Makes popping sounds)* Fried my soul. But it isn't her at all. I'm tired of my job at the law firm. I'm bored. *(Beat)* There are just too many decisions to make: mustard vinaigrette or the house special? BMW or Volvo? Paper or plastic?

(David suddenly gags and begins to choke. Greg watches with disdain; George is fooled. He cautiously approaches David while glancing with fear at the border.)

GEORGE *(Whispers)*: David?

(David continues to gag.)

David? Are you OK? *(To Greg)* Something's the matter with him, Greg. Come and look.

(George touches David with his foot. David doesn't move. Then, suddenly, he grabs George's leg and bites it. George screams and shakes him loose. Greg and David laugh together. Then David looks around him.)

DAVID: Oh, no. Did I fall on my sapling?

GREG: I hope so.

GEORGE: That wasn't funny. I'm going home. Even if I have to walk.

(David gets up and approaches George. David spits on his hands and smooths George's hair back in place. This is a tender action. Then he suddenly strikes him.)

Hey!

DAVID: Remember our agreement? The three of us stick together. Right, George? Right?

(George doesn't answer.)

GREG: Lay off him.

DAVID: What?

GREG: I said lay off him.

DAVID: What did Greg say?

GREG: Greg said: "Fuck you."

(David takes a moment to register this, then sings at Greg.)

DAVID:
On the border, Greg's getting nauseous.
On the border, he's just too serious.

GREG *(Pushing David backward with the lines that he sings)*:
On the border, you're playing frat-boy-king.
On the border, your education's nothing.

DAVID *(Pushing Greg back with his lines as he sings)*:
On the border, it's your American half-dream,
one side upriver, the other downstream.

GREG *(Winning)*:
On the border, too many tricks in your head.
On the border, you just might wind up dead.

(There is a silence for some moments as Greg and David stare at one another. Then George begins applauding and continues until he gets their attention. David grins and casually picks up his clothes off the floor and slings them over his shoulder. He crosses to the car; Greg follows him.)

GEORGE: What a show!

DAVID: You liked that, didn't you?

GREG: I'd never have guessed.

GEORGE: You are a poet.

DAVID: Ah, but a poet born from grief. And everyone believes a poet, especially a poet who . . .

GEORGE: I had to memorize a poem once for class.

DAVID: . . . indulges a little, elaborates a bit for the show.

GEORGE: Want to hear me recite it?

GREG: So the radishes were only an elaboration?

DAVID: Only an elaboration?

GEORGE: The poem I learnt was about an idiot who sawed off his arm.

GREG: So you lied.

DAVID: The radish episode is true.

GEORGE: I just got to say that that was a pretty disgusting thing to do to your sister, David.

(David shrugs.)

GREG: I'm sorry about your sister. She always had a nice word for me.

DAVID *(Casually)*: You never met her.

(Greg shrugs.)

GEORGE: Do you think they're sorry? *(Motions to border)*

DAVID *(Whispers)*: Frankly, dear, I don't give a damn.

GREG: So what did you choose in the end?

DAVID: Why, I choose Marlboro, of course.

(David and Greg laugh together, as though at an inside joke.)

GEORGE *(Angered)*: You two are so cool, aren't you? Big
  jokers with broken hearts.
DAVID *(Looking at his watch)*: It's time to move fence lines.
GREG: Yep. *Los peces* aren't biting here.
GEORGE: Well, I can do it too, you know.
DAVID: You've got asparagus for brains, Georgie. I said
  let's go.
GEORGE: You just watch. Old George will surprise you.
  *(Moves across stage, whistling and glancing shyly at the
  border/public)*
DAVID *(Claps softly)*: That was wonderful, George, now zip
  your fly and let's go.
GEORGE *(Confiding)*: But it's different for me, 'cause mine
  is a secret.
DAVID: George. Old buddy. You're just blocking the view.
GREG: Shhh. George has a secret. Mustn't tell. Mustn't tell.
DAVID: All right. But there's nothing that long-toothed
  border wolf hates more than a pitiful performance.

(Greg and David howl.)

GEORGE: Just ignore them. *(Beat)* Lookie what I can do?
  (Grabs barbed wire and twists it. Holds his hands up) See?
  (Beat) You got to forgive them. They want to be hon-
  est. They're OK guys. I grew up with them.
DAVID: This is a warning, George. If you step on that
  sapling . . . Move it. To the right.

(George does so.)

Farther. Farther.
GREG: Farther.
GEORGE *(Moves closer to public)*: Is this OK? *(Beat)* I don't
  want them to hear some of this, so I got to speak soft.
  I was a kid when it started growing. It was the size of
  a penny, right in the middle of my back. It just
  popped up one day when I was standing in front of
  this billboard waiting for the school bus. On the billboard was a picture of a camel, sitting on a beach

with sunglasses, smoking a cigarette. The camel had this smile on his face I'd never seen on any human face before: this smile of slap-happiness, of some just-do-it secret. And that's when I felt it pop up on my back: the hump. The camel's hump. *(Does a curious rotating motion with his shoulders)* Most kids would have got scared, but I wasn't surprised. I just kept it hid under my jacket so as not to scare my friends. *(Beat)* By the time I was a grown man I had a genuine camel's hump on my back.

GREG: His fuckin' hump again.

GEORGE: When it quit growing I started waiting in front of the mirror for the rest of it, for the smile. I was patient, too. But it didn't come. I started smokin' two at a time, to hurry it up a bit but the smile still held out on me. So there I was, a camel's hump without a smile, like a dick without balls. *(Itches his back)* Don't believe me? *(Turns around and lifts his shirt. We see nothing)* Then what the hell is that? A pimple the size of a pup?

DAVID: It's an infected pore.

GREG: Another stripper. Yawn.

DAVID: Hey! Look out. I saw something move over there.

GEORGE *(Pulls his shirt down fast)*: Don't touch. It's *my* hump. *(Beat)* Now my daddy, he had—

DAVID: Not another father story.

GEORGE: —no hump, no smile and, after the mines, only one lung to smoke with. But he was a G-O-O-D man. *(Beat)* I was into four-legged animals back then, so he took me hunting. I was seven. We sat on the tail of the truck, oiling the rifles. It was so cold I couldn't feel my hands in my gloves. I walked behind him. I must have stepped on every damn twig in the woods. He kept smacking the cap off my head— *(Smacks self in head a few times)* telling me to shush up. Finally, we saw one. A buck. He was the size of a horse with antlers like Christmas trees. *(Dramatically)* His breath circled up out of his nose like ropes. *(Snickers at friends in car area)* Not bad, huh?

DAVID: George, I sense another boredom riot. If you don't pick up the rhythm, we might have to cancel. How about a questionnaire to liven things up? Let's see a show of hands. How many of you have enjoyed—

GEORGE: Shut up.

DAVID *(Continues)*: —a Big Mac so conscientiously that you had to hurry off to the restroom after the meal to beat off?

(Not to be discouraged, George returns to his monologue.)

GEORGE: My daddy whispered: *(Shouts)* "If you make a noise, I'll kill you." The barrel rose over my . . . No . . . How about this: the cold, black barrel rose over my daddy's shoulder—

DAVID *(As though counting hands)*: Which of you had the guts to switch from Coke to Pepsi out of respect for Schwarzkopf?

(George now raises the invisible rifle and aims it at his friends.)

GEORGE: —and he took aim. The buck raised its head. Its long tongue licked its gray nose. And then I saw it. *(Does so)* Wham. For the second, maybe last time in my life, that smile, that smirk of oblivion and party time. And then it hit me: that was my camel. Not a buck but my camel. *(Lets out a wild yodel)* That's just what I did. Then that camel burned rubber. The shot rang out. My father spun, and out went my lights.

GREG: This one's especially for you, David: do you recycle? *(Beat)* Only your milk jugs? Tsk, tsk.

DAVID *(To Greg)*: You don't respect your environment.

GEORGE: When I woke I saw leaves above me, then my daddy's face, the spit dripping down his chin, right into my eye. He made me crawl back to the truck on my hands and knees, with the barrel of his gun at my ass. But I didn't mind a bit. I was happy. My camel had got away. And I'd been born again by that smile. *(Beat)* Watch this. *(Walks and chews like a camel)*

DAVID: Hey, Greg, were you SDSS? *(Whispers)* Rat-tat-tat-tat. I was.

GREG *(Whispers)*: Secret Desert Storm Supporter? You know, David, that's what I've always appreciated about you liberal types. I mean, recycling not only your clear glass but your green glass as well.

GEORGE: Beautiful, huh? That stride. The stride of a camel. There is nothing else like it.

DAVID: Hey, I care, while you, you've made no choices for the future.

GEORGE: I paste billboards now, and take care of my little bro. But don't think I'm one of those broken-hearted give-ups. I'm watching out for that smile again. You see, unless you are a certain kind of American you miss the smile, and all those people out there, sneaking their way in here, are out to steal that smile. But over my dead body. That's what I say: over my dead body. *(Itches hump furiously)* It's a sport. *(Beat)* Want another peek at my hump? *(Begins to lift shirt teasingly)* Fuck off. Go get your own. *(Beat)* I'm a camel. *(Chews again)*

(David moves in on George's space. He pushes George onto all fours and puts his foot on George's back. George doesn't resist.)

DAVID: You, sir, are obviously malfunctioning. Your father shoved a gun barrel up your rectum, so you are also anal retentive.

GEORGE: Anal what?

DAVID: And if a gentleman such as this is anal, it only follows that he'll work the border.

GEORGE: Oink, oink.

DAVID: I never saw a yellow ribbon tied around your tree, George. And I know for a fact that you don't save your newspapers. Did you know that it takes ten years for a seed to become a sapling?

GEORGE *(Shouts)*: This is my story. Mine. Get the fuck out!

GREG *(To David)*: You know, David, this is what gets me. How come you always get to interrupt? Whenever you want?

DAVID: Because you let me?

GEORGE *(Struggles to his feet)*: Fuckin' traitors. Both of you. You're no better than a pair of beaners. Fuckin' beaners, both of you.

(Beat.)

DAVID: George, Greg. This is why I must constantly interrupt you. It's my duty. You see, people like me, we don't call them beaners, wetbacks or greasers. We who aren't of your, shall we say "constipated class," we call them illegal aliens, immigration offenders or, for those of us, like myself, still religiously inclined, "poor souls." Try and show a little understanding. I mean, I've used my education to figure it out: we stagnate their economies with our IMFs and can't-pay-them-off-ever loans, so they've got to try and cross and work for Roto-Rooter. Why can't you two be a little more sympathetic? Citizens like myself are trying hard to *(Sings)* "reach out and touch someone"? This tree, for instance. *(Kneels beside the sapling, sings:)*

I'm the Robin Hood of Saplings,
I watch over the small trees
and when I see one broken
it brings me to my knees.

(Beat.)

At the end of the day, you're still an ignorant man, George, and so are you, Greg, sorry. You don't care about the future, about the air the children of tomorrow will need to breathe. You're selfish, poor, a measly excuse for a working class.

GEORGE: Fuck you. I'm upper working class.

(David moves to George, smacking him across the face with each word he speaks. He does this with measured boredom; George is passive.)

DAVID: You *(Smack)* poor, *(Smack)* ignorant *(Smack)* bigot. *(Beat)* Feel any better?

(George nods.)

I understand you, George. Your psychological make-up is painfully clear. Nevertheless, you deserve to be punished, as you went ahead and did your show against my better judgment. You're going to have to drag.

GREG: No.

DAVID: George?

GEORGE: I don't want to. It hurts.

DAVID: Learning is painful. *(Takes a small piece of barbed wire from his pocket)* Open your mouth, George.

GREG: I said no.

DAVID: I heard you. A powerful word, isn't it? "No." "No." "No." Though it depends on who's saying it. *(Beat)* I'm not correcting you, Greg. I'm correcting George.

GREG: I don't want blood on my shirt. That's my shirt he's wearing.

DAVID: Take off the shirt, George.

(George begins to do so after a moment's reluctance.)

GREG: Put it back on, George.

(George starts to.)

DAVID: George.

GEORGE: I don't want to drag. It hurts.

GREG: Get back in the car, George.

(No one moves.)

Not tonight, David. Just this once, do me a favor. I don't think I've asked for one in a while.

DAVID *(After a silence)*: Put the shirt back on, George.

GREG: Thanks. I mean it. Thanks. *(Beat)* Thanks, thanks, thanks. Why am I always thanking you? You pull this every time. Why do you get to decide when and how we do our stuff, where we have to stand?

DAVID *(Ignores Greg)*: No drag, got it, George? But repeat after me: "I am the ignorant one—"

GEORGE *(Repeats with toleration rather than obedience)*: "I am the ignorant one—"

DAVID: "—the humped one—"

GEORGE: "—the humped one—"

DAVID: "—the . . . the . . ." *(Snaps his fingers so Greg will give him his line)* Isn't anyone helping out anymore?

GREG: Looks like things are going to hell pretty quick, heh, David?

GEORGE *(Screams)*: I want to finish my story!

DAVID: I give up.

GEORGE: So I hunt Mexicans. It's not a personal thing. Why should I like them? *(Turns to David)* But I like you. You wear nice clothes. You let me mow your lawn.

DAVID *(Sniffs under his arms)*: My armpits are odor free.

GREG: You don't itch your crotch in public.

GEORGE: I mean, how could I hate you when you gave me your old Adidas and bought my flag for me at Kmart?

DAVID: So there are no inappropriate feelings?

(Greg shrugs.)

GEORGE: Naw. *(Beat)* Well, how did you like it?

(They ignore him.)

DAVID *(To Greg)*: It's ten o'clock.

GREG: Shut up, George. Let's shift.

GEORGE: Just a fuckin' minute. After you guys went you got some fuckin' feedback. It's my turn now. I get my minute in the sun.

DAVID: But really, Georgie, a camel?

GEORGE: Yeah. A camel.

(Greg laughs with David.)

GREG: A camel? I'm tired of this. It's time to move.

GEORGE: Yeah. A camel. Is a camel worth any less than a radish? Than a half-breed with a heart split in two?

DAVID: Have you ever stopped to consider the size of a camel's turd?

GEORGE: OK, OK. But you guys are screwed, because my camel could eat your radish any day. But, you know, I had a rhythm going, and you just moved in, without even asking, and fucked it up.

GREG: You're pathetic, George. You didn't have a rhythm going. You never had a rhythm going.

DAVID: Don't be too hard on him. He's mentally challenged.

GREG *(Turns on David)*: Is he? Well, let's not forget you're only hanging out with us, Mr. Educado, due to our good graces. But you know, I think it's time we sent you back to your hot tub.

DAVID: Please. Not that. Let me stay with you fellows. Let me get some dirt on my boots, some oil under my fingernails.

GREG: I've been thinking. All these years I wanted to ask you, but I figured better not because you're my friend. But I want to know. Now. What else? What else from the root family, huh, David? Is it only radishes, or do you get hot over tubers as well? Most of all, did you have the guts to try them out on yourself before you did your sister in?

GEORGE: What's a tuber?

DAVID: A tuber is a situation like this one. Stuck in the ground with no place to grow. Snore, snore. You two Boy Scouts are getting so predictable I'm going to have to go back to playing tennis at the club.

GREG *(Sniffs David)*: You know, I've never liked the way you smell.

DAVID: You mean I've practiced all these years for nothing?

GEORGE: What the fuck is up here?

DAVID: Did I ever mention to you two that I finally hired myself a maid?

GEORGE: A beaner?

DAVID: Only the best. Guess what I named her, Greg?

GREG: Maid.

DAVID: Getting warmer.

GEORGE: Cleanie-beanie?

DAVID: Colder.

GREG: I'll tell you what the difference is, David. Like all of them in your club: you wear deodorant, but you can't hide the stink. A real handicap.

DAVID: I gave her a special name. *(Beat)* In honor of Greg, of course.

GEORGE: You see, Greg? He likes you. *(Beat)* Watch this trick: I can eat a rock.

GREG: No. No. I don't want to see you eat a rock. I don't want to see you swallow a beer cap. I don't want to see you put a centipede down your pants. Stop trying to act like a funny guy. You're no more worthless than the rest of us.

GEORGE: I'm not?

GREG: No, you're smart. Sometimes.

GEORGE: I am?

DAVID: This is . . . This is . . . Words fail me.

GREG: As a matter of fact, you're a winner.

GEORGE: A winner?

GREG: Who spots the most beaners on a weekly basis?

GEORGE: Me?

GREG: Yes. You. Who spots the least?

GEORGE: David.

GREG: And you know why? Because he gets paid not only for the beaners he turns in, but for the ones he lets cross.

GEORGE: Lets cross?

DAVID: Greg.

GREG: As a matter of fact, he gets paid a bonus for the athletic types he lets through. The ones that can do the hard labor.

GEORGE *(To David)*: That's not true, is it, David?

DAVID: Hey Greg. About that money you owe me.

GEORGE: You get paid for letting them cross?

DAVID: I think I'll need it by tomorrow.

GEORGE: Why? Why?

GREG: Because David knows he's got to let in just enough beaners to work dead cheap so he can—

DAVID: —maintain my standard of living? It's a very good standard, too. Don't forget it.

GEORGE: I can't believe this.

DAVID: But there's another reason you've left out, Greg. I want to share.

GREG: Share?

DAVID: Certainly. This is the melting pot, isn't it? If we keep everyone out, we'll lose the mix.

GEORGE: You lied to me, David. You never did that to me before.

DAVID: So has Greg. He knew all about it.

GEORGE: Greg?

GREG: If it weren't for David, we wouldn't even have the deal with the feds to begin with.

GEORGE: Well, fuck you. Fuck you both, I'm going home.

DAVID *(Takes George's face in his hands)*: Hey, I'm still your friend. I've taken good enough care of you so far, haven't I? Who helped you out on your electric bill last month? *(Beat)* You see? I'm still your friend.

(George pulls away, but he's less angry now.)

That's right. I am. And I'll tell you what. Just to show you I'm respectable about it, I'm inviting you over so you can finger my new maid's teeth. It will tickle your innards. No charge.

GREG: You really fell for that molar story, didn't you, you *hijo de la gran puta*, son of a bitch.

DAVID: Something tells me that lately you've begun to feel uncomfortable about our relationship.

GREG: No. This isn't a friendship thing. We've always been amigos. Father, Son and the Holy Ghost, right?

GEORGE: I want to be the ghost. Hey! Look! There's three of them!

(David pays no attention to George. Greg is torn between helping George and confronting David.)

DAVID: Then Simon says, "What is it?"

GEORGE: Oh, shit. They're going to charge. Come on, Greg!

GREG: It's how you like it out here.

GEORGE: I like it out here. *(To border)* Go back! Go back! We're not ready for you!

DAVID: Oh, please. Are we going to have another "David thinks he's got gold for shit and only hangs out with us, hoping it will rub off" episodes? Or how about the rerun where you curse me and George for feeling up the chicks we catch just because you haven't got the stomach to join in.

GREG: I never wanted to join in. I just wanted the ten bucks a hit.

GEORGE: Will you two cut the shit and look alive before we lose these guys?

DAVID: Shut up, George. *(To Greg)* Or perhaps you never joined in because of the difficulty you have in getting an erection that will last more than three seconds.

GEORGE: I don't want to talk about Greg's dick!

GREG *(Refuses to let David "get" him)*: If the feds ever changed their minds, if they ever wanted to burn us . . .

GEORGE: They fucking crossed.

DAVID: You think they don't know what we're up to? You really are confused.

GEORGE: A hundred feet away from us and we're letting them cross. That's thirty bucks down the drain.

GREG: Well, if they ever did decide to burn us, they'd burn me and George, not you. Not you, because you've got a Lawn-Boy rider and a concrete pool.

GEORGE: Let's talk about my show. I want to talk about it!

DAVID *(To Greg)*: My, you are breathing rapidly. You must be ill. Should we call it quits for the night? But we still haven't guessed what I named my maid? *(No response from Greg)* I named her Evalina. *(Beat)* I did it for you. And all I get in return is a—

GREG *(Interrupts)*: You named your maid Evalina? Evalina? Is she one of the chosen ones you let through? I bet she loves her job, doesn't she, cleaning your toilet the same way she brushes her teeth?

DAVID: Teeth. Teeth. It's got into your subconscious, hasn't it, son?

GREG: Tell us how you caught her, David, tell us what you said to her to make her feel safe. Tell us. Which fence line?

DAVID: You're tiresome.

GREG: Did she walk across or did she crawl? What was it like? Hey, David, was it like this?

(Greg crawls from the border. Though he pretends to be a Mexican woman, it is important that his voice is not affected. He does not try to "sound" like a woman, instead he speaks with his own voice. He may affect a slight accent but then drop it when the action gets more violent.)

Hallo! Hallo! Gringo. Do you have a job for me? Gringo. Gringo. Can you help me?

(As Greg speaks, David begins to circle him, joining in the game.)

DAVID: How can I help you, miss?

GREG: Oh, Mister Gringo. I want to work. I like work.

(David trips Greg and pushes him to his knees.)

DAVID: So you like to work?

(George gets into the game. David and George both interrogate Greg.)

GEORGE: What kind of work?

GREG: Anything. I need money. *Dinero. Dinero.*

DAVID: What for?

GEORGE: What for?

GREG: For pretty clothes?

DAVID *(Smacks Greg in the head)*: Stupid answer. Try again. Why do you want money?

GREG: I'm hungry. *(Beat)* I'm starving.

GEORGE *(Picks up a handful of dirt)*: Then open up. I got a McDonald's for you.

(George forces dirt in Greg's mouth. Greg spits it out and attempts to rise. David forces him back onto his knees.)

DAVID: So you want me to give you a job, heh, sweetheart? Why don't you get a nice job in your own hometown?

GEORGE *(Kicks Greg)*: Yeah. Why do you want to come over here and take mine?

DAVID: You better answer old George, miss, or he'll throw you to the border wolf. *(Beat)* Answer him, you bitch!

GREG: Because . . . Because . . .

DAVID: Answer him.

GREG: Because there's no jobs in my hometown. The Yankee pays better over here than the Yankee does over there. *(Beat) Putas. Todos los* Yankees.

DAVID: Did you hear that, George? Cursed at me in Mexican. The bitch.

(David slaps Greg.)

GEORGE: The bitch.

DAVID: But I'm a nice guy. I'll give you a job. You can come home with me. But are you clean?

(Greg holds up his hands to show David that his hands are clean.)

Not your hands. I mean what you've got between your legs. Show me.

GREG: No.

GEORGE: Show us.

GREG: No.

GEORGE AND DAVID: Show us!

GREG: No!

(David throws Greg on his back and straddles him. George pins Greg's arms down and puts his hand over Greg's mouth so he can't speak.)

DAVID: So you want a job? Well, if you're going to work for me, you can't wear those dirty shirts.

(David rips Greg's shirt open. Greg struggles.)

GEORGE: Nice tits. Look at her tits.

DAVID: What's a girl like you doing in a mess like this? But I will have to give you a tip for your troubles.

(David takes out some dollar bills and stuffs them in Greg's mouth so he can't speak.)

GEORGE: Touch her, David. Hurt her. Twist her tit.

(David twists Greg's nipple; Greg screams through the bills.)

DAVID: It's not nice to shout.

(Greg struggles and manages to throw David off of him. Now Greg sits on David. George has backed off. Greg spits out the bills on David's face. There are some moments of silence as David and Greg become aware of their new positions.)

GREG: So you want a job, huh? *(Strikes him hard)* I'm talking to you. You want a job?

GEORGE: Do it again, Greg.

(*Greg strikes David again.*)

GREG: Well, if you're going to work for me, you can't wear those fancy shirts. (*Rips David's shirt open. David is passive, as though stunned*) Nice, *chica*. Really nice. Here in America—

(*George pulls on David's hair and spits on him.*)

—we know how to appreciate a nice piece of foreign work. (*Beat*) How does it feel, baby? How does it feel to be on the bottom, with your ass in the dirt? Want to come home with me and scrub my tub? I'll buy you a green apron.

(*Some moments of silence. As David speaks the following, Greg's power leaves him.*)

DAVID: You know, Greg, I've been meaning to ask you— (*Beat*) did you ever get that GED diploma you were working for? You really should, you know. Not that there's anything wrong with not even having a high school diploma, but it is important to be an educated man. That way, you've got more choices. You can move up in the world.

(*David pushes Greg off of him. David cleans himself off. Neither George nor Greg resists him. Then David notices the sapling.*)

You fucking clodhoppers. I can't believe it. You stepped on my sapling. Squashed it.

GEORGE: I didn't do it. Greg stepped on it. He did it.

DAVID: Broke its back. You sons of bitches. With your big, dirty, stinking boots. (*Beat*) This night is over. We're calling it quits.

GEORGE (*Yells*): But I want to have a good time!

GREG (*Calmly, not shouting*): Aren't you? Aren't you having a good time, George?

DAVID *(Gazing at sapling)*: I don't like to see things die. *(Beat)* Do you remember the taste of your first girl, Greg?

GREG: No. I don't.

DAVID: But you must. How can anyone not remember the taste of their first girl, when you're leaning over to kiss her . . .

GREG: I don't remember.

DAVID: . . . when you're leaning over to kiss her, and her mouth is shining like glass, and her chest is rising and falling when she breathes, rising and falling like the wing of a bird. *(Beat)* But then you hear it again. And it stops you cold. *(Begins to sing:)*

Wrigley Spearmint Radish, Radish, Radish.
Wrigley Spearmint Radish, Radish, Radish.

(Greg watches him some moments, then begins to shout at David until he drowns him out. Greg continues.)

GREG: Stop. Stop it. Just stop it. *(Beat)* You think that's how it happens? Yeah? You think that's what I remember when I remember my first girl? No, I remember this:

(Greg slowly, gently runs his finger over David's lip. David does not move or respond.)

Evalina. She used to run her finger over my lip like that, and then there was no better place to be than right there where she touched me. *(After a moment of silence, he moves away)* But that's not how the story gets told, is it, David? Well, I'll tell you right now that I can one-up your radish, you motherfucker. Just watch this. *(Turns to public again, starts speaking fast)* Hey! Hey! *Dame dos cuchillos.* Throw me a couple of knives. Right here. Think I haven't got it in me? Well, half of me is *Mejicano.* The other half of me is WASP. *Como sabes* which side is which? My mother used to tell me: *"Este lado es Mejicano.* This side is Mexican, *(Slaps left breast)* the side with the heart." *(Beat)* My father made OK *dinero.* He helped me get a loan on my car. *(Turns to David)* Are you listening? *(Back to public/border)* I met my first girl when I was working at the grocers on 17th and Chestnut. She was Chicana.

DAVID *(Shoves him)*: You already told us your *(Beat)* emotional dentistry saga, Greg. No second chances.

GREG *(Shoves him back)*: I figured, like father like son. And she was legal, nice trailer, two-parent family. *(Beat)* Then she got pregnant. I brought her home to meet my father.

GEORGE: Hey, I didn't get a second shot. This isn't fair. This isn't fair.

GREG: He called us into his office. I told him: *"Voy a casar con esta chica, Papa."* It used to piss him off when I spoke Spanish. So, no, I didn't say it like that. I said, "I'd like your permission to marry, sir." He just nodded. Evalina smiled. She'd been so damned loco scared he'd say no. Then he put his hand on Evalina's head and took hold of her long braid. *(Beat)* Then he gave her arm a quick twist and she was lying on the floor. She was so surprised, she couldn't make a noise.

(Lifts his foot and balances. George and David are now listening to him.)

No. It's not good enough.

(Suddenly Greg grabs David by the collar and swings him to the floor.)

She was so surprised, she couldn't make a noise.

DAVID *(Protesting)*: Hey!

GREG: Shut up.

DAVID: I'm not taking part—

(David breaks off as Greg kicks him violently.)

GREG: Shut the fuck up! I said: she was so surprised that she didn't make a noise. *(Lifts his foot)* And then he did this.

(Greg puts his foot on David's throat. David is passive. Greg speaks as his father.)

"This isn't the first time I've had to do this. Don't worry about it, son, it's just like getting your finger pricked. Ask your mother." *(Beat)* And then he brought his boot heel down, hard, on her abdomen. *(Makes a sound of air escaping from his lips)* That was the sound that escaped from Evalina's lips. Can you make that sound, David? *(Jerks David by the hair)* Come on. Try it.

(Greg makes the sound again. David is silent. Then Greg steps over and away from David.)

Then there was no sound. *Nada. Nada.* I could feel the warm slide of piss running down my leg into my shoe. *Cuando Evalina se despierto*, I drove her home. She was already bleeding it out. *(Beat)* Over breakfast the next morning he asked me . . . he asked me . . . *(Breaks off)*

DAVID *(Without malice)*: He asked you if you'd decided to postpone the wedding.

GREG: Yeah. *(Beat)* Well, it was a year later. I hadn't been home in a while. I came by to visit my mother. Father was out on patrol. We were just talkin' shop while she was doing the wash. I asked her why she never had any more kids after me. She just shrugged. I came right out and told her about me and Evalina, about almost having to marry, about Father helping us out. I watched her pour a whole bottle of detergent in the wash. Then she said, like she might be saying, "That's the third load today," "I thought mine were the only ones." Then she hit me.

(Greg moves to David, takes David's hand, and uses it to smack himself in the face. David tunes in to the role and now plays Greg's mother, but with no affectations in his voice.)

DAVID: And you did nothing? *(Smacks Greg again)* And you did nothing? *(Smacks Greg again, harder)* And you did nothing?

GREG: The kid would have been three-fourths beaner, Ma. Not a hundred percent, like you, but three-fourths. Three-fourths. An almost. A not quite. A partly. A fuckin' percentage. And he'd never be able to grow up and be like his father, Ma. Like I can never grow up and be like you, no matter how hard I try. *(Moves to George)* She spit at me.

(Greg is expecting George to spit at him. When he doesn't, Greg pushes him.)

(Louder) She spit at me. Hey! *(Pushes him)* Hey!

(George spits in his face. Greg turns his story back to the public.)

That's right. *(Quietly)* When my father walked through the door that night, "bang," my mother shot him in the throat, bull's-eye through the Adam's. *(Sings:)*

Oh, Evalina, no llores mas por mi
porque vamanos to the border
con cervezas 'cross my knee.

So I'm here. The border. It keeps me in line. I mean, what if I just gave up this huntin'? I might start going weird. I might start feeling sorry for Evalina again, go track her down. Find out where she went to.

DAVID: Enough of this, old boy.

GREG: I might even take that gun of his I've got hidden under a floorboard in my room.

GEORGE *(Becoming more agitated)*: Stop it!

GREG: I might go out hunting. But maybe not for beaners this time.

GEORGE: I can't listen to you anymore!

GREG: And what if I got even weirder and went after some of you too. I don't know. I mean, you saw him lift his foot over her belly, didn't you? *(Laughs, turns to David and George, and says calmly)* And you did nothing? *(Turns back to public/border)* And you did nothing? *(Beat)* And you did nothing?

GEORGE: Shut the fuck up!

GREG: I mean, he was the law, your law, and she was just the cheap labor.

(George punches Greg. Greg falls down.)

DAVID: Get the fuck back in the car or this will be the last time we take you shopping.

(Greg gets up, obeying David, and goes to the car. Then he snatches the gun and aims at them.)

GEORGE: No, Greg. Put that down

DAVID: Stay calm, big boy. Take a deep breath.

GREG *(Speaks calmly and with complete assurance)*: Shut up. You're both dead. *(Beat)* Hey, I look good, don't I?

DAVID: Brilliant.

GREG: I've never been more brilliant in all my life. *(Beat)* You're finished. Both of you.

DAVID: Listen, Greggie.

GREG: No. I'm not going to listen. You're going to listen.

GEORGE: Jesus, Greg.

DAVID: You're not playing the game.

GREG: But I am. *(Beat)* Trust me. *(Beat)* Hey, let's play one more time? Which one should we play, David? Once upon a time in the land of radishes?

DAVID: Listen to me a minute. If you'd just—

GREG *(Interrupts)*: No. Not that one. We're tired of that one. So tell me, David, how do you spell relief? *(Beat)* My story is about halves. *(Lifts shirt)* Will you look at this? Split down the middle. But which side is which? I mean, when the moment hit you, when the crisis struck, which did you choose, Hostess or Sara Lee? JVC or Sony? I mean, isn't that the simple beauty of it: who can afford to hire a maid and who can't afford not to be one?

(George moves slightly, as though he is thinking to run for it.)

GEORGE: Let me go, Greg. I got to get home.

GREG: Hey, don't you want to play a game? This is your game, David. I say the words and you try and put your mind to work somewhere else so the words won't get to you. Now, think hard about the first time you put your tongue in someone else's mouth, or map it out in your head how you're gonna change things in your neighborhood. Or how about this one: picture how your sister looked when you left her lying there in the park, saying: *(Softly)* "No." *(Beat)* "David. No." "David. No." *(Slaps David in the face, though not hard. David is passive)* "David. No." *(Beat)* Now, I dare you not to switch out, not to turn off. OK? "I pledge allegiance, to the flag, of the United . . ." Hold it. Let's start over. Make it harder this time. *(Pokes him with the gun)* Hey. Pay attention. Isn't this what you taught me?

(Greg puts the gun in David's hand and places the gun at his own forehead. They are both holding it now.)

Come on, David. Show us your stuff. *(Kneels)* "I pledge allegiance, to the flag of the United States of—"

(Greg knocks David so that David says the rest with him.)

GREG AND DAVID: "—America. And to the Republic for which it stands, one nation, under God, indivisible, with *(Beat)* liberty and justice for all."

(Greg stands. He takes the gun back from David.)

GREG: "David. No." *(Beat)* The show's over. *(Beat)* O-V-E-R! *(Beat)* George, get out of here.

(George doesn't move. Greg speaks gently.)

Hey, now and then, you were funny. I mean it. *(Beat)* So go home, Camel-boy. *(To David)* But I can't let you off that easy, David. Yeah, I like you. But I'm your nightmare now, your very own one-hundred-per-cent, all-American, pure beef wetback, and I'm gonna stay right here, light up this border, *(Beat)* but how about from the other side this time. *(Beat)* Y de ahora en adelante ya no voy a hablar mas el ingles. Yo necesito mis proprias palabras para . . . para . . . luchar. Si, ya se que has escuchado todo eso antes, pero esto vez . . . Watch out!

(Greg pushes David to kneel. David does not resist. Greg pulls David's head back by the hair and kisses him violently on the forehead.)

Listen. Something just had to give. It's nothing personal. *(Raises gun to David's temple. Greg speaks calmly and slowly)* We were always friends.

(There are some moments of silence as we wait for the shot. Nothing happens.)

Escucha, David. With all that *inteligente* you bought— *(Holds the gun up in front of David's face)* can you read this? Right here? Can you read it? It doesn't say

Taiwan or Japan this time. On the barrel, you can read it if you squint. You see what it says? *(Steps back)* It says: MADE IN THE USA. *(Beat)* Here. *(Holds out gun to David and George)* You can have it back.

(Neither George nor David moves. Greg drops the gun at their feet. He begins to exit. As he leaves the stage, blackout.)

END OF PLAY

SLAUGHTER CITY

1996

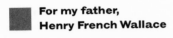 **For my father,
Henry French Wallace**

PRODUCTION HISTORY

Slaughter City had its first performance on January 17, 1996, at the Royal Shakespeare Company. The director was Ron Daniels, design was by Ashley Martin-Davies, lighting design was by Hugh Vanstone, sound score was by Glyn Perrin, sound was by Monkey and Tony Brand, movement was by Struan Leslie, fights were by Terry King, dialect coach was Charmian Hoare, company voice work was by Barbara Houseman and Andrew Wade, the stage manager was Michele Enright, the deputy stage manager was Nick Chesterfield and the assistant stage manager was Lucy Bovington. The cast was as follows:

ROACH	Lisa Gaye Dixon
MAGGOT	Sophie Stanton
BRANDON	Alexis Daniel
COD	Olwen Fouéré
TUCK	Rudolph Walker
TEXTILE WORKER	Mairead Carty
SAUSAGE MAN	Robert Langdon Lloyd
BAQUIN	Linal Haft

In March 1996, *Slaughter City* was produced by American Repertory Theatre, Cambridge, MA. The director was Ron Daniels. Set and costume design were by Ashley Martin-Davies, lighting design was by John Ambrosone, sound design was by Christopher Walker, original music was by Glyn Perrin and the stage manager was Jay McLeod. The cast was as follows:

ROACH	Starla Benford
MAGGOT	Judith Hawking
BRANDON	Jay Boyer
COD	S. J. Scruggs
TUCK	Terry Alexander
TEXTILE WORKER	Phoebe Jonas
SAUSAGE MAN	Alvin Epstein
BAQUIN	Remo Airaldi

CHARACTERS

ROACH, an African-American worker, mid-thirties
MAGGOT, a white worker, mid-thirties
BRANDON, a white worker, early twenties
COD, a white worker of Irish descent, mid-thirties
TUCK, an African-American, mid-forties
TEXTILE WORKER, a woman, twenties
SAUSAGE MAN, a white man, energetic, somewhat elderly
BAQUIN, a white company manager, fifties

TIME

Now and then.

PLACE

Slaughter City, USA.

SETTING

Should be minimal and not "realistic."

I came to the cities in a time of disorder
When hunger ruled.
I came among men in a time of uprising
And I revolted with them.
So the time passed away
Which on earth was given me.

I ate my food between massacres.
The shadow of murder lay upon my sleep.
And when I loved, I loved with indifference.
I looked upon nature with impatience.
So the time passed away
Which on earth was given me.

In my time streets led to the quicksand.
Speech betrayed me to the slaughterer.
There was little I could do. But without me
The rulers would have been more secure.
    This was my hope.

—Bertolt Brecht

"To Those Born Later"

ACT I

PRELUDE

The stage is empty but for a woman textile worker, her back to us, working over her cloth. She speaks as if in a trance. Cod is elsewhere on stage, watching her work. We are in a textile factory setting, "somewhere" in the past.

TEXTILE WORKER: Pull the cloth, punch it down, cut three out, and trace. Hurry, hurry, don't slow down, keep your cheer and grace.

COD: Could you look up for a second? Hey.

TEXTILE WORKER: Pull the cloth, punch it down, cut three out, and trace.

COD *(Calls)*: Is anybody out there?

TEXTILE WORKER: Hurry, hurry, don't slow down, keep your cheer and grace.

COD: The doors are locked. *(To Textile Worker)* I'm talking to you.

TEXTILE WORKER: When I daydream, my hands sweep the cloth—

COD: What floor are we on?

TEXTILE WORKER: —like water over the keys of a piano.

(We hear the distorted sound of a siren in the distance.)

COD: We've got to get out of here.

TEXTILE WORKER *(Touches his face gently)*: Oh, what eyes you have. Black eyes. Like my eyes.

COD: I haven't got any eyes. I'm not even born yet.

(The woman turns back to her cloth to work. Transfixed, Cod watches her.)

SCENE ONE

Lights up on Maggot, Roach and Brandon working. They are hosing down the heads of carcasses which are suspended above them, and slicing off bits of gristle from the bone. When the workers work, the feeling should be one of the intensity of industrial labor here on earth and perhaps also in hell.

ROACH: Maggot? *(No answer)* Maggot? Come on, sweetie. I said I was sorry. It was just a joke, wasn't it, Brandon?

BRANDON: A masterstroke, an okeydoke joke.

MAGGOT: A just plain you-haven't-got-any-brains-left-for-God-to-suck-out-of-your-skull joke.

ROACH: Did you eat it?

BRANDON: Didn't even pause till she got to the claws.

ROACH: Maggot? Come on.

MAGGOT: Not unless you buy me three packs of brand name smokes and on third shift you snap guts and let me scale.

ROACH: You know I won't snap guts.

MAGGOT: I've been snappin' guts since I was seventeen.

BRANDON: Princess of Excrementis.

MAGGOT: Just because I turned you down three years ago for a Dairy Queen date . . .

BRANDON: That was before I realized that what you need is a dull blade, baby, a blade that won't cut meat.

(Bell sounds, which means a short break for the workers. At the moment the bell sounds, all work/assembly line movement stops. Maggot flexes her hands, which are hurting her.)

ROACH: Two packs of generics, and I'll go third shift on the night you want off, 'cept Saturday—

BRANDON *(Interrupts)*: Hey! Here it comes: I'm startin' to itch.

(Cod enters, headed for the kill floor. He is a slim, young Irishman, who is stronger than he looks. Brandon jumps in front of Cod and pretends to sword fight.)

Unsheathe from your scabbard, you scoundrel, you fleabane, you scabrous snake.

(Cod does not respond.)

Look at this, ladies. Not a peep. Why, they're no fun, these bacterial spots. And, Lord, how they—

MAGGOT AND ROACH: Itch, itch, itch.

BRANDON *(Like a commercial)*: Are you covered with raised, roughened or unwholesome patches?

MAGGOT AND ROACH: Scratch, scratch, scratch.

BRANDON: Do you sometimes feel a little down, like a crust of hard blood and serum over a wound?

(The three workers circle Cod.)

MAGGOT AND ROACH: Are you characterized by crustaceous spots?

BRANDON: Then you need Local 226.

MAGGOT: Only Local 226—

ROACH, MAGGOT AND BRANDON: Don't need you.

(They stand in a circle around Cod.)

You know what Scab stands for?

MAGGOT, BRANDON AND ROACH: Stupid Cunts And Bastards.

(Cod spits on the ground at their feet.)

ROACH *(Speaks)*: It's raining, it's pouring . . .

MAGGOT AND ROACH: The scab's gone a-whoring!

MAGGOT: Watch you don't bump your head.

BRANDON: Or you won't be back in the morning!

(Maggot begins to sharpen her knife, the others do the same. Roach hums a tune and then the three workers sing the following. When one of them sings, the others hum.)

I'm gonna cut you, Scabby, gonna cut you deep
with my sweet, blue kisses, gonna send you off to
    sleep.

MAGGOT:
I'm gonna slice you, sweetheart, gonna slice you
    wide—

ROACH:
—with my hot, fast lips I'm gonna take you for a ride.

(Bell sounds again. The workers move back to their jobs. Cod stands silently, watching them.)

SCENE TWO

Baquin in his office, with Tuck, a supervisor.

TUCK: Mood. The mood?

BAQUIN: Yes. What's the mooood in the packhouse?

TUCK: Sickly. Yeah, a sickly mood in there.

BAQUIN: Well, their boycott of our products has put a dent in our sales, but a dent is a dent. We can survive a dent. What we need is a mooooove. *(Clears his throat)* A turn in the right direction. Some better weather. What do you say we . . . What's your name again?

TUCK: Tuck. Supervisor Tuck.

BAQUIN: Yes, well, fellows come and go here. Mostly Affirmative Action types. They don't always last—

TUCK *(Interrupts)*: Affirmative Action didn't get this job for me.

BAQUIN: I didn't mean to imply. No. Not you. But then, why you? What makes Buck special?

TUCK: I started on the kill floor, sir. About fifteen years ago. I worked my way up. Now I take night classes at Bellarmin. Just about got my degree.

BAQUIN: Where do you see yourself in five years?

TUCK: Do you like your job?

BAQUIN: Clever! Very clever.

TUCK: Yeah. But I've also been cut. *(Shows his arm)* Sliced. *(Shows his torso)* And hacked. *(Shows where a finger is maimed)*

BAQUIN: Now, don't get sentimental. We've got a business to run. Special interests are slicing our hearts, gutting innovation, shredding our ability to compete—

TUCK: You've got two Mercedes.

BAQUIN: That's what I mean. Fellow that runs IBP's got three. *(Laughs)*

TUCK: They won't go easy for the mechanical sharpener, and seniority rights are still top of the list.

BAQUIN: Seniority rights. I need capable workers. A worker is like a nose. It runs good, runs on time. But like all things, it gets stuffed. You pick it. It gets stuffed again. It starts costing too much to pick. What do you expect me to do? Be their grandmother and carry out their snot rags in their old age?

TUCK: I would get rid of some troublemakers.

BAQUIN: I've done that.

TUCK: There are some more.

BAQUIN: Tell me something, son, I heard a rumor the other day that some of our boys in the packhouse aren't circumcised. The Board doesn't like it. It's not good for packhouse reputation. *(Beat)* What about you? *(No answer from Tuck)* Well, if you're not, you should go get it done. Those little hats collect dirt. And you don't seem like the kind of man to collect dirt.

TUCK: No . . .

BAQUIN: What we need is to raise the spirits around here. We need to give the union the feeling that it has a voice. That the boss listens. That we're a team.

TUCK: They want a new contract and a guaranteed pace.

BAQUIN: That's not a team concept. Let's start a reading circle. Management will supply the books. We'll discuss literature. Start with Thomas Hardy. *(Beat)* What about an environmental program? We could get a committee together to discuss *Partula affinis*. *(Holds up a glass bowl)* It's the only current member of a small and exclusive club of species that have been wiped out by man.

TUCK: What is it?

BAQUIN: A snail.

TUCK: Looks like snot.

BAQUIN: It's the last single snail of its kind. I bought it from the University of Virginia. Under the table deal. They get our sliced meats thirty percent off. It's a hermaphrodite, this one. If it wants to, it can mate with itself. When this small mollusc dies, its species will enter the eternal night of extinction. Hard to imagine, isn't it? *(Beat)* Do you think we could stir up some interest? An after work hobby?

TUCK: They're pretty tired when they get off work.

BAQUIN: Imagine. The ultimate loneliness. To be the last of your kind. *(Beat)* Who's that kid, the one always sparking trouble over the knives? College kid. Full of spunk.

TUCK: Brandon.

BAQUIN: Find a reason to fire him.

TUCK: He's one of our best with a knife.

BAQUIN: Then promote him. That should turn him around.

TUCK: By the way, he's back. The guy with a sausage grinder, old hand-held thing. Nasty. He's waiting in the hall to see you. He won't leave. Says he started the Company.

BAQUIN: Nonsense. No one started this Company. It's been here since . . . the beginning of time. *(Beat)* Now, give me a check on their . . . on their . . . mooooood again. *(Clears his throat)* At the end of the week.

TUCK: I'll do that, Mr. Baquin.

BAQUIN: That a boy, Buck.

(Tuck exits. Baquin sits at his desk and clears his throat again. He speaks aloud, though he is alone.)

At the end of the week. Give me a report on their . . . *(Looks around, in some distress. Tries again)* At the end of the week. Give me a report on their . . . general well-being.

SCENE THREE

Brandon is showing Roach how to pull loins, one of the toughest jobs in the industry.

BRANDON: Reach and pull. Reach and pull. Got it? *(Beat)* Half the men I know can't pull loins.

ROACH: For a number one pay bracket a whole week, I'm damn sure gonna try.

BRANDON: Now, you got seven to nine coming at you a minute. When the horn goes for the speed up, you get up to twelve.

(He puts his hands on hers to show her. She pulls away.)

ROACH: Just show me, OK?

BRANDON: The important thing is you've got to dip your knife before each cut. Like this. And swing the blade out over the loin like this. You have to be quick. Real quick.

ROACH: I got it.

(They pull loins side by side.)

BRANDON: You've got . . . nice quick arms.

ROACH: Why don't you go on back to college where you belong?

BRANDON: 'Cause I like the pay.

ROACH: That's the difference between you and me, besides the color: you like the pay. I need it.

BRANDON: When I started working here, I vomited every Monday morning. They dropped me down on the kill floor pulling black guts, cleaning chitterlings. Hog shit in my nose, in my mouth, all day long. Then I was trimming jaw bones. Lost half a thumb, see? Moving up. Moving up in the pay bracket. Ten cents more. Fifteen cents more. All the time waiting to get to the knives. Then I was head boner. Slipped a disk twice. Twenty-five cents more. Then moving up again to a scalder. Forty cents. Then forty-five. Hot. That was too damn hot. Then I was bung dropper. Too fucking intimate, cutting the assholes out of hogs. One guy slipped his bung and cut my left thigh to the bone. Then I was splitter. Top-rate bracket. Bingo. New used car. Two-bedroom apartment, one for me, one for my television. I like it. I like the money.

ROACH: You like the money. We're making less now at the top pay bracket than we were at the lowest ten years ago.

BRANDON: But that's gonna change for me, 'cause I'm moving up to formal combat with the meat, straight into that neat, clean seat in the sky.

ROACH: You don't give a damn about the contract, do you?

BRANDON: Sure I do. While I'm here. I'm not budging on knife-sharpening time. The twenty minutes we got now isn't enough.

ROACH: It's about more than knives.

BRANDON: Not to me. What they want is to hire some distempered dildo who doesn't know that one knife is as different from another as two women are different. And this guy is gonna sharpen my knife for me? That fatuous ferret will fold that edge over without even knowing it, and I'll have to break my back all day long cutting with a dull knife.

ROACH: Seniority is the priority.

BRANDON: You never used a loin knife till now. Look. The edge of a knife is like a thin piece of hair. What the steel does is it stands it up, so if you angle that steel wrong, you're going to fold that edge over.

ROACH: Hmmm.

BRANDON: I was thinking maybe you *(Beat)* and me, we could take a stroll. Nothing too fancy, a twirl through the park, a couple of cartwheels 'cross the Belvedere?

ROACH: I already said no. I'm fifteen years older than you.

BRANDON: Maybe you don't dote on white boys.

ROACH: I don't dote on boys period.

BRANDON: You're caught up on this color thing.

ROACH: Since the day I was born.

BRANDON: Well, get over it, Roach. Cast it behind you.

ROACH: Just scale it off me like a fish. Right. Why are you here? Why don't you toddle on back to the U and get some more of that financial aid. Though I doubt you'll learn to figure this side of the fence even if you sit bare-assed on the barbed wire.

BRANDON: Light the candles. It's gonna be another pity party! And guess who gets the gifts? *(Chants:)*

'Cause I'm a little white boy,
and the world's my wind-up toy.
I'm the power of the nation.
I'm the source of all creation!

(Double bell sounds for a break. Roach looks at her watch.)

ROACH: Isn't it about time you changed your diapers?

BRANDON: Every day I wake up, and people like you are telling me that the world's a rabbit in my hat, right? That I'm the boss. I can't even get my fuckin' knife sharpened the way I want to. Feel this one they did on the machine.

(He takes her hand to make her feel it. She pulls away.)

ROACH: Don't touch people who don't want to be touched.

BRANDON: Tell me something. Who got to you first and ruined it for me?

(Calmly, Roach slaps him.)

If you can keep up *(Beat)* I'll steel your knife for you.

(Roach doesn't respond.)

At least until you get the hang of it.

ROACH: And what, Mr. Nice Guy, do I have to do in return?

BRANDON: Like ice cream?

ROACH: Depends.

BRANDON: On what?

ROACH: On the cone.

BRANDON: When I said I liked . . . It wasn't a line. Your arms. They're *(Beat)* stalwart and sturdy.

ROACH: They get the job done.

BRANDON: I like to eat mine out of a cup.

SCENE FOUR

Supervisor Tuck stands watching Cod sweep/mop up offal.

TUCK: It's an odd name. Cod. Know what it means?

COD: No.

TUCK: Look it up. I did. It's a fish. From the cold North Atlantic. *(Beat)* Not too bad here, is it? Though I never liked hogs myself. Small eyes.

COD: That transfer you mentioned? I'd rather stay in one place.

TUCK: In Latin your name is *Gadus morrhua.* Don't you think "Gadus" has just a bit more status to it? And status might be what a guy like you needs, Gadus. Gadus?

COD: Yeah.

TUCK: You missed a bit. To your left. *(Beat)* Did you know you were once thought of as a nigger, Gadus? Now don't take offense. I know white folks don't like being called nigger. It gets them confused. *(Beat)* Why are you making those puny strokes. Watch me. *(Takes the broom/mop and makes some masterful and fancy sweeps with it)* History, Gadus. You ever read? That's where you'll find the key. When you Irishmen came over here in the 1800s, after that British potato problem, you were called a dark race, low-browed and savage. *(Tuck gives Cod back the broom/mop)* Oh, yeah. You were more feared than us blacks. You were the Celtic Beast, and you chased the women and raped the chickens. That's a fact. You lived side by side with us in the slums. Chums we were, you and me. Chummed up and slumming it together. Then you were given a raise. That raise was the right to call us "nigger" and the right not be called a "nigger" yourself. So you see, whiteness don't have to be a color, Gadus. It can be a wage. *(Watching him mop)* That's it. Use your shoulders. Pull and push. Pull and push.

COD: The kill floor. I like it there.

TUCK: We'll see. We need you where we need you. *(Beat)* Hold your head up. Don't stoop. A man like you shouldn't stoop. Gadus?

COD: It's just that you're standing in the way and I can't get to it.

(Tuck doesn't move.)

TUCK: Do you dream, Gadus? I dream. But a dream is like the waves a fly makes struggling on the surface of the water. When the fly stops struggling, so does the dream. *(Beat)* Gadus? You're all wet.

COD: It's the heat, sir.

TUCK: It's only seventy in here.

COD: It's hotter than that.

TUCK: Push and pull, Gadus. Push and pull.

SCENE FIVE

Maggot and Roach are trimming ham bones.

ROACH: A Scab's a Scab.

MAGGOT: That doesn't mean he don't have a cute ass.

ROACH: It's Scab ass, honey. And that sort of ass never changes its spots. You just like the underdogs. You ever been with someone with a nice colored ass?

MAGGOT: I was with a French guy once.

ROACH: French is white. *(Beat)* A lot of the Scabs they brought in here were black. When we said we'd come back to our jobs without a contract, they fired most of those Scabs. Just trash. *Black* trash. *(Beat)* I see our boys with their Local 226 T-shirts on, and they are calling them Scabs everything they can think of but racial. 'Cause it's not allowed. 'Cause we are above that. But I can hear that word behind our white boy's teeth: *(Whispers:)* nigger. Nigger. *(Beat)* That word ever get stuck up behind your teeth, Maggot? When you're cursin' and yellin' at those Scabs and you're madder than hell, you ever feel that word on your tongue?

MAGGOT: How long have we been best friends, Roach?

ROACH: If promotion time comes, who are they gonna promote, you or me?

MAGGOT: Neither of us is gonna get promoted.

(A light flashes. This signals a speed up. The workers work faster.)

ROACH: They're not supposed to speed up till after lunch.

MAGGOT: You ever done it with a white man?

ROACH: How white are we talking?

MAGGOT: Ice white.

ROACH: I'm going up to Green River this weekend.

MAGGOT: You won't sleep with a man because he's white!?

ROACH: I got a new set of spinners, yellow tails. Want to come?

MAGGOT: Got no money for gas.

ROACH: Shhh. Look who's coming for supper.

(Cod enters with huge meat hooks and chains. He wipes them down and stacks/hangs them.)

Aren't you in the smoke department this week?

COD: Injecto pump's down.

MAGGOT: You look like a nice, young man. Where did you find it in that puny little soul of yours to cross our picket line when we were out on strike? Give me a straight answer.

(The following dialogue is fired back and forth rapidly.)

COD: I have kids to feed.

MAGGOT: Not with our jobs.

COD: It's not your job if you're out there.

MAGGOT: All they want to do is use you like a piece of junk.

COD: Where are you gonna work where they aren't gonna treat you like a piece of junk?

ROACH: Come back on that one, Maggot. We need a comeback.

(Maggot is silent.)

Two points for the Scab!

COD: You two talk this bold to the Company?

MAGGOT: We haven't got a new contract 'cause lowlifes like you crossed the picket line.

COD: I haven't got any kids.

ROACH: Always sounds better when you bring in the kids.

COD: I want to join your local.

MAGGOT: You can't join a local once you cross their pickets.

ROACH: Trying to change his spots.

COD: A man can have a change of heart, can't he?

ROACH: You're no man, Spotty, and you'll never be part of this union.

COD: I used to be union. A foundry worker. Long time ago . . . No. A miner. Harlen County . . . Kentucky . . . No . . . That's not right. It was the . . . yeah . . . the Colorado coal strike. A few years back.

ROACH: Wait a minute—

MAGGOT: So sometimes you're union and sometimes you're Scab?

ROACH: The Colorado Coal Strike. That was in 1914—

COD (*Interrupts*): You know, the guy whose job I took stands outside the packhouse, all day, uptight, calls me a meat-fucking Scab. At 5 A.M. when I walk in, I look the other way. I've never touched a hog alive. Here, I touch them in pieces. I stroke them from the inside out, where they're wet; it's not right.

MAGGOT: Oh, my. What a big mouth you have, Granny!

(Maggot kisses Cod on the mouth. He doesn't respond. She kisses him again. He pushes her away violently.)

COD: I didn't choose this place. You understand that? It chose me.

(Cod exits as the women watch him in silence.)

SCENE SIX

The packinghouse is dark and empty. We see a figure wandering alone, carefully looking over the packhouse. He is turning what looks like a small musical organ, but it's a hand grinder for sausages that is hung about his neck. He speaks to the space around him. He has a light German accent.

SAUSAGE MAN: I came across the ocean, from Zwei-brucken, in the late 1800s. I ground meat in my own backyard. I didn't have a pot to piss in. Sausages. I made sausages. All the little bits of bone and gut and cartilage that the rest of the world threw away, I made into something useful. Something edible. And

I wrote the song. The sausage song. I wrote the lullaby that rocked this city to sleep. *(Sings:)*

Fischer's, the Sausage Makin' People,
makes it fun to be hungry.

With my two hands I created an empire out of a single sausage. And I fed you. I fed you! And what do I get in return? No one is happy making my sausages anymore. But still I grind and grind. I fill the skins with meat. I make it fun to be hungry. *(Grinds his grinder faster)* Ah, what a sound. The sound of hundreds, thousands of sausages filling up the empty spaces in the world. Sausages filling up the empty spaces in our very souls. I love that sound. Like the world in my hands. Like the world going to pieces in my hands.

SCENE SEVEN

Brandon, Roach and Maggot working at metal tables.

BRANDON: I don't trust him. He's fractious.

MAGGOT: The man's got passion.

ROACH: Only for himself.

MAGGOT: If we strike again, he'll join us.

ROACH: If we strike again, the replacements will turn their backs.

BRANDON *(To Maggot)*: You really want to stick your neck out for this yokel?

ROACH: He won't be a part of my union. What's left of it.

MAGGOT: You're a tightass, Roach.

ROACH: Yeah? He's a Scab and you're an itch and if you two get to scratching someone is gonna bleed.

MAGGOT: You wouldn't know an itch if it crawled up your leg and bit you.

ROACH: An itch is something a dog gets.

(Maggot barks like a dog, then she picks up a piece of meat and takes a bite out of it.)

You white girls are disgusting. You take a joke so far it'll kill you.

BRANDON *(To Roach, to interrupt the women)*: So . . . when are you gonna succumb to my sugar cone, baby?

ROACH: You're making me nauseous.

BRANDON: "I find my heart inside my ribs aroused by your impertinence."

MAGGOT: Brandon.

BRANDON: Homer.

MAGGOT: Give it up.

BRANDON *(To Roach)*: Come on, darlin', I'm hankering. I'm baffled and balked. Just give me half a wink.

ROACH: What a charmer!

MAGGOT: Could charm the shit out of a dead rabbit's ass.

BRANDON: Not much up top, Maggot, and less down below. For a fruit tramp baby, you're a seedy specimen.

MAGGOT: Listen, little man. You don't, can't, won't ever get me hot, 'cause I got a clit the size of a small rodent and I'd just snap you in half like a corn-nut.

ROACH *(To Brandon)*: If we vote on letting him join, will you back me up with a negative?

BRANDON: I'll back up, bend down and roll up just as far as you want me to. Well?

ROACH: I'll go for a Coke with you, Brandon. A Coke. For an hour.

MAGGOT: Look who's using the itch.

ROACH: But I'm not gonna let you watch me sip it.

BRANDON: Why not? I want to see you sip it. I want to watch that liquid ascend through the straw, up into your moist and marvelous— Fuck! *(Cuts himself on his knife)* Look at that! Look at that, goddamn it. Just try it, he says. Just try it. Machine gives it a good edge. Fuck his edge. *(Shouts to someone offstage)* Fuck your edge. *(Beat)* They're going to replace us. Then they won't need the top-rate knife boys. The mechanical will do it.

ROACH: You better check that at the clinic.

BRANDON: And a mechanical won't ask for a raise. Well, we'll see about that. *(Shouts to offstage)* We'll see about that! One more time and you won't have any knives left to steel.

(He is furious now and drops to his knees, hacking at the floor until the knife is ruined. He throws it aside. Silence. Then he speaks quietly:)

That'll fuck your edge.

SCENE EIGHT

Baquin and Tuck giving the Sausage Man a tour of the facilities.

BAQUIN: Ah, Baquin's the name, meat's the game. And you are? . . .

SAUSAGE MAN: I make sausages.

BAQUIN: Ah. Hobby perhaps, or old-style deli? Well, you've come to the right place to see how slaughtering and packing are properly done.
(Meaning the packhouse) So, what do you think?

SAUSAGE MAN: It makes me sad.

BAQUIN: Ah yes. I know. Do you think I haven't spared a thought for the cow, trembling at that final moment, those big, brown eyes?

SAUSAGE MAN: It's not the cows, dear sir.

BAQUIN: Oh, the pigs . . . well, the toys are cute but the real thing . . . Just think of that book about the pigs who take over the farm . . . um . . . Tuck?

TUCK: *Animal Farm*, Mr. Baquin. Napoleon and—

BAQUIN *(Interrupts)*: Right! A great writer, Joyce. If we gave pigs—and I'm sure the cows would be right behind them—if we gave them their declaration of rights . . . Well, who knows, we might all end up as sausages!

SAUSAGE MAN: The workers, the shop-floor, the union . . .

BAQUIN: They love our sausages!

SAUSAGE MAN: I'm troubled. Deeply troubled. Too much talk and idleness. Kid gloves, cowardly tactics. Not how we used to do it. Those times then are here, now. I know the rules. I can say yes, no, stay, go. Open, close and fire! And this Company? Ah, if I had ulcers, they'd be the size of oranges by now. Look at you!

(Baquin inspects himself.)

You're not even triple-stitched. I bet you let your socks wear thin before you throw them out!

TUCK: Should I get rid of . . . ?

BAQUIN: PR, Tuck. PR.

SAUSAGE MAN: What we need is to kindle a spark, ignite a little imagination around here. Have you ever felt your blood boil? It's extraordinary.

BAQUIN: I eat lots of bran. Keeps my stress level under control.

SAUSAGE MAN: There's too much sympathy nowadays.

BAQUIN: For the cows? The workers? The pigs?

SAUSAGE MAN: It was different; it used to be an ironclad operation, lock, stock and barrel. It's a shame.

BAQUIN *(Without a clue)*: I know what you mean.

SAUSAGE MAN: It saddens me.

BAQUIN: I, too, am deeply touched. Nevertheless, I think you're a bit out of date. If you want to start a competitive business, you—

SAUSAGE MAN *(Interrupts)*: Out of date? I'm your future.

BAQUIN: What?

SAUSAGE MAN: Oh, I'm having no fun at all. Something must be done.

BAQUIN: I agree completely, Mr. . . . ?

SAUSAGE MAN: I made the finest sausage links . . .

BAQUIN: Mr. Links, you know, it's an age-old conundrum with us in the meat-packing business: where does our sympathy go? I confess, I try to steer clear of those big, brown innocent eyes—but man cannot live by greens alone. It thins the blood.

(Sausage Man starts to leave. Baquin follows him.)

Age-old, I confess, yes, and we run a tight ship here and the hands, well, we can't let sympathy out and about or the cows and the pigs, Napoleon—right, Tuck?—well, they'd be ruling the roast . . . the roost . . . And be sure to pick up some literature on your way out, we're the professionals.

(Sausage man is "gone.")

Ah, the muddled Old School. Never get a business off the ground these days.

SCENE NINE

Brandon alone after everyone has gone home. A makeshift, bloody bandage on his hand, he stands on a work scaffold, then jumps down and clears the space for his "dance." He places his cassette player in the center of the space and then begins to run, jump and dance around the stage. The feeling is one of a body taking complete control over the space around it. There is part of a wrapped carcass hanging from the ceiling. Brandon cuts it loose with his knife and it falls. He turns off the music to begin the second part of his "show." He circles the carcass, then takes off his shirt and speaks. All this movement should be stylized. Brandon has done this sort of "show" before.

BRANDON: "Let sorrow split my heart— *(Slashes the wrapper open to expose the meat)* if ever I did hate thee."

(He gently undresses the carcass and sings to it:)

I got a mouth like a spider
and a web for you I'll spin.
Just open up a little wider,
with my spinneret, I'm comin' in.

(He throws away the knife and begins to kiss and nip at the carcass. He then holds out his arms. Roach appears elsewhere on stage and watches Brandon. He is not aware of her.)

See the light comin' off my feathers, Love? See it? I'm an angel, and I'm gonna reach my wing so far inside you, I'm going to disappear.

(He pushes his hand, then his arm, inside the carcass. This should be both sensual and frightening. Roach picks up the knife. She comes up behind him, takes him by the hair and holds the knife to his throat. She is in complete control.)

ROACH: Oh, but that's not enough, my cherub. No. This piece of meat wants your sweet face inside her, your whole head inside her.

(She crushes his face into the carcass, then turns him on his back so she's straddling him, knife still at his throat.)

You like this dream, lover boy? What happens in the end? Does she come like he needs her to, like a train, blasting off, straight up to the sky?

BRANDON: He'll never know 'cause she doesn't want him.

ROACH: This is a sad picture if this is how you want me. In case you haven't heard, we don't like to be cut when we come.

BRANDON: I fuckin' hate you, Roach. I fuckin' hate you, 'cause I want you so bad it's like a knife up my ass.

ROACH: If I could I'd turn it, college boy.

BRANDON: Tuck is gonna promote me.

ROACH: Promote you?

BRANDON: Office work.

ROACH: You've only been here a couple of years.

BRANDON: They want me off the kill floor.

ROACH: Always the fuckin' white boys get promoted.

BRANDON: I can talk, Roach. Hear how I can talk? I pick up words, all kind of words, big words, small words. I pick up words like a dog picks up fleas. *(Beat)* But I can't read. How am I going to do office work when I can't read? *(Beat)* Shit. My face hurts. Damn it.

ROACH *(She touches his forehead)*: You've got a fever.

BRANDON: Keep your hand there.

ROACH: You got to get to the hospital. You got blood poisoning.

BRANDON: You're poisoning me.

ROACH: Right. Come on. Get up.

(She helps him to his feet.)

BRANDON: I'm twenty-two years old. I've never been with a woman.

ROACH: What are you saying?

BRANDON: Look at my mouth.

ROACH: So?

BRANDON: No. Look at it. The white marks. Like a halo around my mouth.

ROACH: Pretty.

BRANDON: I quit going to school when I was fifteen, 'cause the words were upside down. Somersaulting. I couldn't keep them in line. I left home and went and lived with my boss. He let me have a corner in his garage. He owned a chain of jewelry stores. I swept, stacked, cooked. One day I dropped a box with some china in it. He hit me until I passed out. When I came to, he was sitting beside me. He had a lure box with him. He said I'd cursed him. I couldn't remember, up till then I'd never said a thing but: "Yes, sir." He said he'd make sure I never spoke against him again. He took some fish line and a hook out of his box and he sewed my mouth shut. That's why I never could kiss a girl. Because it's always bleed-

ing where the line went through. How can you kiss a
girl when your mouth is always bleeding?

ROACH: Your mouth isn't bleeding.

BRANDON: Yeah, it is. I can taste it.

ROACH: There's no blood on your mouth.

BRANDON: Every day I can taste it.

SCENE TEN

Cod is soapboxing the workers as they clean up their work. The
workers laugh at Cod; they think he's ridiculous. Brandon is
somewhat crazed with fever.

COD: What we need around here is some direct action.
Shall I tell you what direct action means?

BRANDON: Go to hell . . .

COD: The worker on the job shall tell the boss when and
where the worker shall work—

MAGGOT: Not again. Christ.

COD: —how long, and for what wages and under what
conditions.

ROACH: This is gettin' tedious.

COD: The working class and the employer class have nothing in common? IWW? Industrial Workers of the
World? *(Beat)* OK. How many of you don't have
arthritis from workin' the cold and wet? Maggot?
You've got carpal tunnel in both your hands.

MAGGOT: Been operated on twice.

COD: Roach? Back so bad from lifting you got to roll out
of bed in the morning?

ROACH: Why do you think we went on strike to begin with?

COD: How about you, Brandon? So tired after a split-
double, chasin' half-crazed steers at midnight you just
can't get that erection you need for Saturday night?

BRANDON: Fuck your dog, your cat and any other carniv-
orous animals you own.

COD: Fucking? Well. Yes. Now, fucking is a key, no matter with who or where or how, and each time a worker fucks in this world, the possibility for their taking power increases, just a little.

MAGGOT: Oh, Scabby's talking dirty!

COD: Because coming is the body's way of saying fuck you to the rules and regulations.

BRANDON: Fuck you.

COD *(Continuing)*: It's catching! Fuck you to the bowing and scraping we live by just to eat. When a worker comes, when we come, it's our body's way of saying: "I am radiant and I am fearless and I will not be disposed of; I am not a piece of meat."

(Cod has got their attention now.)

Whatever we win or lose here is what meat workers will have to accept all over the country, at Swift, Armour, IBP, Hormel. *(Sings:)*

So fold up your arms and sit where you stand,
they're gonna hear us across the land

BRANDON: So you like to soapbox?

COD *(Sings)*:

We're sick of getting nothing but an ear of shit,
this time it's enough and we say quit.

BRANDON: A little exhibition to flaunt your wares?

COD: We have a world to win.

BRANDON: Could be a world to lose. But since you like to play, let's play. A little game. You and me. You believe all it takes is to sing a few words and the boss is going to hand you the plate? All right. Show me some fortitude. Make me afraid.

COD: Sorry about that office job, Brandie. I know you were counting on it.

BRANDON: Lovely touch. And precise. But let's get back to the matter at hand. Let's say I'm running this packhouse. I'm running this whole joke. *(Tears off his apron and throws it aside)*

MAGGOT: Sup's got two warnings on your file, Brandon.

BRANDON: And I'm clean. I haven't been standing in blood all day. No gut in my hair. Hands don't shake. My back is straight. Mouth tastes like I just brushed my teeth. Nice. But here you are. Just your average guy, cutting out hog asshole fifteen hours a day, piss running through your veins, gums swimming in steer blood.

ROACH: Strike three, and there won't be nothing the union can do for you anymore.

BRANDON: No. How about a bitch. Can you play a bitch? I bet you can. And I'm the boss. *(Takes up a knife)* Now, convince me.

(Brandon struts about like a "boss." Then he turns on Cod. Through most of the scene the women are mesmerized. They are watching themselves in Cod. They are silent and motionless.)

That's all very well said, young woman: "Nothing in common," but we have everything in common. I need you to do work, and you need me to have work. We're linked, from birth until death. Star-crossed lovers igniting in the dark. *(Beat)* Oh dear, your apron's loose. Let's just give it a little tuck.

(He runs the knife up and down Cod's body, sensually.)

You like it here, princess?

(He knocks Cod down.)

"Where be your gibes now? Your gambols? Your songs? Your flashes of merriment?"

(He hits Cod.)

We always try to make you feel at home.

MAGGOT *(To Brandon, but also about her own past)*: Get your
fucking hands off—

COD: We have nothing to lose.

BRANDON: What did you say?

(He hits Cod.)

MAGGOT: No!

BRANDON: I didn't quite catch that?

MAGGOT: Don't.

BRANDON: You're mumbling. Girls shouldn't mumble.
Nasty habit.

ROACH: Brandon!

BRANDON: Listen, young lady, I offered you that nice little
office job, with a window to look out of. *(Starts to
laugh)* But you couldn't handle it. *(Hits Cod again)*
No. I mean, this little bitch couldn't even read! Can
you believe it? That's what he said. That's what he
said to me: this little bitch can't even read!

*(Brandon raises his arm to strike Cod again, but Roach's voice
stops him. She plays the "boss" to get Brandon's attention.)*

ROACH: Can you believe it? This little bitch can't even
read! How do you sign your name, then, baby, with
what's left of your thumb? Can't you even defend
yourself like a decent woman?

(Brandon is silent. He sinks to the floor.)

I didn't think so. You see, you're never gonna learn
nothin', never gonna make nothin', never gonna be
nothin'.

BRANDON *(Whispers)*: I can do it. I know I can do it.

ROACH: You're just a piece of gut got stuck to my shoe
when I walked by.

(Brandon sits silent and numb. It is obvious that he is ill.)

I know, Brandon. I know it better than you. 'Cause
that's what they've been saying to me all my life.

(Tuck enters.)

TUCK: What the hell's going on here? *(Sees Cod has been hit)* Brandon's initiating the new crew again? Well, that's a "bingo." You're out, boy.

COD: No. Brandon was. He was showing me. How to—I slipped.

TUCK: Really? *(To Brandon)* On your feet.

(Brandon doesn't respond.)

ROACH: Get on the phone, Tuck, and call an ambulance. He needs medical attention.

(Roach helps Brandon to his feet and leads him out. Tuck moves quickly to call an ambulance.)

COD: Local 226 is one of the last in the industry.

MAGGOT: Would you shut up already!? There's no difference anymore, union or not. Things just stay the same. Scrabblin' for something better is like scrabblin' for heaven. You only get there when you're dead.

COD: All we have to do is fold our arms, and the whole thing will stop.

MAGGOT: You really believe that?

COD: No. Not most of the time. But it's living under water like this.

MAGGOT: Yeah. And when you yell, it doesn't make a sound.

COD: Only bubbles.

MAGGOT *(Shrugs)*: What do you think about when you're working the meat? My hands do this thing called work, but I let my mind go somewhere else. 'Specially when the manager, that Baquin guy, comes to call. He likes to keep us neat, to tighten my apron when it gets loose, smooth the wrinkles down. *(Beat)* Does that excite you? Thinking about him touching me against my will?

COD *(Puts his hand out into the air, touching it)*: Feel it? It's heatin' up in here.

MAGGOT: I don't mind the heat.

COD: That's how it starts.

MAGGOT: It's the smell I can't get used to. *(Beat)* You're
sweating.

COD: It's a hundred degrees in here. Who doesn't sweat?

MAGGOT: Maybe you're sick.

> *(Maggot tries to touch Cod's forehead to check his tempera-
> ture, but Cod jumps back, terrified at being touched.)*

COD: Don't. *(Beat)* Please.

MAGGOT *(Amused)*: Did you like it that time I kissed you?

COD: I wish I could say no.

MAGGOT: Take off your shirt. I want to see if you've got
the kind of chest I like.

COD: What kind of chest is that?

MAGGOT: I'll know it when I see it.

COD *(Turning away)*: Things aren't always the way you see it.

SCENE ELEVEN

*Sausage Man appears, wandering in the empty packhouse. Cod
sits nearby, huddled in a corner, dejected and alone. The Sausage
Man knows Cod is there, and his words are partly a performance
for Cod.*

SAUSAGE MAN: What happened to the dream? Our
dream? I made one sausage, then two, then three. I
could live off of two and sell the third as surplus. The
dream as simple math. Make more than you need.
Sell the excess. With a little extra cash, hire someone
to make the sausages for you, while you deal with the
papers and the cash. What is unjust about having
another human being work for you? I employed
hundreds. I gave them free trimmings. But they bit
the hand that fed them. Chomp. Chomp. They did
not respect the math. The math of the dream.

Myself, I am an innovator. I make something from the refuse in this world. And there will always be refuse in this world, so there will always be a place for me. It's just a matter of time, that's all.

(Sausage Man nears Cod.)

Tsk, tsk. I should have guessed. Daydreaming again. Wasting precious time.

COD: I hate it when you send me in as a Scab instead of union; it takes twice as long to even get them to listen.

SAUSAGE MAN: A little extra challenge. You'll manage. You always do.

COD: Oh, leave me alone. Please.

SAUSAGE MAN: You're not ill, are you? *(Feels Cod's forehead)* You shouldn't sit on the floor. It's damp. *(Takes off his jacket and puts it around Cod's shoulders)* You should take better care of yourself.

COD: A mollusc. In the ocean. A limpet. That's what I'd like to be.

SAUSAGE MAN: But they're so small. You might get eaten by a sea gull.

COD: Limpets live near reefs. They have this endless, tremendous ocean all around, but they stay their entire lives on one rock. And they never move from that rock. And if you try to pull a limpet off its rock, it hangs on. And the harder you pull, the more tightly it hangs on.

SAUSAGE MAN: How 'bout a walk? That'll cheer you up.

COD: I can't even imagine that kind of determination.

SAUSAGE MAN: Tsk, tsk. That's not very ambitious. A limpet? And what would you do then? Suck at a rock? For eternity?

COD: Yeah. And I'd be a part of it all. A part of the ocean. I'd watch the tide go in and out. I'd eat algae, digest sand, be witness to shipwrecks and sharks. The birth of an octopus. The death of a sea cow. My mate would be a starfish, and we'd grow old together.

We'd even die. Imagine that? And millimeter by millimeter I'd travel that single rock. And after all those years—who knows?—maybe I'd even leave a scratch, some kind of mark on the stone to prove I was there.

(A noise somewhere that startles Cod. He clings to the Sausage Man, frightened.)

What? What? Where are we?

SAUSAGE MAN *(Holding him)*: Shhh. We're still here. Shhh.

COD *(Still clinging)*: Where? Where?

SAUSAGE MAN: My child, why are you always lost? You've got to learn to locate yourself. Listen: this little piggy went to market. This little piggy stayed home. This little piggy—

COD: OK. Stop it. Stop it. I know where we are. But why a slaughterhouse? *(Looking Sausage Man over)* I preferred you as a Pullman, a Carnegie or a Rockefeller, delving into mines, reeking of money, not meat.

SAUSAGE MAN: But you complained about the mines. Too much coal dust in the nose. And then you caught a cough, remember? That was a nasty cough you had.

COD: Yeah, and we were ready to blow that mountain wide open. The fuse was lit. But you yanked me out just before the explosion. Just in time.

SAUSAGE MAN: It might have been serious.

COD: Was it serious?

SAUSAGE MAN: Nasty. Sticky. There was a mess to clean up.

COD: What's the point if I never get to see things through? Damn you.

SAUSAGE MAN: That's it. Get angry! Tantrums make you hotter quicker.

(Cod turns away.)

Oh, come on now: kiss my forehead, child. *(Beat)* There's a life's work in this industry. Martyrs to be made. Reputations to be saved.

COD: I want something else. Anything. Forget the limpet then. Send me to an island. I'll rally the coconuts and crabs. I'll give you a good tussle. Only let me stay. In one place. Whatever the final outcome.

SAUSAGE MAN: I won't risk losing you.

COD: Then I'll refuse.

SAUSAGE MAN: It's your nature to resist. I can count on you. That's hard to come by in this late century. That sort of certainty. This city needs you.

COD: No. I need this city. Without you.

SAUSAGE MAN (*Holds out his arm for the jacket*): The jacket, please. It's the only one I have.

(*Cod moves away.*)

Come now. I'm not a very convincing Mr. Fisher without the threads, now am I? Do you want to be the death of me?

COD (*Sniffing the jacket*): This jacket stinks.

SAUSAGE MAN: It's authentic. Mr. Fisher died in it.

COD: Yeah? Well, all right then: meat this time it will be! (*Holds up the jacket*) And how would you like your jacket sliced, sir?

SAUSAGE MAN: The sewing's a triple-stitch. Take a look. Rather fine, isn't it?

COD: Fine did you say? One jacket, finely sliced, coming up. (*Takes a knife from his pocket*) No fat on this one. (*Makes a neat, clean slice through the back of the jacket*)

SAUSAGE MAN: Now that's too bad.

(*Cod throws the jacket at Sausage Man's feet. Sausage Man puts it on. The rip down the back is visible.*)

Irreparable damage. No sense.

COD: I beg you.

SAUSAGE MAN: You're a fighter, Cod, not a beggar. Get out there and stir, spark, sputter. The laborer against my system! It's glorious. It's heroic. And we have all the time in the world. Do you know what that sounds like?

COD: I know what it tastes like. *(Spits on the floor)* Like ashes on my tongue.

SAUSAGE MAN: Listen. *(Turns his grinder. We hear strange, sad and sensual music)* That's the music of all the time in the world. Hear how it weeps, how it grieves and longs to be silent. But it can't. It must sing forever. Just like you. Dance to it, my child. Dance to your music.

(Cod stands transfixed as Sausage Man slowly turns in a circle, like a figure in a music box, dancing to the music.)

SCENE TWELVE

Baquin, Tuck, Maggot and Roach in Baquin's office.

BAQUIN: It's not the taste of our meat we're selling, but its appearance, its attitude. How the meat is colored, how it shines, how it carries itself with a straight spine, even if it's boneless. *(To Tuck)* Don't slouch. Bring me the soap and water. Good. A man won't get ahead if he slouches. But what's really getting the Company image down is smudge, the smudginess of the workers. They aren't laundering their uniforms regularly.

TUCK: It's tough keeping a uniform clean down there, sir.

BAQUIN: One of your jobs is to make sure the work force looks decent. Would you say this work force looks decent? Look at the smudges, the wrinkles, the rips in the cloth.

TUCK: New uniforms were due six months ago.

BAQUIN: Nonsense. These uniforms are new. I ordered them myself. They simply haven't been cared for. We must cultivate a passion for cleanliness. The problem is that some of us simply lack passion, and passion is a clean impulse, not a dirty one. And where there is passion lacking, dirt will be lurking. *(Beat)* Take off the uniforms, please.

(Maggot and Roach look at each other in disbelief. They don't move.)

My dear ladies. Those uniforms are Company property and the Company wants to wash its property. Right now. *(Beat)* Take them off.

(The women turn away and begin to unbutton their uniforms. Roach turns to Tuck as she undresses. He turns to leave. Baquin silently stops Maggot's hand so that she stops undressing. Until she has removed her uniform, Roach doesn't realize that she stands alone in her slip.)

BAQUIN: Just a minute, Buck. I might need your help. Give them the soap and water.

(Tuck places the bucket of soap and water between the two women.)

ROACH: I can do this in the bathroom.

BAQUIN: This is private space here. Feel completely at home.

TUCK *(Turning to leave again)*: I need to check the pressure gauge on hog box number six, sir.

BAQUIN: That can wait. Now wash.

(The women don't wash.)

(Shouts) Wash!

(The women take the sponges and begin to wash.)

That's right. Get those smudges off. Scrub hard! Put that whiff of daintiness back in the cloth, restore that *Odiferous mundi*. That's Latin for World Odor. The smell of worldliness and cleanliness. And we do need world odor. Order. Don't you agree, Chuck?

ROACH *(Throws down her sponge)*: We're finished.

BAQUIN *(Looking Maggot over)*: Yes. You are, Maggot. *(To Roach)* But you can't be.

(He takes the sponge from Maggot and gently cleans a spot on her uniform) What do you think, Maggot? Is

your friend clean? *(Continues sponging Maggot, slowly nearing, but not quite touching, her breasts)*

TUCK: She's clean, sir.

BAQUIN: It's hard to tell. *(Sets a chair in the center)* Roach, could you help us out? Please. Step up here so we can see things better?

(After some moments Roach steps up on the chair.)

Just as I suspected. There's dirt behind your knees.

TUCK: But, sir—

BAQUIN: Surely you can see it? Can't you, Maggot?

(Maggot does not answer but looks away from Roach.)

Exactly. Well put. Smudges are attracted to the backs of knees. Finish the job.

TUCK: Sir?

BAQUIN: Scrub behind her knees.

ROACH: Go on, Tuck. Follow your orders.

(Tuck kneels before Roach as she stands above him. He doesn't wash her. She sings.)

Every day one more dolla in my hand,
slip through my fingers like a grain of sand

BAQUIN *(To Tuck)*: Let me see your nails.

ROACH *(Sings)*:

One day soon don'tcha know, I'll be free
livin' in the sun so don't you worry 'bout me

BAQUIN: A supervisor must keep clean, short nails.

ROACH AND TUCK *(Sing)*:

—O Lord, God hear me callin', take my hand

BAQUIN: Show me your hands.

(Tuck puts his hands in his pockets.)

ROACH AND TUCK *(Sing)*:

—Won'tcha take me, take me to the promised land

BAQUIN *(Shouts)*: I said show me your hands!

ROACH AND TUCK *(Sing)*:
>—O Lord, God hear me callin', take my hand
>Won'tcha take me, take me to the promised land.

(Some moments of silence.)

BAQUIN: Well, yes. Well. Tuck. I'm ravished. I'm going to catch a bite to eat. Please have their files ready. I'd like to look them over when I get back. *(Beat)* Would anyone like a cup of tea before they return to work?

(No response from the workers; Baquin shrugs and exits.)

SCENE THIRTEEN

Cod in the men's changing room. Maggot enters. Cod has his shirt pulled up, and we see bandages around his lower back that he is just finishing adjusting.

COD *(Looking over his shoulder)*: Ladies' changing room is across the hall.

MAGGOT: What's the bandage for?

COD *(Pulls down his shirt)*: Slipped on the kill floor. Got a steer horn in my ass. Cracked three ribs.

MAGGOT: Wait. Just wait. A minute.

(She approaches him. He does not turn around.)

Can I touch your back?

COD: I'd rather you didn't.

MAGGOT: Oh.

COD: It's not that I don't like you.

MAGGOT: Sure.

COD: I wouldn't want you to make a mistake; I'm not the kind who sticks around.

MAGGOT: Save it.

COD: Look, you seem like. An interesting girl. Nice. If I could stay here a while, I would. But it's not up to me. I'm out of here, *(Snaps his fingers)* just like that, when he blows the whistle. Could be today. Could be tomorrow, and my time's up. And I don't leave a trace.

MAGGOT: I've heard *that* before.

(Maggot is hardly listening to Cod. She's moved closer to him but hasn't touched him. Instead, she stands there and from a distance feels the warmth coming from his back.)

I can feel the heat coming off your body like . . . You know, if I died, I think I'd like to lay my head down on something like you.

(Cod moves away.)

COD: Who's thinking about dying?

MAGGOT: We don't have to think about it. We're already dead.

COD: Yeah. Most of the time. But then there's that minute or two, once or twice a year. Once or twice a decade, when you think, maybe this time something is gonna change.

MAGGOT: Nothing ever changes here. You just break down after so many years, and they sweep you out back with the rest of the scraps.

COD: Whatever happened to that animal called hope?

MAGGOT: First it got stunned, then it got slaughtered. Seems like for years I just wake and work and shit and sleep. It's a good life. Nothing to disappoint me. *(Beat)* You know, when I was a kid there were only two things I wanted in the world. A V-8 pickup and a boyfriend who'd let me drive. You wouldn't think that was a lot to ask for in life, would you?

SCENE FOURTEEN

Roach and Maggot at the end of the day in the changing room. Roach has her rod and lure box with her. She opens the lure box and sorts the lures, getting ready for the weekend.

MAGGOT: The truth is, my uniform was cleaner than yours.

ROACH: Get your narrow white ass out of my face—

MAGGOT: Yeah? You look like garbage. You never take your uniform home and bleach the stains out, like I do.

ROACH: You know what I was thinking when I stood on that chair? No. You don't know. You have no idea.

MAGGOT: What was I supposed to do?

ROACH: Not one word. Didn't call my name. Didn't say, I'm here by your side. Nothing.

MAGGOT: You didn't do nothing either. Should I've let him get me like that too? Then we could've both played the dog. Oh yeah. That woulda been "right on, sister." *(Beat)* I couldn't have been that kind of friend to anyone.

ROACH *(Examines lures while ignoring Maggot)*: Ah, the rapalla. Looks like a knife in the water.

MAGGOT: I thought I could, but I guess I can't.

ROACH: Nickname: "Stab in the Back." *(Holds up another lure)* Double-headed jig. I call her "Old Two-Face-Strikes-Again."

MAGGOT: I'm not making my bills.

ROACH *(Holds up another lure)*: Big Eyes: The Zephyr Puppy. Commonly know as: "The Traitor."

MAGGOT: I don't want to sell the truck. Could sell the tires.

ROACH: Oh, she plays it coy.

MAGGOT: Goddamn it, I'm tired.

ROACH: But she's got nine silver hooks, nine pretty lies just waiting for you.

MAGGOT: You don't know what that's like. I can't even get myself off anymore 'cause my hands start to shake so bad when I go into repetitive motion.

ROACH: Whoever named it carpal tunnel never had it. Sounds like a fish.

MAGGOT: I was on probation last summer, remember? You piss too often, you chew your lunch too slow, your sausages aren't bent the right way. Well, I got called down to the office. My scales were off about half a point. Manager said he'd have to let me go. I said I needed the job. He said how bad. I said bad. He said show me. *(Beat)* I showed him. *(Beat)* Across his desk between two fern plants.

(They are silent some moments.)

ROACH: I hate ferns.

MAGGOT: Whatever it was you wanted me to do that day, I just couldn't do it. I guess I'm not who I thought I was.

ROACH: That makes two of us.

MAGGOT: You know, when I was a kid I couldn't sleep at night, thinking about dying. Now I think about dying the way I fix a bowl of cereal in the morning; I could take it or leave it.

ROACH: You remember Mr. Morton? Our second grade teacher? You used to get jealous, 'cause he would take me fishing and he wouldn't ever take you.

MAGGOT: I remember: teacher's pet.

ROACH: Yeah, well, he liked fishing the way I liked it, and sometimes after school he'd take me down to the stream. He was the first white man who ever treated me like a child likes to be treated. Like I had something special about me that only he could see. *(Beat)* When Mr. Morton cast a good line, his ears would go red. Red as a worm.

MAGGOT *(Sings)*:
Oh, my love is like a red, red, worm.

ROACH: They say a worm has seven hearts and that if you break it up in the right places, two or three of the pieces will live. Problem was, I never knew where the hearts were or where to put the hook in. That's why I mostly use artificials now. *(Casts her rod as if out into the audience and reels it back in)* Twelve-pound line. Eight-pound line. I was using a six-pound line that day and I landed a four-pound smallmouth bass. You remember the picture? That fish was longer than my arm! Almost snapped my line. Mr. Morton and I skinned it right there and cooked it over the fire. I can tell you I was proud that day. And Mr. Morton was proud of me too. He kissed me on the mouth four times, one kiss for each pound of that bass. Have you ever made your teacher that proud of you? I liked him better than my own father because he took me fishing, and my own father never had time because he was always at the packhouse splittin' hogs. *(Beat)* Four times. On the mouth. He said he wanted to know what my kind . . . tasted like. *(Beat)* That's how proud he was. That's how. Yes. And I closed my eyes, because if a worm has seven hearts it could have eight and I wanted him to know I could take it. And I took it. Right there in the grass beside the stream. *(Beat)* But once it's cut you never can tell just which parts of the worm have been killed and which parts will crawl away and start over because all of the parts are moving. All of the parts are trying to live. Funny. How you can look at a body and see nothing but the whole of it. But I know. I know which parts went on and lived and which parts gave up and died. *(Maggot just watches her in silence)* Yeah. I *know* what it's like, girl. I just don't let it lead me. *(Beat)* Damn it. I oughta punch you in the mouth *(Beat)* but it's the weekend and you and me are going fishing!

SCENE FIFTEEN

Cod and Sausage Man in the empty packhouse, at night.

COD: Let go of me.
SAUSAGE MAN: You're becoming tiresome, Cod.
COD: I need to stay here.

SAUSAGE MAN: Tiresome is not fun. You're meant to be my rival, not a driveling pup!

COD: Just a little bit longer.

SAUSAGE MAN: Well, well. I think you've finally fallen in love. How sweet. How infantile. Tell me, has she seen you out of this garb?

COD: This garb? You think I'd have had a chance in hell of catching their attention—of catching anyone's attention in the last fifteen decades—if I hadn't worn this garb?

SAUSAGE MAN: Come now. You've always enjoyed a nice cut pair of trousers.

COD: Listen to me: she could keep me here.

SAUSAGE MAN: Ah, yes. The strength of a woman's love to break an old promise? I like it. But what are you waiting for? Why don't you sweep her up in your arms?

COD: Because if I touch what I desire—I'll destroy it. Just one touch and . . . toast.

SAUSAGE MAN: That's right. You can't touch her. Not like *that*. And don't you forget it.

COD: I hate these hands.

SAUSAGE MAN: You can't change the past, Cod. It's like you, condemned to repeat itself.

COD: Yeah. And I'm always at your mercy, because once upon a time someone somewhere agreed that yours was the only game. But what if there were another way?

SAUSAGE MAN: Imagine that! How exciting.

COD: What if, over time, all this friction, all this fire, began to burn a hole in your playground?

SAUSAGE MAN: That's my Cod! Keep tossing those dice.

COD: Then we'd just walk through that hole to the other side. And from the stink and wreckage of your death, we'd build something new.

SAUSAGE MAN: Give it your best shot!

COD: But I never get to stay around long enough to see what's left, do I?

SAUSAGE MAN: Don't be sour. You're a spark for eternity. What else could you ask for?

COD: What else? What else? *(Beat)* Just for one single moment to be without heat. To shiver. Watch my fingers turn blue. To be *(Beat)* cold. Yeah. That's what I'd like. To be cold like . . . snow.

(Sausage Man grinds his sausage machine. As he does so, it begins to snow inside the packhouse.)

SAUSAGE MAN: To be cold like snow.

(Cod looks up in amazement and lifts his arms to catch the snow like a child.)

In your dreams, my friend. Only in your dreams.

ACT II

SCENE ONE

Cod, Maggot and Roach are listening to Baquin, who stands in the center of the workroom, Tuck at his side. The workers all have their arms raised.

BAQUIN: Let's try it again. Ready? And a one, two, three, go!

(Baquin and Tuck do jumping jacks. The workers stand with arms raised but they don't jump. After eight jumps or so Tuck stops. Then Baquin stops.)

Not just your arms, but your feet too. You've got to moooooove . . . You've got to moooooove. *(Clears his throat)* Jump up and down. Like I do. You've got to learn to take care of your bodies. Your body is a temple. It belongs to God. Your body is God's property. Respect God's property. Respect God's temple with its rooms, oh, gorgeous rooms— So jump! Leap! Exercise your gifts. Raise your bodies to the cause, make yourselves stars of motivation, coordination, innovation! *(Beat)* Now. Let's try it again. And this time make an effort. And a one, two, three, go!

(Everyone does jumping jacks in unison for some moments. One by one they stop—first Roach, then Maggot, then Cod, then Tuck, then Baquin.)

Now take a deep breath. In, and out. In, and out.
Well, I feel refreshed. How about the rest of you?

*(No response. The workers stare at him. Baquin exits, then
Cod and Maggot. Tuck and Roach are alone.)*

TUCK: It's Miss Roach, isn't it?

ROACH: Miss Lyles. Roach is my first name.

TUCK: You taught the recorder lessons after work for
employees?

ROACH: That was Maggot.

TUCK: Could I ask where you got your name?

ROACH: Little girl gave it to me when I was seven. I col-
lected bugs. The day I met her I only had a roach in
my bug box. So she called me Roach. That was
Maggot. Maggot calls me Roach.

TUCK: That's a name that won't get you very far.

ROACH: It's not my name that's holding me back.

TUCK: And Maggot?

ROACH: When I met her she looked whiter than any white
kid I'd ever met. She reminded me of a maggot. The
whiteness of maggots.

TUCK: Yes. I can see how it came to you. White friend.
That sounds like a contradiction.

ROACH: Sometimes it is.

TUCK: Well, Roach. What do you know about snails?

(Roach just looks at him.)

Partula affinis. It is the last snail of its kind. This
packing Company is going to start a committee to
raise funds for a search in the South Pacific. For a
mate. I'd like you to head the steering committee.
We'll call it the Salvation Nature Alliance Involving
Laborers. S-N-A-I-L. SNAIL. *(Beat)* The board's hot
on the idea. They've asked me to sell it.

ROACH: We get a new contract signed, and I'll get you
members for SNAIL.

TUCK: You do trimming, right? Number three pay bracket? How would you like ham pumper or pickle maker?

ROACH: Can we speak off the record?

TUCK: Of course.

ROACH: Last year the Company tried to sell us piano lessons after work. The year before, it was ice skating for management and employees on Sunday afternoons. Free of charge. Well, let me tell you something: we're at war here. And we will not shake your hand and we will not skate with you and we will not sing Christmas carols with you for the holidays. We have nothing in common, Tuck. Nothing. And it's a sorry thing when people like you don't even have to be forced to the hook. No. Worms like you jump on the hook, take the spear right in their gut and then wriggle and say they like it. You may be a supervisor, Tuck, but you're still a nigger, and when he's through with you, you'll go out with the rest of the garbage. *(Beat)* I'll see you there.

TUCK: How about a smoker? Top pay bracket. Or a cooker? You can have your pick. *(Beat)* It's not a color thing anymore, Miss Roach. It's a money thing, a class thing.

ROACH: Yeah. It's a money thing all right, and I haven't got any. But I have got a class and you, my brother, are not in it. But you might be again one day. Because the color thing never quite rubs off. You know it and I know it.

(He touches her hair, briefly.)

TUCK: I'm sorry about the uniforms. It wasn't my idea.

ROACH: When I see you back on the kill floor, then we'll do some talking.

TUCK: Frankly, I don't like snails myself.

ROACH: Don't get in our way.

SCENE TWO

Maggot, Roach and Cod are working in the refrigeration unit among large hanging carcasses, stamping the meat. They all sing together. The song is less celebration than a song of exhaustion and despair.

MAGGOT, ROACH AND COD:
>We stick and slit and shackle and head
>We snap and trim and pull and scald
>We scale and stun and scrape the meat
>We pack it all for you to eat.
>
>If there's a hell it's as hot as this
>Standing all day in the blood and piss
>We work in the war zone and the wages we pull
>Aren't enough to keep a dog's tit full.

(Brandon enters, moving slowly, like someone who has recently been ill. He steels his knife, very slowly.)

BRANDON *(To Cod)*: Let me see your knife.

(Cod hands the knife over. Brandon examines the blade.)

You sharpen this?

COD: Yes, I did.

BRANDON: Manually, I see.

COD: Yes.

BRANDON: Good for you. But you've folded the edge over. Cutting with a knife like this you'll pull your back out. Look. It won't cut.

(Brandon reaches for Cod's hand, but Cod pulls back. Brandon rolls up his own sleeve and drags the blade down his arm. It doesn't cut him.)

See what I mean? *(Holds the knife up between them)* The edge of a knife is like a thin piece of hair. If you angle that steel wrong, you're going to fold the edge over.

COD: I'll work at it.

(Cod returns to work.)

BRANDON: So the Company won't talk?

MAGGOT: Sent them three proposals. They said no.

ROACH: And no and no.

COD: They'll bring in replacements if we strike again.

BRANDON: So it's "we" now, is it? *(Beat)* I heard about the new proposal while I was . . . out. So we've offered to cut knife time in exchange for seniority rights?

ROACH: We had to give them something. We're fucking tired. Half voted to throw in the towel. Next time we vote, it'll be over. And so will we.

BRANDON: We're not going to eat their contract. Ever. Isn't that what we said? *(Speaks even slower)* See how a few . . . few . . . thousand wa . . . wa . . . watts to the brain can make a fell . . . fellow . . . rea . . . rea . . . rea . . . sonable? *(Suddenly jumps and does a perfect cartwheel, ends up face to face with Roach, speaking fast, in rhythm)* So. Have you made a decision

'tween makin' the dip
to sip the straw
or having a dip on a cone
while I sup with my cup
and smile my way up?

MAGGOT: We didn't miss you, Brandon.

SCENE THREE

We are back in the workroom with Cod and the Textile Worker. It is the same dream/scene as the prelude. The Textile Worker is the central focus, but we also see Maggot, Roach and Brandon working slowly, in silence. They are not aware of the scene going on around them, though they chant with the woman.

TEXTILE WORKER *(Chants)*: Pull the cloth, punch it down, cut three out, and trace.

COD: Hey! I'm talking to you!

TEXTILE WORKER: Hurry, hurry, don't go slow, keep your cheer and grace.

COD: I know you can hear me.

TEXTILE WORKER: Pull the cloth, punch it down—

COD: Look at me!

TEXTILE WORKER *(Turns to look at Cod, but looks in another direction away from Cod, as though she sees him elsewhere)*: I am looking at you. I'm always looking at you.

(Smoke begins to trickle in from a crack in the floor.)

COD: No. No.

TEXTILE WORKER: Yes. Look at your hands. They're beautiful. *(Holds up her own hands)* Like mine once were.

COD: Can't you see what's happening?!

TEXTILE WORKER: Your hands are like two flames.

COD: Do something!

TEXTILE WORKER: All the water in the world can't put their fire out.

(Cod drops to his knees and tries to cover the smoke with his hands to keep it from coming in.)

COD: There's no fire. There's no smoke. Not here. So pull the cloth, punch it down.

(Sausage Man enters with his sausage machine.)

ALL THE WORKERS: "Cut three out and trace."

SAUSAGE MAN: The doors have been locked.

TEXTILE WORKER: "Hurry, hurry, don't be slow—"

SAUSAGE MAN: From the outside.

ALL THE WORKERS: "—keep your cheer and grace."

SAUSAGE MAN: To keep track of employees. The fire trucks are on their way. The fireman will say his ladders could only reach the seventh floor. Is this the eighth?

COD: Let us out. Open the fucking doors!

SAUSAGE MAN: I don't have the key. I lost it years ago. *(Beat)* It's already happened. You can't change it. Why upset yourself?

COD *(Turns to the other workers)*: Help me with the doors. We'll break them down.

(The workers go on working. They can't hear him.)

You stupid bastards.

SAUSAGE MAN: They can't hear you.

TEXTILE WORKER: My hands sweep the cloth like water—

COD *(To the workers)*: Do you want to die?

TEXTILE WORKER *(Continuing)*: —over the keys of a piano.

COD: Are you just going to stand there and burn?

(Sausage Man cranks his grinder, and the fire increases. The workers go on working.)

SAUSAGE MAN: They won't ever be able to hear you. Because you're always somewhere else, my child.

(Cod sinks down to the floor, the sound of the fire drowning out his voice as he screams:)

COD: Isn't anybody out there!

SCENE FOUR

Tuck is alone on stage in Baquin's office. The chair Roach stood on earlier is center stage. Tuck sees it, circles it. He slowly gets undressed, then stands on the chair, as Roach did earlier. He stands still for some moments, as though in another place and time. In his mind, he hears Roach singing a line of the song she sang in Baquin's office. He gets off the chair, picks up his clothes. He tips over the chair with one finger, then casually exits.

SCENE FIVE

*Cod and Brandon in the cafeteria. Brandon is seated, engrossed
in eating.*

COD: It's a scandal.
BRANDON: Make yourself at home. Food's not that bad.
COD: OK. Then as food it shall be.
BRANDON: It is food.
COD: Not always it isn't.
BRANDON: What is the "it" we're talking about here?
COD: It's no longer an "it," it's an "isn't."
BRANDON: You're ruining my lunch with your gibberish.
Can't a man have—
COD: A man should have.
BRANDON: —a peaceful . . . intermission? *(Returns to his
food)*
COD *(Picking food off Brandon's plate)*: Not this canned pea,
not this frozen carrot, in fact, not even this . . .
BRANDON: Lumpagravy.
COD: Right. Not one piece of anything comes into being
without us.
BRANDON: So, what's new?
COD: Not even this tray. *(Takes Brandon's tray)*
BRANDON: Wait a minute.
COD: What you see here is dead.
BRANDON: It's a pork chop.
COD: Labor. Dead labor, of past and present.
BRANDON: Get out of my lunch.

> *(Cod lifts the tray and balances it between them, then swiftly
> slams it onto the table, face down. Brandon watches,
> stunned.)*

COD: Without the tray, the mashed potatoes slide into the
cheesecake, the milk swamps the peas. This is the situation we're in today. Without the tray, and the tray
being the union here, we're without a world that
gives us definition and power. We're no longer a

community of carrots and peas and mashed potatoes— *(Grabs up a handful of the squashed food in his
hand)* but a handful of slops. And they'll use us to
feed the hogs.

BRANDON *(Picks the pork chop out of the mess)*: *Voilà!* The
pork chop's the enemy, right?

COD: You got it.

BRANDON: What's the Big Bad Boss doing down here in
the mess with the rest of us?

COD: No, no. The pork chop is the enemy in disguise. The
pork chop's no better off than the peas. The pork
chop's—

BRANDON: The Scab.

COD: Bingo.

(Brandon eats the pork chop.)

What you see here is deregulation so that workers
have no way of protecting their rights. When we
make a stink 'cause we're offered part-time jobs with
twelve-hour shifts, big business just ups and moves
over the border or across the sea. It's the sort of
unsavory wage situation you see here when your
milk and gravy meet the cheesecake and it begins to
dissolve.

BRANDON: If we were having Jell-O, it wouldn't have
made a whole lot of difference.

COD: There's always room for Jell-O, because we're one of
the only industrialized nations where illegal firings
and the hiring of Scabs are common practice.

BRANDON: Those fucking pork chops.

(Cod picks up forks and hands one to Brandon.)

COD: We're back to the Depression. Eat. No. Back to the
Victorian age. *(Eats from the table)* Robber Barons are
again free to trade—eat!—over our dying bodies.
Everything and nothing has changed.

(Brandon, to his own surprise, eats from the mess as well.)

But guess what? *(Pounds on the food with a fork)* No matter how many times they pull the tray out from under us, smash, mash and pulverize our communities— *(Takes another bite)* We're still here.

BRANDON: And we're still eating.

COD: Right. *(Beat)* You have the cheesecake. *(Looking the food over)* If you can find it.

SCENE SIX

Cod and Maggot are on break. Cod is checking over his belt tools.

MAGGOT: A 1965 baby-blue F-100 Ford, long bed, with a V-8 so hot I can blow the pants off the highway in third gear.

COD: Must be some truck.

MAGGOT: Yeah. Only it's sitting in my yard right now with a main seal leak and bad mounts. I'm doing the bus these days. You a compact man?

COD: I know a good truck.

MAGGOT: Well, you don't know my truck. I'm the only one who can drive it, 'cause it's three on a tree and it sticks in second.

COD: Fords are temperamental.

MAGGOT: Yeah. The engine sweats, foams just a little at the edges. The trick isn't in your hand, really; it's in your groin. You got to rock your hips at just the right rhythm to lubricate the hitch on that second gear.

COD: I could drive a truck like that.

MAGGOT: Ever changed gears with your mouth? Not too tight and when the pressure's right and just about to blow, you open it up, wide, and shoot across that highway with the windshield shattering over your head like snow and the sun pouring down your throat like water. And there's no turning back.

COD: Ford, huh? A person could go to hell for driving a Ford. They'll put a stick shift up your ass, and the Devil will cruise you all over his Island singing, "Ford gives you better ideas." All through eternity.

MAGGOT: Should have figured you were Chevy.

COD: A '58, V-8, short bed with chrome hubs, AM radio, four on the floor and no hitch. But not everyone can drive a Chevy. You got to have the proper wrist action or you'll burn the gears. And if your hands are dry— *(Spits in palm)* you won't get the grip you need. *(Takes out a screwdriver or other sharp work tool)* You drive a Ford soft, but a Chevy's got to be treated rough. It's what a Chevy likes, 'cause it's an immoral engine and it can take it. Slap it some gas in first and, when you have the speed up and the friction between the rubber and the road is sending sparks down your spine—

(Cod sticks the screwdriver into the ground or box between Maggot's legs. This should be done suddenly and should frighten anyone but Maggot. Cod takes hold of the screwdriver as though it were a stick shift between Maggot's legs.)

—then fast into second, straight on and hard. *(Moves stick into second)* Now third's a risk. Third is going down on the engine. But you got to keep up the speed. And speed isn't a motion, it's a texture. And it's not dry. No. Speed is wet. Speed is an ocean, and third's a deep gear, a diver's gear, only for the brave at heart gear, and I open up the vents 'cause my cylinders need some air, and then down, down— *(Moves stick into third, closer to Maggot's crotch)* and lock into third.

(Some moments of silence.)

MAGGOT: And what about the last one: fourth gear?

(Cod unsticks the screwdriver and turns away to finish checking his tool belt.)

Hey! What about fourth gear?

COD: I never tell a girl how to get into fourth gear. She's got to find that out herself. I will tell you it's not about breaking the sound barrier. It's about breaking light, just like breaking ice under your wheels.

MAGGOT: Never met anyone like you.

COD: I'm not surprised. Want to see a trick?

(Cod touches the floor with his hand. His hand imprint starts to smoke.)

MAGGOT: Aren't we the Boy Scout!

COD: With some women it works.

MAGGOT: Son of a bitch.

COD: Don't think so; never knew my mother. She died in the fire . . . in Peoria, Illinois. A coat factory. No. That's not it. It was the . . . No . . . Yes . . . the . . . Triangle Shirtwaist Company . . . in New York City, some time ago. Turn of the century.

MAGGOT: Just when were you born?

COD: The fire started in a rag bin on the seventh floor, swept through the eighth, ninth and tenth floors. Mostly young women. My mother jumped. A lot of them did. They went in pairs. Holding hands. Nothing below them but concrete. My mother landed on top of some others. She wasn't crushed up like the rest of them. I was inside her. She was dead, but I wasn't. When the doctors found out I was in there, they ventilated her for five months. It was an experiment. They'd already filled out her death certificate. Then they cut her open and took me out.

MAGGOT: I heard about that fire.

COD: Yeah. I was born from a dead woman.

MAGGOT: That fire happened over eighty years ago.

COD *(Wryly)*: It's a hell of a way to come in to the world.

SCENE SEVEN

Brandon sneaks into the women's changing room. He's not sure what he's looking for. He sees a woman's work dress. He smells and touches it sensually, in much the same way as he did the meat in Act I, Scene Ten.

BRANDON: "I have lain in prison . . . Out of my nature has come wild despair—"

(He takes the dress in his arms. Roach enters, watches unobserved for some moments.)

"—an abandonment to grief that was piteous even to look at." *(Beat)* No. Not on your knees. *(Tries again)* My darling, my dreams are dark, dark, dark. *(Beat)* Damn. Don't bring up color. *(Tries again)* When I am with you, I feel the . . . the shadows of our desire floating and . . . light, no . . . floating and . . . luminous above us, delirious with . . . with . . . intercourse. Intercourse? Shit. *(Beat)* Can I hold your hand?

ROACH *(Makes herself known)*: Now I like this show better than the last one, cherub. But you could use some lessons. *(Beat)* Put the dress on.

(They watch each other some moments.)

I mean it.

(Brandon glances quickly over his shoulder to make sure they're alone.)

BRANDON: Please, sir. Avert your eyes. *(Takes off his clothes, turning away to do so)* No peeking!

(Roach watches him undress and put the dress on as he speaks:)

Oh, I'm just a girl, a waif like a wafer you could snap in two, just a gosling in distress, an egret with no inlet to satisfy my pitiable appetites.

ROACH: Shush up, baby doll. Or I'll tear your fucking heart out with my teeth.

BRANDON: Oh, no, no, no. *(Beat)* Oh, yes, yes, yes.

(Roach is silent.)

Well, go on, you brute. Tear me into tiny, little pieces.

ROACH: I forget the script.

BRANDON: Now you force me.

ROACH: I force you.

BRANDON: Yeah. (Beat) Please, please, pretty please.

(Roach approaches Brandon and takes hold of his dress collar.)

ROACH: Isn't this the part where I . . .

BRANDON: Exactly.

ROACH: And I do it all the way down . . .

BRANDON: You got it.

ROACH: I won't be able to wear it again if I do that.

BRANDON: Don't worry, darling, I've got one at home I can lend you . . .

ROACH: Shut up.

(Roach rips the dress open so that Brandon's chest is exposed. This should be done how we've seen it in countless melodramatic films.)

I could get into this style.

BRANDON: And now you . . . go on . . . now you . . .

ROACH: Chew your mouth up, right?

BRANDON: And the eternal flames of hell engulf us.

ROACH: I don't think so.

BRANDON: Trespass matures the soul.

ROACH: It wouldn't be a game out there, Brandon.

BRANDON: This is the nineties.

ROACH: A Puerto Rican friend of mine had some teeth kicked out for dating a white girl.

BRANDON: My friends won't mind; I don't have any.

ROACH: What's the deal? Does it make you feel bad 'cause I'm black?

BRANDON: You want me.

ROACH: You're a boy, Brandon.

BRANDON: You want me and you hate me for it.

ROACH: This is a kid's game. I'm not playing.

BRANDON: You're a coward.

ROACH: I just like things simple.

BRANDON: Look. These are the facts. I like your mouth. It's the only place on earth I ever felt like laying a foundation to make a home.

ROACH: This wouldn't be simple.

BRANDON: I have this dream sometimes. And in the dream the scars on my mouth are gone, and my mouth is . . . like it's . . . scorched, seared, and then you kiss me and your kiss is so cold. *(Gently runs a finger over her lips)* Like an apple in the snow. *(Roach removes his hand)* When I wake up from that kiss, my pillow is always wet and I'm crying like a baby.

ROACH: A kiss is a dangerous thing.

BRANDON: It's a dangerous thing to live without it. *(Beat)* Are you afraid of me?

ROACH *(Laughs)*: I'm afraid of me.

BRANDON: I won't give it up.

ROACH: No. I don't think you will. All right. *(Takes one of Brandon's knives)* I'll give you a kiss. If.

BRANDON: If?

ROACH: If you can take this knife from me. *(Beat)* But if either one of us bleeds, if either one of us gets so much as a paper cut, it's over. And we'll never talk about us again. Agreed? *(Beat)* Agreed?

BRANDON: Yeah. Completely.

(Roach puts the blade between her teeth. Slowly and carefully she passes the knife from her mouth to Brandon's mouth. In doing this, they are also in a kiss. During this transfer,

Brandon is pushed to his knees. He holds the knife between his teeth as he kneels.)

ROACH: That's where I like my Tarzan. On his knees.

SCENE EIGHT

Maggot and Roach on break. Maggot is smoking. Roach drinks a glass of water. They hardly hear what the other is saying.

MAGGOT: I've been thinking about trading the Ford.

ROACH: He's a kid. But he's a smart kid.

MAGGOT: You ever had a Chevy?

ROACH: He's not really a kid, I mean, he's twenty-two. That's about . . . *(Counts on her fingers)*

MAGGOT: A Chevy can take a lot of rust.

ROACH: Not so bad.

MAGGOT: And the front end won't go out at a hundred thousand.

ROACH: But he's awfully white. Don't you think he's awfully white?

MAGGOT: He's Irish. They don't get much sun.

ROACH: A bit young and a bit white.

MAGGOT: How much older are you, about a decade?

ROACH: Thanks.

MAGGOT: I love you, you know.

ROACH: What's out there will keep coming between you and me. If you ever forget it, we're finished. When it comes down to it, they're going to try and break one of us, and, more likely than not, it's going to be me. And you're going to stand by and watch.

MAGGOT: I couldn't get a job anywhere else.

ROACH: You couldn't get a friend like me anywhere else.

MAGGOT: That's for sure.

ROACH: So has he got a spotty ass?

MAGGOT: I haven't got that close yet. *(Beat)* I've had some crushes, you know, pretty serious before. But I never felt like the ones I knew could reach down inside me, grab a hold of my tailbone and turn me inside out, like a shirt.

ROACH: I know what you mean.

MAGGOT: And Cod's got this smell . . . Ahhh . . . A smell like . . . like something that's just about to burn.

ROACH: I kissed Brandon the other day.

MAGGOT: No!

ROACH: It was . . . interesting.

MAGGOT: Interesting? What's he taste like?

ROACH: Like nothing. *(Beat)* Nice.

MAGGOT: This one's over my head.

(Roach turns around.)

ROACH: Yeah. It is. *(Beat)* Close your eyes.

(Maggot does. Roach tilts Maggot's face up.)

Brandon tastes . . .

(She pours the water slowly and gently onto Maggot's face.)

Like this. Like water. Like drinking one, two, three glasses of water.

SCENE NINE

Roach and Maggot are still standing together in the shadows. Sausage Man appears. No one sees him but Cod.

SAUSAGE MAN: It's time for you to go.

COD: Not yet.

SAUSAGE MAN: I can feel the heat coming off your body a hundred years from now. Why don't we go there?

COD: I'm not leaving this time.

SAUSAGE MAN: You're trying my patience.

COD: Hey, all of you. Look at this son of a bitch!

(Neither Roach nor Maggot hear Cod.)

SAUSAGE MAN: I've let you stay far too long already.

COD: Check this joker out!

SAUSAGE MAN: Listen, I'm getting tired of playing rivals.

COD: Go back to the hell you crawled out of.

SAUSAGE MAN: I want you to come work for me. On my side this time. We'd make a good team. You're sensitive. You listen to the meat. You'd know how to coax it into my grinder without a struggle. Without a strike. We could start anew.

COD: This time it's going to be different.

(Roach exits. Maggot remains on stage, finishing her cigarette. Cod turns away from Sausage Man.)

I can't touch her. I can't. You know that. I can't touch anyone like that. I'd burn them to a cinder. Turn their heart to a chunk of coal. But in my head. No. That you can't stop. In my head I touch her over and over. Again and again.

(Cod approaches Maggot closely; Maggot is unaware of Cod.)

And her skin is cold and sweet. Ice forms at the corners of her mouth. Just before we kiss. And across the world it's winter. In the fields. Inside the houses. Even under our tongues. Winter.

(Maggot exits.)

But, even in my own head, I can't make her touch me. Because I don't know what it's like to be touched. What? What? Does it cut or maul? Scratch or tear? Tell me. Is it pain? You don't know. But it must be pain, because my heart is a cheap toy and it breaks inside my chest each time I try to imagine: what would it feel like to have her hand on my breast, her fingers along my spine. Her hard mouth against my hip. And what would it be like to stop moving at that touch? To stand still and listen? Just listen. To the pulse in her wrist. No rage, no hurry, no you and me, no struggle. Just her blood, to and fro, in her wrist, against my ear. *(Beat)* I am alone. I have never been anything but alone. Let her touch me. And I'll know where I am.

SAUSAGE MAN: What a sermonizer the decades have made you. You'd've made your mother proud. But reality won't be changed, Cod.

COD: It's nothing more than a bucket of clay, and this time we're going to shape it.

SAUSAGE MAN: It might go bad if you push me. Things aren't ripe yet.

COD: Yeah, well sometimes history's just not ready for you and so you give it a shove.

SAUSAGE MAN: Snap of my fingers and you're toad's dust.

COD: But then there's no conflict. And if there's no conflict, then I won't exist. And neither will you. *(Beat)* You can send me anywhere, but you can't make me fight you; I quit.

SAUSAGE MAN: Damn you. Damn you! *(Beat)* All right. If you won't play, then you'll have to pay. But how much?

(Sausage Man gestures to the shadows, where in the darkness we see the shadow of the Textile Worker working. She shines with a strange light.)

How much will you pay? *(Beat)* Listen. "Pull the cloth, punch it down, cut three out, and trace." Can you hear her? She's talking. Oh, yes, and laughing. Because it's Friday and it's almost time to quit work.

(Cod puts his hands over his ears so he won't hear Sausage Man, who seems to be physically hurting him by recounting the story.)

And she feels you kick inside her, and she whispers something to you, and she is happy because she's managed to borrow a crib from a friend and because the woman sitting across from her is telling a joke about "Jack be nimble, Jack be quick, Jack tripped over the candlestick." Stupid, stupid Jack. Now flames are coming up through the floor boards at her feet. Can you hear her, Cod? She's not laughing anymore. No. She's making another sound now. Listen.

(We hear the sound of tremendous pressure being released, the sound of something bursting forth from its restraints. Then we hear a terrible scream of pain from offstage. At the same moment Cod and the Textile Worker shout:)

COD AND TEXTILE WORKER: No!

SCENE TEN

Brandon is lying on the floor. Roach and Cod are beside him. Maggot paces.

MAGGOT: Ten minutes. They said ten minutes.
ROACH: Where's the fucking first aid! He's not breathing.
COD *(To Maggot)*: Call the fire department.
ROACH: He's not breathing!
COD: Tell them we got an ammonia line break at hog-box number six.

(Maggot exits.)

ROACH: That's it, Brandon. Breathe. Breathe. Slow. Breathe slow.

(Brandon's lungs make a terrible sound as he tries to breathe.)

COD *(Shouts to offstage)*: Maggot? Get him some water. Maggot?

(Brandon tries to speak but can't.)

ROACH: Shhhh. Just breathe.
BRANDON *(Begins to struggle)*: Fuck.

COD *(Shouts)*: Maggot?! *(To Roach)* Keep his head back.

> *(Cod takes out a knife.)*

ROACH: What the hell are you doing?

COD: His windpipe's gone. I'm punching a hole so he can get some air.

> *(Cod cuts into Brandon's neck to make a hole so he can breathe. This is a medical procedure, and Cod knows what he's doing.)*

ROACH: Where are they?

COD: Keep his head back.

ROACH: Maggot!

> *(Cod strips off his shirt to put it under Brandon's head.)*

COD: It will help him breathe.

> *(His shirt removed, we see that Cod wears chest wraps to hold down her breasts. Cod is a woman. Brandon tries again to speak.)*

ROACH: Shut up. Don't talk.

> *(Maggot enters. She sees Cod.)*

MAGGOT: Jesus Christ.

COD: Have they shut down the mains?

ROACH: Ssshhhhh.

> *(Roach kisses Brandon, gently on the mouth.)*

MAGGOT: I don't know.

ROACH: Stay with us.

> *(Sausage Man slowly walks across the stage. Only Cod sees him. Sausage Man kneels beside Brandon, removes the knife, and gently blows into Brandon's neck as though blowing out a candle. Brandon is dead.)*

Baquin in his office. Tuck paces back and forth.

TUCK: Damage is at a minimum. They were able to shut down the mains within minutes.

BAQUIN: He should have been wearing safety equipment.

TUCK: We don't have any.

BAQUIN: Nonsense. I filled out an order.

TUCK: We've got no sprinkler system, most of the extinguishers are shot.

BAQUIN: That wasn't his job.

TUCK: Half the safety exit doors are bolted shut.

BAQUIN: The boy was out of line.

TUCK: He had the assignment.

BAQUIN: Call the insurance company. I want them to know that he wasn't wearing the required safety equipment.

TUCK: We don't have any safety equipment.

BAQUIN: He was careless.

TUCK: I changed three of those gauges myself two days ago. That ammonia is so cold in a liquid form and it touches you and it's like taking a lit match—

BAQUIN: The board is breathing down my neck.

TUCK: —tttssshhh—it will burn you that quick.

BAQUIN: Just make sure the papers know why it happened.

TUCK: Mr. Baquin. *(Beat)* That's what it does in a vapor form in your lungs.

BAQUIN: I don't appreciate your *(Beat)* tone in this time of crisis. You've done well considering your . . . your beginnings, Buck. You've been given a chance—

TUCK: I earned—

BAQUIN: You earned? You've worked at opportunities offered by this Company. The bottom line here, boy, is— *(Holds out his hands to Tuck)* don't bite the hands that feed you.

TUCK *(Looks at Baquin's extended hands, then his own)*: See these hands?

BAQUIN: Look clean enough to—

TUCK *(Interrupts)*: Oh, they're clean enough. So clean I can't even see them anymore. I used to have hands. Good, strong, black hands that did what I told them to do. They were smart and skillful, good at whatever job I asked them to do. That didn't mean they still didn't complain and ache and bruise and bleed. They very near went for broke at some jobs. But they were mine, and they had a knowledge, a vocation, and when I went home at the end of the day, my hands went with me, and sometimes they played and strayed—strayed to other hands, caressed other hands, along and down and in between—

BAQUIN: Just what the hell do you—

TUCK *(Interrupts)*: Now I got this almighty position. Promotion: but no hands may apply. You know what my hands do now? They hold a clipboard, or they hang at my side. And at the end of the day when I go home, I go home without them. *(Beat)* A man without hands. What do you think, Mr. Baquin? On payday, how do you think he counts his change?

(Baquin is at a loss. He stares at Tuck for some uncomfortable moments.)

BAQUIN: I see. Yes. Well. I'm sorry. Now listen to me closely: if the papers pick up on that . . . that Cod character. Christ. This industry is bringing in the likes of him. Fire him. Her. Whatever.

TUCK: Cod can do the work of two men on the kill floor.

BAQUIN: A person like that shouldn't be handling meat. If the public gets a hold of this. It's unsanitary. It's unnatural.

TUCK: What's unnatural is that we figured she was a man so we started her off at the top. If we'd known she was a woman—

BAQUIN *(Interrupts)*: What are you saying? You've got to learn to articulate—

TUCK (*Interrupts*): But what's really unnatural, Mr. Baquin, is for a twenty-two-year-old boy to have his lungs burned out of his chest.

BAQUIN: A man like you needs to speak clearly, to have command—

TUCK: I changed three of those lines myself. It could've been me instead of him.

BAQUIN: Nonsense. You would have been wearing our safety equipment.

TUCK: That's the truth of it. It could've been anybody in this fucking packhouse. Anybody but you, 'cause you don't change lines. No. You'll never change lines.

(*Suddenly Tuck picks up the bowl with the snail in it and smashes it to the ground. Baquin remains calm. They look at the broken glass between them.*)

SCENE TWELVE

Maggot, Roach and Cod enter with heavy chains. They begin to link them. At some point Sausage Man enters and watches them all from the shadows.

COD: We could take this place over *after* the funeral.

ROACH: No. We do it now. Before they get wind of it and lock us out.

MAGGOT: I figured the next time we saw you it would be in a skirt.

COD: A girl can't chase a steer if she's wearing a skirt.

MAGGOT (*Knocks Cod over*): A girl can't chase a man if she's wearing a jockstrap.

COD: I don't wear a jockstrap.

MAGGOT: Well, thank God for that.

COD: Except when I go out on the town and want to make the effort.

ROACH: You are one confused girl.

COD: I've never been more certain.

MAGGOT: Get this, Roach: she was born from a corpse.

COD: I was born from a fire.

MAGGOT: You've been lying to us all this time. Pretending you were what you're not.

COD: You're the one who pretended.

ROACH: What's the matter, Maggot? She's got the same ass you were mooning about.

(Maggot holds her knife to Cod's cheek.)

MAGGOT: So are you a bastard or a bitch?

COD: Depends on the job.

(Sausage Man appears and watches them.)

MAGGOT: You think you're something special?

(Maggot makes a small cut on Cod's cheek.)

You bleed like the rest of us. *(Throws the knife down)* That's for not thinking you could trust us.

COD: It wasn't a matter of trust.

MAGGOT: No, it was a matter of money.

COD: And a matter of balls. Working like a man, I feel more like a gal. Know what I mean?

ROACH: We've got eight minutes till we take over and lock ourselves in.

MAGGOT: Which changing room are you gonna use?

ROACH: Anybody that wants out better go now.

COD: Want to see a trick?

MAGGOT: I've seen enough.

COD: No you haven't. It's just beginning. *(Holds out her hand)* Go on. Touch me.

(Maggot touches Cod's hand. A small flame erupts. Maggot jerks her hand back.)

SAUSAGE MAN: I think it's time I took things back in hand. *(Exits)*

ROACH: We got three minutes till we lock the doors. Help me with the chains!

(Roach collects the heavy chains.)

MAGGOT *(To Cod)*: Have you got the guts of a woman or a man?

COD: I've got guts. Years of them. More than enough for both of us.

MAGGOT: Then I dare you: take off your shirt.

COD: Really? What do I get in return?

MAGGOT: Name it.

COD: You knew what I was.

ROACH: Let's get on with it.

MAGGOT: I want to see if you've got the kind of chest I like.

COD: And what kind is that?

ROACH: One minute to lock.

MAGGOT: I'll know it when I see it.

(Cod strips off her shirt. She is still wearing the bandage.)

ROACH: Forty-five seconds.

COD: Things aren't always the way you see it.

ROACH *(Exiting with the last of the chains)*: Thank God for that.

COD: All right. You can look, but don't touch.

MAGGOT: What if I want to?

COD: You could get burned.

ROACH *(Offstage)*: Thirty seconds.

MAGGOT: That's what I want.

(Cod unwinds a piece of the bandage and hands it to Maggot, who circles Cod, unwinding the bandage, as Roach counts down.)

ROACH *(Offstage)*: Ten, nine, eight, seven,

ROACH *(Offstage)* AND MAGGOT: six, five, four, three, two, one. Lock.

(The bandage is unwrapped and drops to the floor. Now Maggot can see Cod's breasts. At this moment of revelation, we hear the deafening sound of many heavy doors being pulled shut and locked, continuous echoes of doors locking

and locking. Maggot reaches out and touches Cod's breast. Maggot and Cod kiss.)

Baquin is alone and talking to himself.

BAQUIN: Tuck. You're a good man. I want you to go in there, right now, and check on our workers. Let me know what their moooooooooo. Their moooooooooo-ooo. *(Stops speaking, begins to chew his cud much as a cow would)* Oh, Tuck. My dear Tuck. Come back to me. You can't leave. Please, please, come back. It's lonely in here. The ultimate loneliness: to be the last of your kind.

(Sausage Man enters. Baquin is startled.)

You're not Tuck.

SAUSAGE MAN: You're not happy making my sausages anymore.

BAQUIN: Oh, yes I am.

SAUSAGE MAN: No. You aren't. This is a terrible disappointment. Production has all but stopped. You see? *(Cranks his sausage machine)* It's empty. I've run out of bits and pieces. No bits and pieces, no sausages.

BAQUIN: How can I help you?

SAUSAGE MAN: Get those doors open so we can move in there and crank things up again.

BAQUIN: It's out of my hands.

(Sausage Man nears Baquin, who becomes nervous. Sausage Man steps on something, then looks at the bottom of his shoe.)

What's the matter?

SAUSAGE MAN: Looks like a bit of snot got stuck to my shoe.

BAQUIN: Oh no, oh no.

SAUSAGE MAN: Its time for a little intervention.

BAQUIN: The eternal night of extinction.

SAUSAGE MAN: Why, they've frightened you, haven't they?

BAQUIN: Nonsense. This strike is illegal. I'll call out the National Guard. *(Calls)* Tuck! Get in here. Tuck!

SAUSAGE MAN: Shhhh. I can see it's time. Time for some new blood. Would you like some grass?

(Sausage Man pulls some grass from his pockets and holds it out to Baquin. He also reveals a cattle prod, which he's been hiding behind his back.)

BAQUIN: It's not my fault. That mob in there are tearing me limb from limb. They're cutting me to pieces. They're frying my bacon. The whole industry is being grilled to hell.

SAUSAGE MAN: It's fresh grass. I picked it myself.

(Baquin sniffs the grass. Suddenly, he chomps at it, chews hungrily.)

That's it. That's it. Yes. They've been cutting you to pieces. I can see that. Into little tiny pieces that are so small no one will have any use for them. No one but me.

BAQUIN: Stay away from me.

SAUSAGE MAN: I can turn you into something useful.

BAQUIN: No, thank you. I'm not in the moooooooooooooo-ooooooooooo.

(Baquin clears his throat but nothing comes out but the sounds of a cow. He begins to chew his cud again. Sausage Man moves in on Baquin and begins to poke him with the cattle prod.)

Mooooooooooooooooooo?

(Baquin's "moo" is cut short when he's charged by the cattle prod. Sausage Man "herds" Baquin as they exit. Sausage Man makes soft, little clucking noises to encourage Baquin.)

SAUSAGE MAN: Yup . . . Yup . . . Yup, yup.

SCENE FOURTEEN

Upstage Roach speaks to a murmuring crowd.

ROACH: My friends. Welcome to Slaughter City. This is a place where things go and go and go. Now, this is a place where things stop. Machinery stops. Cows stop. Pigs stop. We stop. And, most importantly, the profits stop. And, whenever the profits stop, things heat up fast. Brandon's death was only the beginning. From now on, anything can happen. And we're going to have to be ready for it.

(Roach exits. Cod enters from one side of the stage, and Sausage Man enters from the opposite side. Baquin's tie hangs from his grinder.

Sausage Man puts his grinder down in front of Cod.)

SAUSAGE MAN: I've been thinking it over. You're right. Why play by the old rules? If you want to stay: okay. Then it's the two of us here, together. Through to the bitter end. Who knows? This might turn out to be the opportunity we've been waiting for. But will both of us be here afterwards to mop up the mess? *(Laughs with true delight)* What a gamble! What a risk! I feel like my old self again. As you said, sometimes history just isn't ready for you, so you give it— *(Lights a match)* a shove.

(Sausage Man drops the match into the top of the grinder. It makes a small flame. Cod stands watching, transfixed. She speaks as though in a trance.)

COD: I'm with the Knights of Labor . . . No . . . With the United Mine . . . *(Shakes her head, trying to locate herself)* No. I know where I am.

(Sausage Man laughs.)

SAUSAGE MAN *(Sings)*: "Oh where, oh where can my little dog be?"

COD: I'm in a chicken processing plant. Somewhere in the broiler belt, in 1891 . . . No. It was 1991 . . . A long time ago. Decades and decades from now.

SAUSAGE MAN: They died on the assembly line.

COD: Yes. That was in . . . Hamlet. In . . . South . . . in North Carolina.

SAUSAGE MAN: The chickens burned.

COD: The doors were chained shut. From the outside.

SAUSAGE MAN: Cluck. Cluck. Cluck. Moooooooooooo.

COD: That was at the Triangle Shirt Waist Company . . . A whole century from now. On the seventh . . . No! The chains were on the outside . . . No, no . . . The chains are on the inside. And this is somewhere else!

SAUSAGE MAN: This is nowhere else. And there was a fire.

COD: Yes. There was a fire.

SAUSAGE MAN: See you on the other side? *Bon voyage*, my friend.

(Split scene: the Textile Worker is standing on the window ledge. She is dressed in a long, flowing dress from a time before her time. A strange light lights her. She looks radiant.

Throughout the following Cod is still trying to locate herself.)

COD: There was a fire.

TEXTILE WORKER: It started in a rag bin.

COD: On the seventh floor.

SAUSAGE MAN: The workers burned.

(Sausage Man moves away and watches Cod.)

COD: Yes. *(Beat)* No!

TEXTILE WORKER: And this is the eighth floor. I'm standing at the open window, and the heat is so big behind me that it's melting the dress off my back. My hair starts to burn. I know I'm going to jump. That way I'll have a few more seconds. Alive. *(Overlapping slightly with Cod)* And I want—

TEXTILE WORKER AND COD: —a few more seconds.

TEXTILE WORKER: Women are jumping out of the windows around me and below me, on the lower floors. From up here, they look like handkerchiefs falling to the ground.

SAUSAGE MAN *(Making the sounds of a fire truck)*: Ding, ding, ding.

COD: Yes. The fire trucks. In the distance.

TEXTILE WORKER: The ledge I'm standing on has started to burn under my feet. The soles of my shoes are gone. *(Beat)* I lean to jump, holding my belly where my four-month-old child is still alive within me, for a few seconds more. And then— *(Sausage Man appears besides her)* he's there and he tells me:

SAUSAGE MAN: I can save your child.

COD: No!

TEXTILE WORKER: And I say, yes, yes, and I make the promise:

(They all chant the "promise.")

SAUSAGE MAN: "If the child is my spark—"

TEXTILE WORKER AND COD *(Slightly overlapping)*: "—forever and ever—"

SAUSAGE MAN: "—to light up the dark—"

TEXTILE WORKER AND COD: "—whithersoever—"

SAUSAGE MAN: "—I choose to send her—"

TEXTILE WORKER AND SAUSAGE MAN *(Chant together)*: "She'll live."

TEXTILE WORKER: And I agree to everything. Because I know her already. Because I want her to live.

COD: There was a fire.

TEXTILE WORKER: And then I jump.

SAUSAGE MAN *(Angry now)*: The workers burned!

COD: No! This is now. Not the day after. This is this hour.

TEXTILE WORKER: And in those seconds, with the wind rushing by me, tearing my dress from my body, I remember only one thing, being asked once, as a child: "If you had five seconds left to live—"

COD: This hour.

TEXTILE WORKER: "—what would you do?"

COD: I'm not going to leave.

TEXTILE WORKER: I didn't answer the question, because as a child I didn't know.

COD: We have to do something . . . We have to . . . Yes.

TEXTILE WORKER: But I know now. And so I do it.

COD: Because this is right now.

TEXTILE WORKER: I laugh.

COD: And it's . . . right here in front of . . .

TEXTILE WORKER: I laugh, because I feel her move inside me like a flame. *(Opens her arms as if to jump)* I laugh, because I know she will never die.

(Cod has located herself. She shouts out, as though she were already somewhere else, as though her voice were crossing a great distance of time and place between herself and her fellow workers.)

COD: Fire!

(We hear the sound of flames and burning. Maggot and Roach rush in, having heard Cod's shout of warning. Maggot and Roach see the fire and move toward it to put it out. The fire roars up brightly all around them as they continue to fight it.

Blackout.)

END OF PLAY

SELECT BIBLIOGRAPHY

Barrett, James R. *Work and Community in the Jungle: Chicago's Packinghouse Workers, 1894–1922.* Champaign, IL: University of Illinois Press, 1990.

Bulkin, Elly, Minnie Bruce Pratt and Barbara Smith. *Yours in Struggle: Three Feminist Perspectives on Anti-Semitism and Racism.* Ithaca, NY: Firebrand Books, 1984.

Carr, Edward Hallett. *What Is History?* New York: Vintage Books, 1967.

Castle, Terry. *The Apparitional Lesbian: Female Homosexuality and Modern Culture.* New York: Columbia University Press, 1995.

Churchill, Ward and Jim Vander Wall. *Agents of Repression: The FBI's Secret Wars Against the American Indian Movement and the Black Panther Party.* Cambridge, MA: SouthEnd Press, 1990.

Dyson, Michael Eric. *Reflecting Black: African-American Cultural Criticism.* Minneapolis: University of Minnesota Press, 1993.

Engels, Frederick and Karl Marx. *Communist Manifesto.* New York: International Publishers, 1983.

Foucault, Michel. *The History of Sexuality.* New York: Vintage Books, 1990.

Garber Marjorie. *Vested Interests: Cross-Dressing & Cultural Anxiety.* London: Routledge, 1992.

Green, James R. *Grass-Roots Socialism: Radical Movements in the Southwest 1895–1943.* Baton Rouge: Louisiana State University Press, 1978.

McGrath, Thomas. *Selected Poems, 1938–1988.* Port Townsend, WA: Copper Canyon Press, 1988.

Rachleff, Peter. *Hard-Pressed in the Heartland: The Hormel Strike and the Future of the Labor Movement.* Cambridge, MA: SouthEnd Press, 1993.

Roediger, David R. *The Wages of Whiteness: Race and the Making of the American Working Class.* London: Verso, 1999.

Sinclair, Upton. *The Jungle.* New York: Penguin Classics, 1985.

Stromquist, Shelton. *Solidarity and Survival: An Oral History of Iowa Labor in the Twentieth Century.* Iowa City: University of Iowa Press, 1993.

Williams, Raymond. *Modern Tragedy: Essays on the Idea of Tragedy in Life and in the Drama.* Stanford: Stanford University Press, 1966.

Yates, Michael D. *Longer Hours, Fewer Jobs: Employment and Unemployment in the United States.* New York: Monthly Review Press, 1994.

Zinn, Howard. *A People's History of the United States.* New York: Harper Perennial, 1980.

THE TRESTLE AT POPE LICK CREEK

1998

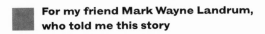 **For my friend Mark Wayne Landrum,
who told me this story**

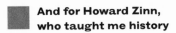 **And for Howard Zinn,
who taught me history**

PRODUCTION HISTORY

The Trestle at Pope Lick Creek was first produced on March 13, 1998, at the Actors Theatre of Louisville as part of the Humana Festival of New American Plays (Jon Jory, Artistic Director; Sandy Speer, Executive Director). The director was Adrian Hall, the scenic design was by Paul Owen, the costume design was by Jeanette deJong, the lighting design was by Greg Sullivan and the sound design was by Martin R. Desjardins. The cast was as follows:

PACE CREAGAN	Tami Dixon
DALTON CHANCE	Michael Linstroth
GIN CHANCE	Marion McCorry
DRAY CHANCE	Michael Medeiros
CHAS WEAVER	Jonathan Bolt

The Trestle at Pope Lick Creek was produced on June 11, 1999, at New York Theatre Workshop (James C. Nicola, Artistic Director; Jo Beddoe, Managing Director). The director was Lisa Peterson, the scenic design was by Riccardo Hernandez, the costume design was by Katherine Roth, the lighting design was by Scott Zielinski and the original music and sound design were by David Van Tieghem. The cast was as follows:

PACE CREAGAN	Alicia Goranson
DALTON CHANCE	Michael Pitt
GIN CHANCE	Nancy Robinette
DRAY CHANCE	David Chandler
CHAS WEAVER	Philip Goodwin

In February 2001, *The Trestle at Pope Lick Creek* was produced by the Traverse Theatre Company, Edinburgh, Scotland. The director was Philip Howard. Design was by Fiona Watt, lighting design was by Renny Robertson, musical composition was by Gavin Marwick, and the voice and dialect coach was Ros Steen. The cast was as follows:

PACE CREAGAN	Julia Dalkin
DALTON CHANCE	Ian Skewis
GIN CHANCE	Pauline Knowles
DRAY CHANCE	Iain Macrae
CHAS WEAVER	Eric Barlow

CHARACTERS

PACE CREAGAN, a girl, seventeen years old
DALTON CHANCE, a boy, fifteen years old
GIN CHANCE, Dalton's mother, forty-one years old
DRAY CHANCE, Dalton's father, a few years Gin's senior
CHAS WEAVER, a jailer, Brett's father, early fifties

TIME

1936.

PLACE

A town outside a city. A jail cell. Somewhere in the U.S.

SETTING

Should be minimal and not "realistic." A piece of the trestle should be visible and awe-inspiring.

NOTE

Accents of the characters should be as "neutral" as possible, an accent from "somewhere" in the U.S.

No overalls for any characters. Being poor and white in 1930s America is not synonymous with poor dress taste, nor Ma and Pa Kettle outfits.

Nothing in the world is single.

—Percy Bysshe Shelley

ACT I

PROLOGUE

Darkness for some moments. Then we see Dalton sitting upstage, in a corner. His back is all we see. Beside him is a small candle. From the light of the candle, Dalton makes hand shadows. We can see the shadows but we cannot discern what they are.

DALTON: This is a horse. *(Makes a hand shadow)* This is a swan. No. Not a swan, shit. A falcon. Yeah. A falcon. No. There's no claw. It's a duck. *(Makes another hand shadow)* Now it's a turtle. There's the shell. But hell. It could be a fish. With a fin.

(He makes another hand shadow. Pace appears. She is there but not there.)

PACE: That's not a fish, Dalton Chance. You should know better. That's a bird. A pigeon. The kind that live under the trestle.

(Dalton slowly turns and peers into the darkness. He doesn't see Pace, though she is visible to us. He calls to her softly.)

DALTON: Creagan? Pace Creagan? Is that you? *(He stands up. He cries out to her)* You go to hell, Pace Creagan!

(Pace tips the candle over. Darkness.)

SCENE ONE

Months earlier, in the past. Pace and Dalton run to meet under the trestle at Pope Lick Creek. Pace gets there ahead of Dalton. They have been running and are both out of breath.

DALTON: You had a head start!

PACE: Nah. You haven't got any lungs in that puny chest of yours. Listen to you rattle.

DALTON: I'm not rattlin'.

PACE: Yeah you are. What've you got in there? A handful of nails.

DALTON: Twisted my ankle.

PACE: Yeah, yeah.

DALTON: So this is it, huh?

(They look up above them.)

PACE: Yep.

DALTON: It's not that high up.

PACE: Almost a hundred feet. From the creek up.

DALTON: Some creek. There's no water: it's dry.

PACE: Don't care; can't swim anyway. What time is it?

DALTON: Coming up to seven.

PACE: Exact time.

DALTON *(Guessing)*: 6:41.

PACE: She comes through at 7:10. Sometimes 7:12. Sometimes she'll come on at 7:09 for ten days straight and then bang, she's off three minutes. She's never exact; you can't trust her. That's what I like.

DALTON: How many times have you done it?

PACE: Twice. Once with Jeff Farley. Once alone.

DALTON: You're lyin'. Jeff Farley never ran it.

PACE: Nope. Never did. Tied his shoes on real tight, took two deep breaths, said, "I'm ready when you are." And then he heard that whistle. Aren't a lot of people can hear that whistle.

DALTON: So you didn't do it twice.

PACE: I would of but he turned tail and ran.

DALTON: So how many times then? Just once?

PACE: Once. And that's once more than you.

DALTON: Yeah. Who was witness?

PACE: No one here to see me.

DALTON: You're lying.

PACE: Whatever you say.

DALTON: Did you run it or not?

PACE: Sure. Once.

DALTON: How come I don't believe you?

PACE: Me and you, we'll have witnesses. Philip, Lester and Laura Sutton will be here at 7:05.

DALTON: No. No way. You said just you and me as witness.

PACE: If you get scared and run, who's to say you won't lie and say I chickened too?

DALTON: You said just you and me.

PACE: It'll be just you and me. Up there. Down here in the creek bed we'll have the three stooges watching us. Keeping tabs. Taking notes. And you can be sure they'll check our pants when we're done and see who's shit.

DALTON: You know. You don't talk like a girl. Should.

PACE (*Meaning it*): Thanks.

DALTON: But you look like one. So I guess you are.

PACE: Want me to prove it?

DALTON: No.

PACE: How old are you?

DALTON: Sixteen. In a couple of months.

PACE (*Nears him*): Well, well. Almost a man. (*Pushes him backward, but not too hard*) Listen to me, Dalton Chance, two years my junior, and shut up. Here's what we're going to do.

DALTON: Just spell it out for me. Once and clear.

PACE: Okay. She's pulling eight cars at seventy tons a piece at eighty-five. Not a big one, as far as they go. But big enough. The engine herself's one hundred and fifty-three tons. And not cotton, kid. Just cold, lip-smackin' steel. Imagine a kiss like that. Just imagine it.

DALTON: How do you know what the train weighs?

PACE: I looked her up. The year, the weight, the speed.

DALTON: So you can read.

PACE *(Ignoring his comment)*: Yeah, well. You and her are coming from opposite sides, right. You've got to time it exact 'cause you need to make it across before she hits the trestle. It's like playin' chicken with a car, only she's bigger and you're not a car. The kick is once you get halfway across, don't turn back and try to outrun her. You lose time like that. Just face her and go.

DALTON: So what if you know it's too close? You go for the side, right?

PACE: There's no side.

DALTON: Yes there is.

PACE: There's no side. Look at it.

DALTON: There's a side.

PACE: What's the matter with you? Look at the tracks. Look at them. There are no sides.

DALTON: So what do you do if you can't make it across before she starts over?

PACE: You make the cross. That's all there is to it.

DALTON: But what if you can't?

PACE: Remember Brett Weaver?

DALTON: That's different. He was drunk.

PACE: He was not.

DALTON: Yes he was. He was drunk.

PACE: Say that again and I'll punch you.

DALTON: The papers said he was drunk.

PACE: Brett wasn't drunk. He was just slow.

DALTON: Slow? He was on the track team.

PACE: That night he was slow.

DALTON: How do you know?

PACE: I just know.

DALTON: Well. I've had a look like I told you I would and I've decided: I'm not crossing.

PACE: I knew it. I knew it.

DALTON: Only a drunk or an idiot'd play that game. Not me.

PACE: You got the heart of a rabbit. A dead rabbit. And now you owe me a buck.

DALTON: No way. I never said for certain. I said maybe. And you said it was safe. You didn't say anything about there being no safety sides. You said it was a piece of cake.

PACE: It is a piece of cake. If you time it right.

DALTON: Forget it.

PACE: You're breaking the deal. Pay me a buck right now or else.

DALTON: I said no.

PACE *(Calmly pulls a switchblade)*: Then I'll hurt you.

DALTON: Put that away. You're warped. That's what everyone says at school: Pace Creagan is warped.

PACE: Then why'd you come up here with me? I'm not even your friend.

DALTON: No. You're not my friend. My friends don't pull knives.

PACE: You were starting to like me, though. I could tell. You said you'd run it with me.

DALTON: I said I might. I thought it could be fun. Warped people can be fun sometimes.

PACE: If you back down everyone will know.

DALTON: I don't care. I don't have a fan club.

PACE: Mary Ellen Berry is coming as witness too.

DALTON: No she's not.

PACE: I asked her to. And she knows you've got a fancy for her.

DALTON: Big deal. I asked her out. She turned me down. End of story.

PACE: She says you're too short.

DALTON: I'm not short.

PACE: I don't think she was talking height.

DALTON: I'm leaving.

PACE: Hey. I told her to give you a chance. She likes me.

She listens to me. I told her you were going to cross the trestle with me. She said, "Oh." You know, like she was thinking things.

DALTON: What things?

PACE: You know. The way girls think things. One, two, three, about face. Change of season. Oh. She said, "Oh," like she was about to change her mind.

DALTON: Mary Ellen's popular. Why would she listen to you?

PACE *(Shrugs)*: I once told her to take off her clothes and she did.

DALTON: And what does that mean?

PACE: It means I can run faster than she can so she does what I tell her to do. And she'll be here tonight. She's coming to watch us cross.

DALTON: You had a look at her? Naked? What's she like?

PACE: I'd say she's on the menu. Front, back, and in reverse. You'd like her.

DALTON: How would you know what I like? You're not good looking.

PACE: Yeah. But that's got nothing to do with trains.

DALTON: So how close were you that time you crossed?

PACE: I'd say I had 'bout eight seconds leeway.

DALTON: Eight seconds. Sure.

PACE: A kid could do it. Look. We won't do it tonight, okay. We'll work up to it. Tonight we'll just watch her pass. Take her measure. Check her steam. Make sure we got it down. Then when we're ready, we'll run her. It'll be a snap.

DALTON: A snap. What if you trip?

PACE: Brett tripped.

DALTON: He was messed up. Even if he wasn't drunk. He used to hit himself in the face just for the fun of it. Brett was mental. He'd hit his own nose until it bled.

PACE: Brett wasn't mental.

DALTON: I saw Brett hit himself. I saw him do it.

PACE: It's none of your business.

DALTON: You were his girl.

PACE: We were friends. I never kissed him. And you're gonna run the trestle. One of these days.

DALTON: How come?

PACE: 'Cause if you don't your life will turn out just like you think it will: quick, dirty and cold.

DALTON: Hey. I might go to college when I graduate.

PACE: You're not going to college. None of us are going to college.

DALTON: I got the grades for it. That's what Mr. Pearson says.

PACE: And who's gonna pay for it? Look at your shoes.

DALTON: Huh?

PACE: Your shoes. If your mom's putting you in shoes like that then you aren't going to college. *(Beat)* Come on. Let's go up and watch.

DALTON: If I can't go to college, I'll just leave.

PACE: Some things should stay in one place, Dalton Chance. You're probably one of them.

SCENE TWO

The present. Dalton in an empty cell. He looks older than his fifteen years, now disheveled. He just stares. And stares. At nothing. After some moments Chas, the jailer, enters. He seems friendly enough. Dalton doesn't acknowledge Chas's presence. Chas slips from one subject to the next, with hardly a pause.

CHAS: On break. Thought I'd sit it out with you. The other guy, across the hall. He's looking for grass in his cell. Thinks he's a moose. Could be some other herbivore but every now and then he lets out this call and it sounds close enough to a moose. Yesterday, a bug. Some kind of a beetle, I think, with huge claws. He used his arms like pincers. Opening and closing them. Opening and closing. For hours.

Wayne was leaning in to give him some grub and the next minute he caught Wayne around the neck. Almost choked him to death. While I was prying him off he's making this sound. A beetle sound, I guess. Sort of like . . . *(Makes a "beetle sound")* Self respect: gone. Was the manager of the Plate Glass Company. A real Roosevelt man. Good to his men, though he laid them off. Then his head went pop one day and he started breaking up the plant. Glass everywhere. Wrecked half the place. Even the WPA says close it down. No one needs glass these days. Might want glass but they don't need it. Mr. Roosevelt, I say, want to buy some glass? Them up high's got the money to want. They don't have to go by need. What kind of a beetle was it, you think? Big pincers. Opening and closing.

How'd the visit go? I know your folks. Nice people. Sorry to hear your daddy's still out of work. But who isn't? Well, I'm not. I'm still here. Could be somewheres else, like Spain shooting some whatyou-callem, but I might get killed and then bein' here looks better. I had a boy like you. You must have known my Brett at school. Big fellow. Fast runner? Moose's easier to identify. Distinctive. My break's about up. So what do you think, kid? How many years do you think you'll get? Or will they hang you? When they hang you the last thing you hear is your own neck break. And if you got a thick neck bone, a strong one, a young one, then it takes a while to break clean through, sometimes hours, and all the while you're dying you're hearing it snappin' and cracklin' and poppin', just like a stick on the fire. So what do you think?

(Chas gets no response so he shrugs and leaves the cell.)

DALTON: A stag beetle. That's what kind it was.

The past. Same as Scene One. Dalton is trying to get the shoes off his mother's feet after she's come home from work.

DALTON: Yeah it does. I read it at the drugstore.

GIN: Just leave it.

DALTON: All your nerves're squashed up in the ball of your foot. Stop wiggling.

> *(Dalton gets one of her shoes off. She relaxes now as he massages her feet.)*

GIN: How's the math going at school?

DALTON *(Teasing)*: You've got seven toes.

GIN: Woman on the right of me, Barbara Hill, laid off Tuesday. Woman on my left, laid off today. Just waiting my turn.

DALTON: You've been there forever. They need you.

GIN: How is he?

DALTON: Quiet.

GIN: Yeah, quiet.

> *(Gin unwraps a small stack of plates. Looks at them. Then wraps them up again as she speaks.)*

It's getting harder to find the plates. Even the Salvation is running short. I don't want to use the blue ones my mother gave me. Might have to one of these days.

DALTON: It'll be okay.

> *(Dalton is finished with her feet. He begins to unpin her hair and then brush it. She lets him.)*

GIN: You got anything better to do with your afternoons than take care of an old mother when she comes home from work? You should be out with the boys. Yelling. Falling down. Doing fun things boys do. What do boys do for fun?

DALTON: You know the trestle up at Pope Lick? Well, I was with a girl there this afternoon, after school.

GIN: Hmmm.

DALTON: Name's Pace Creagan. We watched the train come through.

GIN: Boy got killed up there a couple of years ago.

DALTON: It's not a big train but it's big up close. And loud.

GIN: You kiss her?

DALTON: No way. She's not the kissing kind. Not pretty either.

GIN (*Matter-of-factly*): Not that handsome yourself, Dalton.

DALTON: That's what she said.

GIN: I know the Creagans. They're all right.

DALTON: Even if I wanted to, and I'm not saying I do, I never really—you know, like how people do—kissed a girl.

GIN: Not much to it. Just open your mouth and start chewing. First time I kissed your father it was all wet and disgusting. By the second time I'd started to like him, and then it was like breathing water for air, that smooth.

DALTON: I don't know.

GIN: Neither did I.

(Dray appears. He sits in a corner with a stool. No one speaks for some moments. Dray just sits with his back to them. As they speak, Dalton walks over and lights Dray's candle, casually; he does this all the time for his father.)

DALTON: I need some new shoes.

GIN: I know that.

DALTON: I'll get a job.

GIN: You've got school.

(Dray makes a hand shadow on the wall.)

And no one's hiring.

DALTON: You know, the train that comes through Pope Lick, the engine weighs one hundred and fifty-three tons. That's what Pace says.

(Dray makes another hand shadow. Dalton watches his father. He moves to put his hand on his father's shoulder but his father looks at him, like a warning, so Dalton withdraws his hand.)

GIN: Trains. Yeah. Huge, sweatin', steamin', oil spittin' promises when I was a girl. Always taking someone away, never bringing someone back. I couldn't get used to it.

DALTON: I'm going out. *(Kisses his mother on the cheek, then moves away)* When you were fifteen. Like me, Mother. What did you want?

(Dray makes another hand shadow.)

GIN: Someone to look me straight in the face and tell me flat out that I wasn't going anywhere.

DALTON: Yeah? Well then say it to me. Go on. Say it to me.

GIN *(Quietly)*: Dalton.

DALTON: Say: "Dalton, my boy. You're not going anywhere."

(Gin is silent, then:)

GIN: You're my child.

DALTON *(Quietly)*: That doesn't make any difference.

(Dalton exits.
    Dray stops making hand shadows. He is still.)

GIN *(She just looks at Dray's back)*: Touch me.

(Dray is still. He turns to look at her, then slowly looks away.)

SCENE FOUR

Pace and Dalton at the trestle, a few days later.

PACE: We need to watch her for days and days. Studyin'. Studyin'. And then one night we'll run her.

DALTON: Sure. One night.

PACE: There's a simple reason we're biding our time. Waiting for the moment that counts: we don't want to die. Now repeat after me: we don't want to die.

DALTON: We don't want to die.

PACE: So we'll be patient.

DALTON: Yeah. Until Christmas. I'll be getting some new shoes. And then I'll hook a job. Move up.

PACE: That's against the laws of gravity. Besides, you can't move up when you've got no teeth.

DALTON: I've got teeth.

PACE: You won't in a few years.

DALTON: You've got no determination. No plan for the future.

PACE: Yeah, but I watch.

DALTON: Watch what?

PACE: Things. People. I've been watching. And this is how things are. *(Casually)* You and me and the rest of us kids out here, we're just like. Okay. Like potatoes left in a box. You ever seen a potato that's been left in a box? The potato thinks the dark is the dirt and it starts to grow roots so it can survive, but the dark isn't the dirt and all it ends up sucking on is a fistful of air. And then it dies.

DALTON: I'm not a potato.

PACE: Yes you are.

DALTON: No I'm not. Potatoes can't run. I can. And when we decide to do it, I'm gonna make it over that trestle before you're halfway across. Until then, I'm going home.

PACE: What time is it?

DALTON: 6:51.

PACE: Tell you what. We'll have a practice first.

DALTON: What kind of practice?

PACE: A real kind. Almost. Just to warm up. Pop the bones. Roll the blood over. You know.

(Pace opens the paper bag she has with her. In it are a pair of boy's pants. She starts to take off her dress, not caring a bit that Dalton is there.)

DALTON: Jesus.

PACE: Would you practice running the trestle in a dress?

(Dalton turns around.)

You can look if you want.

DALTON: No thanks. You're not my type.

(Pace continues changing.)

PACE *(Casually)*: Why not?

DALTON: You're loud. Your hands are dirty. You stare. *(Beat)* And you're not pretty, really.

PACE: You said that before.

DALTON: Well, it keeps coming back to me.

PACE: Anything else, kid?

DALTON: There'll be more once I get to know you.

PACE: I'm ready.

(Dalton turns around. Pace is dressed in pants and a shirt, perhaps her brother's. She throws the dress at Dalton.)

Smell it.

DALTON: No way.

PACE: Baby.

(Dalton smells the dress.)

Well?

DALTON: It smells nice. Flowery. Like a girl.

PACE *(Cuffs him as she snatches the dress back)*: Want to know what I don't like about you, Dalton Chance? You're a good boy. A very good boy.

DALTON: So what's that mean?

PACE: It means someone, before it's too late, has got to break you in half. *(Sighs)* I guess it'll have to be me.

SCENE FIVE

The present. Dalton and Chas in his cell. Dalton is turned away
from Chas.

CHAS: Now him over there, he doesn't know who his
    mother is. A turtle doesn't consider those things.
    Want to know how I know he's a turtle? *(Demonstrates,*
    impressively, a turtle, moving its neck in and out of its
    shell) I know what you're thinking: could be a goose.
    I thought of that. But a goose doesn't do this— *(Moves*
    his head slowly from side to side, then cocks his head to one
    side, opens his mouth and eats) A goose doesn't eat like a
    turtle. How you feelin', boy? What're you thinking?
    Still won't talk. Still won't talk. But they got it on
    record when they brought you in: "Yeah, I killed
    her." That's what you said. Why didn't you lie? They
    don't have a witness. Four words. Just four words:
    "Yeah, I killed her." But won't say why. Won't say how.
    What kind of a game are you playing? Well, they'll
    find it out. They know about kids. I had a boy your
    age. Couple of years older than you. Not much to
    him. But he was my son. *(Beat)* To think. He was just
    a kid like you. Scared of nothing. Yeah. Scared of
    nothing 'cause you are nothing. Half of you kids
    wanting to kill, the rest wanting to die. Ordering
    death like it's a nice, cold drink and you're going to
    suck it down in one gulp and then get up and walk
    away from it. Right. Kids. Just want to eat, fuck and
    tear the ornaments off the tree. But only if you don't
    have to get out of bed in the morning to do it. The
    whole damn country's going to hell 'cause of your
    kind. *(Beat)* You should have killed your own self
    instead. That's what they say. *(Beat)* I loved my boy
    Brett. But I never could figure what he was.
    Something kinda small. Like a wheel, maybe. Some-
    thing that spins in place in the dark. He had a gap in
    his heart. He was empty. I know; I was his father.

Sometimes he'd ask me to embrace him. *(Shrugs)* He was my son. *(Beat)* So he'd be here, in my arms, sniffling like a baby. But there was nothing. I was holding him. He was in my arms. But it was like holding onto. Nothing. *(Beat)* What's it feel like to be like that? Huh? What's it feel like to be that empty? *(Begins to take off his shirt)* I'm going to have to hate you, I guess. There's not much choice.

(Chas stands over Dalton. Dalton is shivering and does not respond. Chas puts his shirt around Dalton.)

I'll bring you some dinner. You've lost weight. Hard not to do in here.

SCENE SIX

The past. Pace, Dalton and Gin are sitting together. There is a strained feeling. Dalton wants things to be nice.

GIN: Dalton made a clock for his science project. Didn't you, Dalton?

DALTON: That was last year. This year I made a scale. To measure things on.

GIN: A scale. That's right. I use it in the kitchen. To measure flour. It works really well. You want to try it, Pace?

PACE: I don't do much with flour.

GIN: Oh. But I'm sure you help your mother in the kitchen.

(Dalton speaks before Pace can answer.)

DALTON: Pace likes to sew. Don't you?

(Pace just looks at Dalton.)

She makes her own clothes. Tell her you make your own clothes, Pace.

PACE: I make my own clothes. My mother's not what she used to be.

GIN: That's nice. I mean, about your clothes. What did your mother used to be?

PACE: Hopeful. *(Beat)* Thank you for the tea, Mrs. Chance. It was very sweet.

GIN: That's how we like it here. In our home.

(They all sit in an awkward silence. After some moments, Pace places the large bag she's brought on the table.)

DALTON: Pace said she brought something for you, Mother.

GIN: My, that's nice. You didn't need to, really.

PACE: I made it in science class. Like Dalton did.

(Pace unwraps the bag to reveal a strange mechanical engine. It looks impressive.)

GIN: Oh. That's. Nice. What is it?

PACE: It's a beam engine.

GIN: I see . . .

PACE: The beam engine was the first practical working steam engine. It's simple: fire here at the bottom heats the water, the steam forces up the piston and it's cooled, fast, by spraying cold water on the cylinder. This turns the steam back to water and makes a vacuum in the space under the piston.

GIN: Piston.

DALTON: It's a present, Mother.

PACE: You see, the pressure of air outside the cylinder then pushes the piston back down again. And so on. The crosspiece joining the engine to the pump gives it its name: "beam" engine.

GIN: This is a train you've got here?

PACE: An engine. But it's an older model.

GIN: Looks kind of small to me.

PACE: The original was bigger than both of us.

GIN: Well, start it up then.

PACE: Doesn't work. Did once. Second time, my father he was leaning over it to have a look, caught his beard on fire. Third time: bang. Not a big one but I got a piece of glass in my arm.

GIN: Sounds unpredictable.

PACE: It's the only thing I had of my own to give you. *(Beat)* I didn't get a good grade on it.

GIN: You're two years older than Dalton.

DALTON: Mother.

PACE: Almost.

GIN: He's been seeing a lot of you these past weeks.

DALTON: Can we have some more tea?

PACE: You ever hear of Cugnot, Mrs. Chance? Nicholas Cugnot. Made the first steam machine that moved. Crawled two miles per hour before it blew up. That was in France. 1769, I think. The government put Cugnot in prison. Explosion didn't hurt anyone. Never understood why they put him in jail.

GIN: My son doesn't know a thing about trains.

PACE: I think they were afraid. Not of the machine, but of Cugnot. They'd never seen anything like that moved by steam. Just plain old water *(Makes the sound of steam)* into steam. It must have shaken them up somehow. Just to see it. They couldn't forgive him.

GIN: What do you want with Dalton?

DALTON: Christ. We're just having tea.

GIN: Hush up.

(Dalton shuts up.)

We're a family here, Pace. A regular family. My husband, Dalton and me. Lots of trouble out there, lots of bad weather. But we take care of each other; nothing out there we need. I want you to know that.

PACE: You know the Union Pacific? They're gonna build the biggest steam locomotives in the world. The engine and tender'll weigh over five hundred tons. Colossal. They'll be 4-8-8-4 articulated locomotives with two sets of driving wheels, each with their own cylinders.

(Gin just stares at her.)

I'm sorry. Mrs. Chance. But me and Dalton. It's none of your business.

GIN: Cylinders, huh? Driving wheels. Articulated locomotives. If you're thinking to trick my son—

DALTON: I can't believe this . . .

PACE: Mrs. Chance, I'm not sweet on your son's locomotive system, if that's what you mean. We've never touched each other. I've got nothing to be ashamed of. Though I did tell him to take off his clothes once, under the trestle.

GIN: To take off his—

DALTON: Pace!

PACE: Shut up, Dalton. *(Beat)* And then once on the tracks. A hundred feet up. Wasn't a train in sight. It was kinda chilly that evening, but it was safe.

GIN: I think you better leave now.

PACE: He doesn't like me, really. He says I'm loud.

GIN *(To Dalton)*: You took off your clothes?

PACE: He's your son. He does what he's told.

GIN: Why would you do such a thing? Anyone might have seen you.

PACE: Yeah. I did. And he's not like an engine at all. Nah. Dalton's pale. Real pale. No steam. How's he keep warm? Doesn't know the first thing about cylinders. And he's so light, what keeps him where he stands? On the tracks, slip, slip, slip. No traction. Now, the Big Boys, the new ones, they'll need near ten tons of coal per hour in their firebox. And the grate where the coal'll be burned is bigger than a kitchen.

(Gin just stares at her.)

Imagine it. That's what we're coming to.

Dalton and Pace at the trestle, a few days before.

PACE: Let's start here. On this tie.

DALTON: What tie? The track's up there.

PACE: Imagine it, stupid.

DALTON: Right.

PACE: See, this tie's marked with a red X.

DALTON: Maybe I want to start on this other tie.

PACE: Look. It's tradition, okay. Besides, Brett made this X so let's use it. Now, you crouch down like this. Go on. Yeah. That's right. Like at a track meet. Point your skinny rear to the stars. Got it.

DALTON: I'll count down.

PACE: Now when you say: "Go" we run like crazy to the other side. But don't check your feet. You'll trip if you check your feet. Just trust that your feet know where to go.

DALTON: I hear you.

PACE: You're playin' chicken with the train, so you keep your eyes on the engine headed towards you. It'll look like she's real close but she won't be. If you start when I tell you to, you'll have enough time to make it across and have dinner before she starts over the trestle. Ready?

DALTON: Pace?

PACE: Yeah?

DALTON: My legs are shaking.

PACE: This is practice, Dalton. There's no train down here.

DALTON: My legs aren't so sure.

PACE: On the count of three. Come on.

DALTON AND PACE: One, two, three—

DALTON: Wait! *(Looking over the "edge")*

PACE: Don't look. You'll lose your nerve.

DALTON: It's a long way down.

PACE: Why don't we just walk it. Give me your hand. *(Takes his hand and begins to walk him)*

DALTON: God we're high up.

PACE *(Smacks him)*: Keep your eyes on the other side. Pretend that we're running.

(They run in place.)

DALTON: We are. I'm out of breath.

PACE: We're almost there. Yeah. Yeah. Grease those knees. And now you trip.

DALTON: What?

PACE: You trip.

(Pace trips him so he falls to the ground.)

DALTON: Hey! What the— You tripped me. Hey—

PACE: It might happen.

DALTON: Why'd you—

(Dalton tries to get up. She knocks him back down.)

PACE: You might trip. Anything's possible. We got to be ready for it.

DALTON: But I wouldn't've tripped! You pushed me!

PACE: Don't get up. Just sit there. Like you tripped. Let's say I'm flaggin' behind and you look over your shoulder to see how I'm doing and you trip. And just as you trip you hear her coming around the hill. *(Makes the sound of a train whistle)*

DALTON: You sound like a kitten. It's like this. *(Makes an even better and more frightening whistle)*

PACE: Yeah! And you can hear her cold slathering black hell of a heart barreling towards the trestle and it sounds like this:

(Together they make an engine sound, surprisingly well.)

But you've twisted your ankle.

DALTON: Yeah. And I can hardly stand. It feels like my foot's coming off. *(Makes a painful gasp)* I try to run but I can only hobble. And the train, she's just about to cross.

PACE: And then there I am. At your side.

DALTON: No. I'd slow you down and you know it. You just pass me by. *(Makes the sound of an arrow flying)* Like an arrow. You've got to save your own skin.

PACE: Yeah, but I can't just leave you there.

DALTON: Yes you can.

PACE: You'll be killed.

DALTON: I'll be torn apart.

PACE: So I put my arm around your waist and start to drag you down the tracks with me. It's hard going. We've only got fifty feet or so 'til we're clear.

DALTON: But the train. *(Lets out the terrible scream of a whistle)* So you drop me.

PACE: No.

DALTON: You drop me and run. You run for your life.

PACE: No. I don't leave you. I—

DALTON: You make it across. Just in time. Alone.

PACE: I drag you with me.

DALTON: And as you clear the tracks, you feel the hurtling wind of her as she rushes by you, so close it's like she's kissing the back of your neck, so close she pulls the shirt right up off you without popping the buttons. *(Beat)* And then? And then you hear me scream.

(Dalton lets out a terrible scream. At the same time Pace screams:)

PACE: I save you!

(They are silent some moments.)

DALTON: And then? And then nothing. The train, she disappears over the trestle and on down the track. *(Beat)* You, Pace Creagan, are standing there, breathing hard—

PACE: —My heart jumping jacks, yeah, shooting dice in my chest. Snake eyes. But I'm alive. Alive!

DALTON: As for me, well, you know I'm dead. You're certain. But still you have to go back and have a look. To see what's left. Of course there's almost nothing left.

PACE: Yeah there was. There was a lot left.

DALTON: No. Just some bits of. Meat. And a running shoe. That's all. I'm mashed potatoes now. Just add some milk and stir.

PACE: He wasn't wearing running shoes.

DALTON: Hey. Take a look at my face. I'm talking to you: I'm dead.

PACE: Brett was wearing boots.

DALTON: And now maybe my mom will be able to scrounge up some new shoes for the funeral. If she can find my feet.

PACE *(Calmly)*: Shut up. Just. Shut up. Have you ever put a shell up to your ear?

DALTON: What?

PACE: A conch shell. One of those big ones. It's not the ocean you're hearing. Or even the blood in your head. *(Makes the sound of a shell over an ear)* That's the sound. And it's been going on for years. It's this town. Our future. You and me. *(Makes the sound again)* Empty. No more, no less. Just. Empty.

DALTON *(Disgusted)*: I'm going home.

PACE: Wait.

DALTON *(Leaving)*: Not this time.

PACE: Take off your clothes.

DALTON: Why?

PACE: Because you want to.

> *(Dalton begins to undress. Pace watches him. He's about to take off his underwear.)*

> Stop. There. Yeah. That's enough.

> *(They both watch each other. Pace moves closer to him, but not too close.)*

> Are you cold?

DALTON: A little. *(Beat)* Well. Are you gonna touch me or what?

PACE: No. I just wanted. To look at you.

DALTON: Once you take your clothes off. Something is supposed to happen.

PACE: It already has. *(Beat)* Get dressed.

(After a moment, Dalton starts to get dressed.)

SCENE EIGHT

Gin and Dray. He sits immobile. She uncovers a small stack of plates. She tosses one to him. Suddenly he comes alive and they are tossing a plate back and forth between them as they speak. They've done this before. The plate tossing will occur less as the scene proceeds.

GIN: You've got to get out.

DRAY: I'm movin'. You just can't see it.

GIN: At the WPA office. They're helpin' people find jobs.

DRAY: A handful.

GIN: That's better than nothing

DRAY: I don't know.

GIN: I went by the Council. They got kicked out of the church basement. Got a room in the Watson storehouse. More like a closet than a room.

DRAY: The Council. They're not government.

GIN: No, they're not. Just people out of work. Tryin' to get things going. Lots of talk about the Plate Glass factory.

DRAY: It's closed down.

GIN: Talk about opening it up again. Building it back up. Running it themselves. Machinery's still there. Most of it. It's a mess but it's all still there.

DRAY: We've got what we need. The three of us. Under this roof.

GIN: I know that.

DRAY: Sounds like you're getting involved.

GIN: No. I'm not. I'm just listening.

DRAY: My father worked there when he was a boy. There'd be explosions now and then. He wore eye wear. A lot of them didn't. Once the glass hit him in the mouth. Long thin pieces of glass. He pulled them out his cheeks with pliers, like pullin' fish bones out a fish. *(Beat)* That place doesn't belong to them, Gin. Sounds like communists.

GIN: People, Dray. Just people tired of not working. Tired of waiting for the WPA to hand out the jobs. Tired. Just tired. You know that kind of tired.

DRAY: Can't remember when I wasn't.

GIN: I remember. When you were a boy.

(Dray almost drops a plate, but catches it. He becomes more playful.)

DRAY: You lie, Miss Ginny Carol. I was never a kid.

GIN: Yeah you were. And so was I.

DRAY: Nah. That was just a fancy idea we had about ourselves.

GIN: You didn't bring me flowers like other girls got. You brought me tomatoes.

DRAY: You can't eat flowers.

GIN: And corn. You were nineteen.

DRAY: A bucket of frogs, too. I made you close your eyes and put your hands in it. You didn't scream like most of them did. You went dead pale. I thought I might have killed you. And then you did the damnedest thing: you kissed me. Not on the cheek, either. Smack on the mouth.

GIN: I was in shock. The frogs did it to me. *(Beat)* You hardly kissed me back.

DRAY: I was in shock. Never had a girl put her tongue in my mouth before. We weren't even engaged. You took me to the storm shelter and took off your dress. You pushed me to my knees. I never kissed a girl there before. I never even thought it could be done. You went dead pale. That was the second time I thought I killed you. When you finally let me get to my feet, you had a clump of my hair in each of your hands, you'd pulled on my head so hard.

GIN: I wasn't tired back then. And neither were you.

DRAY: No, I guess I wasn't. *(Beat)* There were two things I wanted when I was a boy: one was to land a good job at the foundry, the other was to have you turn me into a bald man by the time I was old.

GIN: You lost quite a bit of hair over the years. Though not lately, I'm sorry to say.

(Dray misses a plate and it drops and breaks. Silence.)

DRAY: It was mine, Gin. Nineteen years of it.

GIN: Yeah, and what did it give you? A bad arm, a broken collar, burns across your back so deep the bath water stays in them.

DRAY: That job was mine.

GIN: We're still here.

DRAY: Yeah. And you won't ever leave me.

GIN: I won't ever leave you, Dray.

(Silence some moments.)

I heard at work they were hiring a couple of men down at Turner's. You might—

DRAY *(Interrupts)*: I was there this morning while you were at work. They hired three men. Three men. Fifty-two of us they left standing. There wasn't a sound. For the longest time we just stood there watching the door that'd been shut. All that disappointment. Fifty-two men. Fifty-two of us. And weighin' how much? None of us eating big these days. Most of us lookin' lean. Maybe . . . eight thousand pounds, all of us together. That much disappointment. *(Beat)* And not a sound.

(Gin moves to touch Dray, to comfort him. Dray speaks gently to her.)

Don't touch me, Gin. I could kill you.

SCENE NINE

The cell. Dalton lying asleep on the floor in a blanket. He gets up. He thinks he's alone. But Gin is standing over him; he starts.

GIN: Dalton.

DALTON: You're always alone.

GIN: He hardly leaves the house.

DALTON: You'd think this might be special circumstances.

GIN: He's restless. Without you home.

DALTON: He never looked me over when I was there.

GIN: You don't have to look at someone—

DALTON: I don't need your excuses. Neither does he. From what I remember, he didn't look at you any more than he did at me.

GIN: Not long ago he used to hold me.

DALTON: Big deal. Holding someone's a cinch. It doesn't cost. It's easy.

GIN: And the girl. What about her, then. To hold her.

(Pace appears. While neither Gin nor Dalton sees her, sometimes they sense, at different moments, that she is "there." Pace is playful.)

Was that "easy"?

DALTON: That's none of your business. *(Beat)* I don't want you here.

PACE: Was that "a cinch"?

DALTON *(Shouts)*: I didn't hold her!
(Now he is quiet) She held me. Pace did. But it wasn't that. Holding. Sometimes when I was with her, she wasn't there. Alone at night in bed, I could feel her breath in my ears. No.

PACE AND DALTON: That's not it.

PACE: It wasn't just you and me.

DALTON: It was something more. Like at school. At school they teach you. To speak. They say it's math—

PACE: History—

DALTON: Geometry, whatever. But they're teaching you to speak. Not about the world but about things. Just things: a door, a map,

PACE: a cup. Just the name of it.

DALTON: Not what a cup means, who picked it up, who drank from it,

PACE: who didn't and why;

DALTON: where a map came from, who fixed in the rivers, who'll take the wrong turn; or a door. Who cut the wood and hung it there? Why that width, that height? And who made that decision? Who agreed to it? Who didn't?

PACE: And what happened to them because of it?

DALTON: They just teach us to speak the things. So that's what we speak. But there's no past that way.

PACE AND DALTON: And no future.

DALTON: 'Cause after you've said the thing, you move on. You don't look back. You never think to stop and turn.

PACE *(No longer playful)*: But you stopped, didn't you, Dalton? You stopped and turned.

DALTON: She laughed at everything that seemed right.

PACE: And you didn't turn back. *(Calmly)* You son of a bitch.

(Pace retreats somewhat, but she is still "there.")

DALTON: It wasn't just at night. In the day sometimes. Not her voice but the sound of her. I could hear it. Like water running in a pipe. But that's not it. It was more like this. This cup. *(Takes his drinking cup, calmly kneels and breaks it on the floor. His hand bleeds slightly. He sorts through the pieces)* Look. This was sand and heat. Not long ago. Other things, too. Pieces and bits. And now. It's something else. Glass. Blood. And it's broken. *(Picks up a large piece, nears Gin)* I could cut you open with it.

(Gin slaps his face. He's taken aback, put in his place.)

But that's what she did to me. Cut me open and
things weren't just things after that. I was just a kid—

PACE: —like any other. You didn't care.

DALTON: I never even thought about it. But then one day
I wasn't sure. She did that to me. She made me—
hesitate. In everything I did. I was. Unsure. Look. It's
not a cup anymore; it's a knife.

(Pace stands close to Dalton, but he cannot see her.)

PACE: I could cut you open and see my face.

DALTON: And it was true. I could touch myself at night
and I didn't know if it was her hand or mine. I could
touch myself. I could put my hand. I could. Maybe I
was asleep. I don't know but sometimes I put my
hand. Inside myself.

PACE *(Whispers to him)*: And you were wet.

DALTON: I was wet. Just like a girl. It was. Yeah. Like I was
touching her. Just to touch myself. *(Beat)* It wasn't
right.

(Silence some moments.)

GIN: Only time I ever knew things were right is when they
were wrong. Everyone said your father was a mistake.
After I made that one, and it worked out so well, I ded-
icated myself to making as many mistakes as possible
in a lifetime. The only time I was ever sure who I was
was when I was wrong. *(Beat)* I think you loved that girl.

DALTON: Yeah. Maybe that's why I killed her. Please. I
want you to go.

GIN: All right.

*(Pace suddenly kicks a piece of the broken cup. It skids
between Gin and Dalton. Gin looks at the broken piece.*

*Split scene: Dray is alone in another area. Perhaps up
above them. In the dark. He is making awkward but somehow
lovely movements. Then we see he is dancing without music.)*

PACE: There's your cup, kid. Drink from it.

(Dray sings and dances his song.)

DRAY:

When I was still living, when I was a boy
I could sing like the water and dance like a toy.
My love she would kiss me 'til my mouth it was
    warmed.
There was no place on earth where we'd ever be
    harmed.

SCENE TEN

Pace and Dalton under the trestle.

DALTON: There's no one home at my house in the day-time. We could hang out there. Well, my dad's at home, but I'm not sure he counts as someone any-more. Ever since he got laid off at the foundry, he sits with the lights off. He's got a candle burning. Makes shadows on the wall with his hands. Spiders. Bats. You know. Rabbits.

PACE: I guess I'm supposed to think that's sad.

DALTON: You think about kissing me?

PACE: Kissing you where?

DALTON: I don't know. Here. In your yard. Or mine.

PACE: I mean where on you?

DALTON: My mouth. Where else?

PACE: Nope. We're friends.

DALTON: Like you and Brett were friends?

PACE: That was different. He was like my sister or some-thing.

DALTON: Yeah. Yeah. Just forget it, okay. Pace Creagan isn't that kind of girl, anyhow. She pulls knives. She takes off her clothes. She pisses under the trestle.

PACE: Shits there too. I mean, why go all the way home?

DALTON: But she doesn't think about kissing.

PACE: Not on the mouth; that's common.

DALTON: Where else then?

PACE: I don't know. A place where no one else has kissed you, maybe. Everyone in the world has kissed you on the face, right?

DALTON: Keep talking.

PACE: If I ever kiss you, and I'm not saying I ever will, it will be some place even you've never thought of.

DALTON: You mean— *(Looks down at his crotch, with a sort of reserved bravado)*

PACE: No way. You could trick me and piss on me. Look, if you want a kiss so bad, I'll give it to you, but you got to promise to take it wherever I want to plant it.

DALTON: If it's at least ten seconds long, I promise.

PACE: Agreed. Take down your pants.

DALTON *(Suddenly afraid)*: No. Wait. You said it wasn't there!

PACE: It's not. Trust me.

(With some apprehension, Dalton drops his pants.)

Turn around.

DALTON: Pace. I'm not sure—

PACE *(Interrupts)*: Shut up, kid. We got a deal.

(Dalton reluctantly turns around. Pace stands behind him, then drops to her knees.)

Count.

(Pace puts her mouth just above the back of his knee. She kisses him there and holds it.)

DALTON: One, two, three, four, five, six . . . seven . . .

(Pace slaps him and he continues counting.)

. . . eight, nine, ten.

(Pace stands up. Dalton pulls up his pants. They look at each other. Dalton is unsure of what has happened.)

Well. Yeah.

PACE: You happy now?

DALTON: Happy. Sure. *(Beat)* I'm gonna run over to Sean's right now and tell him all about it. How it was great. How long it lasted. How far we went. "Sean, Sean, guess what? She tongued the back of my knee!" Is that what you did with your friend Brett? You kiss him like that too?

(Pace approaches him, then spits on him and wipes her mouth.)

PACE: There. You can have it back. I wish I'd never done it.

(Dalton starts to push her. He's pushing her hard backward but she keeps her footing. The potential for violence to escalate is evident.)

DALTON: Spit on me? You think you can do that? Who the hell do you think you are? Who the hell, Pace Creagan? What's so special about your kiss, huh? I could just take it, you know. I could just take it if I wanted to.

(Pace pushes back. Pace raises her arm to hit him but then hesitates.)

Go on. I'm your friend. Hit me.

PACE: I don't want to hit you. I want you to shut up. You liked it. I could tell. You're mad at me 'cause you liked it.

DALTON: I wanted you to kiss me on the mouth.

PACE: When you were counting. All the while. Couldn't you feel it? Where I was kissing you, it was on your mouth.

(They are quiet some moments.)

DALTON: What I said about Brett. It was stupid.

PACE: Yeah. It was. *(Beat)* But you were wrong the other day. That's not what a train does to you. It doesn't mush you up in neat little pieces. This train. She's a knife. That's why we loved her. Me and Brett. So much beauty she's breathless: a huge hunk and chunk of shiny black coal blasted fresh out of the mountain. *(Beat)* We had a good start. Me and Brett. We both could have made it. 'Course Brett, he was faster. I expected to be running behind. But Brett was worried. About me. He was stupid like that. He turned to look over his shoulder at me and he tripped. I thought he'd just jump up and keep going so I passed him right by. We'd timed it tight, and right then that engine was so close I could smell her. *(Beat)* I thought Brett was right behind me.

DALTON: You left him on the tracks?

PACE: I thought he was running behind me. I could hear him behind me. He didn't call out. He didn't say wait up. I didn't know. Why didn't he call out?

(There is the real sound of a whistle in the distance.)

Not even a sound. Brett just sat there where he'd fallen. And then he stood up, slowly, like he had the time. He stood there looking at her, looking her straight in the face. Almost like it was a dare. Like: go ahead and hit me. You can't do that to a train. You can't dare a train to hit you. 'Cause it will.

(Another whistle, closer this time.)

DALTON: This is stupid. Brett was alone up there. Nobody knows.

PACE: Just stood there like she could pass right through him for all he cared. Like he wasn't going to flinch.

DALTON: Let's get out of here, it's getting late.

(He takes her arm.)

PACE: Let go of me.

DALTON: You're making this up.

PACE: Get off.

DALTON: You're out of your mind.

(Dalton tries to grab her again. She resists and he stumbles. There is the tremendous sound of a train rushing over the trestle above them. Then it disappears into the distance. Dalton's cut his hand.)

Shit.

PACE: You all right?

DALTON: No. Cut my hand.

PACE: Let me see.

DALTON: Just a scratch.

PACE: It's not how you think it is. The train, she doesn't mush you up. An arm here. A leg here. A shoe. No. She's cleaner than that. I walked back down the tracks after the train had passed. She cut Brett in two.

DALTON: Pace.

PACE: You know what I thought? Blocks. Two blocks, and maybe if I could fit the pieces back together again, he'd be. Whole.

DALTON: Will you shut your mouth. Please.

(Pace rips a long strip of cloth from her dress.)

PACE: Use this. Wrap it around your hand. It'll stop the bleeding. *(She bandages his hand)*

DALTON: Thanks. *(Beat)* You going home now?

PACE: I don't know. My mom made a loaf for my brother's birthday tomorrow. Maybe we could weasel some out of her tonight.

DALTON: Okay.

PACE: We're going to do it for real.

DALTON: Yeah. We'll do it. We'll make the cross.

PACE: Both of us. Side by side.

DALTON: That's right.

PACE: A steady run.

DALTON: As can be.

PACE: Does your dad really make shadow animals on the wall?

DALTON: Yep.

PACE: Can you?

DALTON: Never tried.

PACE: That's pretty neat. Not everyone can do that. I can't.

(She stands close to him, face to face for a moment.)

You won't take anything from me that I don't want to give you, Dalton. And that's a fact.

DALTON: All right. *(Beat)* Hey, I'll race you down the hill.

PACE: Nah. I'm tired. *(Beat)* Go!

(Blackout. We hear Dalton's voice in the dark, but as though it were coming from a distance away.)

DALTON: Hey, you—I'll catch you this time!

SCENE ELEVEN

In the semi-dark we see the hands of someone. Two blue hands. They move about in the dark. They "play," trying out their glow in the dark. Then Gin becomes visible.

Suddenly, Pace appears, perhaps somewhere above or behind Gin. Pace is in the same dress we saw her wear in her earlier scenes with Dalton. The tear in the dress is larger. This is the only difference in her appearance. Though Pace is not in front of Gin, Gin speaks to her and looks at her as though Pace were right in front of her.

GIN: Oh. Pace.

(Pace is still. She just watches Gin.)

I didn't see you. I was just. Trying to get used to this. It won't come off. They're lights, almost. It doesn't hurt. Well, it hurts 'cause I scrub them but it does no good. This color's here to stay. One morning I go to work and I come home with blue hands. They changed chemicals again at the plant. All sixteen of us in my section got blue hands. Some of the women, they were upset when it wouldn't wash off. But we had to see it as a wonder, too. During break, we turned off the lights and standing all together, some with our arms raised, others at our side, we looked like a Christmas tree in the dark, with blue lights. Then we all put our arms over our heads like this *(Demonstrates)* and waved our fingers and we were a flock of crazy bluebirds taking off. We started laughing then, and piling on top of each other, imagine it, and most of us women my age, and our hands were like blue snowballs flying this way and that. One of the girls, Victoria, she laughed so hard she peed right where she stood. Another one, Willa, she slipped in it and that had all of us roaring. *(Beat)* Then Laura Townsend said we had all better think again 'cause we had the hands of dead women. Well, that put an end to the fun and we went back to work. The manager said it would wear off but it won't. We even used bleach. We'll have to get used to it. Kind of ugly and kind of pretty both, isn't it? But hands aren't meant to be blue. *(Beat)* You're almost a woman yourself, Pace. Hell, I don't blame him. My husband. We're not. Close. Do you know what I mean? Like we used to be.

PACE: You asked me what I wanted with your son.

GIN: I meant no harm, girl. A mother's supposed to ask.

PACE: I was going to be different. I don't know in what way. That never mattered. But different somehow. Do you know what I mean?

GIN: There's blood on your leg.

PACE: And Dalton would be there to see it happen. That's what I was getting him ready for.

GIN: What are you doing out so late? Where's Dalton?

PACE: He'll be home. He's still out at the trestle. *(Beat)* He's not alone. He's with a girl.

GIN: Oh. Pace. I'm sorry.

PACE: I'm not. I was watching them. At first, I couldn't see them. It was dark. And there was this noise, like water rushing. Right through my head. But then I looked harder and I could see them. He stood over her. He was shaking her. But she wouldn't get up. And he was shouting. Shouting so loud. He wouldn't shut up.

GIN: Dalton wouldn't— No. Dalton's—

PACE *(Interrupts)*: But she wouldn't answer him. The girl just turned her head. She hates him, I thought. And that made me glad. And then he stopped shouting. He gave up and put his head on her breast. *(Beat)* And then, well. I saw it; he kissed her. He kissed her.

GIN: There'll be other boys, Pace—

PACE: And she let him. I never let Dalton kiss me, but she did. And then, I felt him kiss her. I felt it. He was kissing her. Kissing her. But his mouth was inside of mine. And I let him. I let his mouth be inside of me like that, even though I wasn't with him anymore.

GIN *(Moves to comfort Pace)*: Come here, girl. I'm sorry.

PACE *(Stepping backwards)*: Don't touch the back of my head.

GIN: Why not?

PACE: It's gone.

(We hear a door slam loudly.)

GIN: Dalton? Dalton!

(We hear the loud slamming of the door, like a cell. The slamming echoes.
Blackout.)

ACT II

Dalton's cell. It's dark. Then a light appears. It's Chas. Dalton lies sleeping on the ground. Chas stands over Dalton, watching him sleep.

CHAS: Least you could do is turn into a boat. A little one. No oars. I could guess it. I know water.

(Dalton moans in his sleep, like a child. Chas sings to put Dalton back to sleep.)

Rocking on the sea, looking for my soul,
dead man's blood from an old boat hole.
Sail to the left, sail to the right,
sail to the end in the cold moon light.

(The song ends.)

Sleep of the dead. That's you. Creagan. Pace. Ring a bell? In the dead. Of night. What're you thinkin'? Are you there with her or somewhere else?

(Standing over Dalton, he begins to peel an apple. He lets the bits of peel fall across Dalton's face.)

Why do I spend my time on you, huh? Could it be I know our friend across the hall is on his way out of here? The poor man's got no wind in his jail cell. Still, he's doing this— *(Spins his head to the left and*

319

right like a weather vane) He's a weather vane tonight.
(Beat) I'm waiting for you to surprise me, kid. Turn
your head, open your mouth, roll your eyes, swish
your feet and I'll know it: you're a fish of sorts.
Could you do that? Here? Or am I wastin' time, my
time, when I could be over the sea fightin' with
Franco's boys, bullets and dive-bombers whistlin'
and divin', and you here, sweet as baby's breath,
sleeping and moaning over a dead girl. And I'm
sharing my apple. What are county jails coming to.
(Softly chants:)

Apples, apples, buy a veteran's apples,
Sweet and hard as ruby rocks.
Five cents a piece, two dollars for a box.

Apples, apples, buy an old man's apples,
fought for his country, left on his back.
Won't you taste his apples, they're black, black, black?

Whatever you are my boy, I'll find you out. I won't
sleep. And little by little, you'll stop sleeping too.

*(The peels falling on Dalton's face finally wake him. He
screams himself awake. He sits up, not knowing where he is.)*

Another one, kid. That's about three a night now.
You're sweating 'til you stink. Hey. I got a good one.
What's this—

*(Chas gets down on all fours and acts out something con-
torted and disturbing.)*

Come on. Make a wild guess. I'll give you a buck.
And a hint: it's something you can't see, but it's
there from the moment you're born 'til the moment
you die. What is it?

*(Chas repeats the act. This time it's more grotesque. He
comes up close to Dalton, too close, and Dalton backs away,
frightened.)*

Give up? *(Beat)* It's your soul.

(After some moments:)

DALTON *(Quietly)*: Go to hell.

CHAS: He speaks! He speaks! And what does he tell me? Go to hell. Go to hell. That's us in here, isn't it? Just you and me, hour after hour. So tell me. Why'd you kill her? Think she was pregnant? Well, she wasn't. But they say you got a chance if you say you thought she was. Don't you want a chance, Chance? *(Beat)* Why'd you kill Pace Creagan?

DALTON: Don't. Say her name.

CHAS: Pretty name. Strange. Strange girl, too. Lucky she wasn't more of a girl. More of a girl, and they'd hang you for sure. That's what they're saying. Seen her parents since? No. But I have. Like two gray sticks, the man and the wife, so thin with grief they are. As they walk, the wind blows them from one side of the road to the other. You did that to them. You did that, boy. She was a kid. A box of crackers. You opened her up, took a handful and threw the rest away.

(Dalton gets to his feet.)

That's it, boy. That's it. Let's see some life in you. I know what's inside of you. Don't think I don't know. Here? *(Throws his small knife down on the floor between them)* There it is, boy. You can use it. Go on. Show me what you really are. What happened that night, huh? Lose your nerve? You tried though. We know that. Dress all torn up. Head smashed. She must have put up a hell of a fight. I bet you liked that. That's the way you kids like it. All that fightin' hoists your flag, gets you flappin'. Got you so edged, you couldn't hold it in. Couldn't wait. Shot your come all over her dress but missed the target. Oh yeah. It was your come all right. But Pace Creagan died a virgin. That's what the doctor says.

(Dalton moves away from Chas. After some moments, Chas picks up the knife. He speaks gently.)

You want to kill me, don't you?

(Dalton shakes his head no.)

I can see the hate rising out the top of your head like steam. Here, take this. Go on. *(Holds out the knife)* You got to face up to what you are. You're a killer. A kid with a head full of black water. Everything sunk. Everything drowned inside you.

(Chas forces Dalton to hold the knife. Chas forces the knife up to his own throat. Dalton is passive. Chas whispers:)

Go on. It's what makes you whole.

(Chas laughs softly. Then suddenly Dalton shouts and forces Chas backward. Dalton forces Chas to the floor with the knife to his neck.)

DALTON: I don't want to do it. You're just a man. *(Seems as though he could kill Chas at any moment)* I can't even imagine it. Killing someone like you. With her. With Pace. I could imagine it. This what you want to hear? Okay, then. Like her parents, she was just a stick. I picked her up, carried her a little ways, and when I got tired, I broke her—snap—in half. Threw the pieces to the side. Those are the facts. It was that easy. You want a reason? Okay: the only way to love someone is to kill them.

(Dalton releases Chas. But as he moves away, Chas suddenly grabs at his leg. Dalton attempts to shake him off, even drag him, but Chas holds on, lying on his belly. This makes for an irritating—and almost comical—interruption for Dalton's words.)

Goddamn it I did what I was told— *(Drags Chas a little ways)* —became what I was taught: a man with a little piece of future, 'bout as big as a dime. Only there wasn't one—let go of my leg—there never was for most of us. That was the plan and it never was ours. But I bought that plan anyway—get off of me—'cause it was the only thing to buy. Those are the facts. This isn't about who we are. This isn't about what we wanted.

(With effort, Dalton breaks free. Chas lies still on the floor, looking up at him.)

My country loves me. That's why it's killing me. It's killing my father. Those are the facts. Those are the facts of love.

(After some moments, Chas gets to his feet.)

CHAS: You. You're not our children. We don't want you.

DALTON: What you were making earlier? That wasn't my soul. *(Beat)* That was yours.

SCENE TWO

Gin stands with her mother's blue plates behind her back. Dray has cornered her.

DRAY: Give them to me.

GIN: Get out of this house and get your own. These were my mother's. I won't do it anymore. The Salvation was out. The woman there says to me, "What're you doing with all those plates, ma'am." I said, "There's no food anymore. We eat them." I went down the road. I stopped at the dump. Next thing I'm on my hands and knees, digging through garbage to find something for you to break. That's when I started laughing. Laughed so hard two rats flew out from under me.

DRAY: Just give me one.

GIN: Not one. Not two. Not ever again.

DRAY: Gin.

GIN: Go to the jail and visit your son. Get outside. Tear the bricks from the sidewalk if you have to. I don't care.

DRAY: I can't. I'm afraid.

GIN: Of what?

DRAY: That if I go out, they won't be able to see me.

GIN: Who? Who won't be able to see you?

DRAY: People. Out walking in the road.

GIN: Yes they will.

DRAY: They'll walk right through me. *(Slowly takes off his shirt, seemingly unconsciously while he speaks)* My mother used to tell me, "Dray. You are what you do." In the foundry, it's no rest and you've always got a burn somewhere. I never minded. I was doing. I was part of the work. Part of the day. I was. I don't know. Burning. Freezing up. Inside that buzz. Melting down alongside thirty other men. But we were there. You could see us, and we weren't just making steel, we were. I don't know. We were. Making ourselves. We were. I was. All that. Movement. Movement. And now I do. Nothing. So. Then I am. What? Yeah. Nothing.

GIN: Go talk to them. They understand. They'll listen.

DRAY: I won't have anything to do with the Council. I know what they're up to. They're gonna take something that's not theirs. They're gonna break the law.

GIN: Yeah, well sometimes you break the law or it breaks you.

DRAY: Red thoughts, Ginny.

GIN: Yeah. My thoughts are red and my hands are blue.

(Dray begins to methodically rip his shirt into pieces as he speaks. This is a violent act, but somehow he does it calmly, simply.)

DRAY: They were running. Like all of us are. A few months back, up North. You know the story. *(Rips the cloth)* A strike. Out on the street. Thousands of them.

Doing something about it *(Rips the cloth)* like you say. Republic Steel brought the police out. Ten men were killed. All of them strikers. *(Rips the cloth)* Papers said the strikers started it. Weeks later. It got around. They were running away. *(Rips the cloth)* The bullets hit them in the back.

GIN: I never said I wasn't afraid.

(Dray is finished with his shirt, and is very calm.)

DRAY: You can go ahead now. If you want.

GIN: Where?

DRAY: I don't know.

(Gin carefully, hesitantly touches his bare arm. Dray closes his eyes. She touches his chest. He flinches slightly.)

You're cold, Gin.

(She keeps touching him. Now his back.)

But it's nice. It almost burns.

(Beat.)

There. That's enough.

GIN: I don't want to stop.

DRAY: I don't want to either.

GIN: I want you to kiss me.

DRAY: I can't. I might hurt you.

GIN: I don't care.

DRAY *(Gently)*: Get away from me. *(Suddenly furious)* I want you. Can't you understand that? I want you and it's choking me. Look at me: I don't know how to belong to my life. To be here. Not knowing where here is anymore. Am I here, Ginny? What you're looking at—is it me?

(After some moments:)

GIN: I'm going into that plant with the rest of them. I'm going to work with glass. We're going to make it

ours. But I'm a coward. If they come after us, I'll run
too. But I won't live. Like this anymore.

DRAY: You want me to leave?

GIN: I want you to do something.

DRAY: I can't.

GIN *(Calmly)*: I love you. So. I'll leave you behind.

SCENE THREE

*Pace and Dalton at the trestle. Pace is dressed in her brother's
clothes. Dalton holds out her dress to her. Something unsettling
has happened between them, though we don't know what. Pace
takes the dress, looks at it.*

DALTON: Pace. What was that? What just happened.

PACE: You tell me.

DALTON: That wasn't. No. That wasn't. Right.

PACE *(Examining the dress)*: You made it wet.

DALTON: I'm sorry. I didn't mean to.

(Pace throws the dress aside.)

PACE: Dalton Chance, when we're grown up, I want to
stand here with you and not be afraid. I want to know
it will be okay. Tonight. Tomorrow. That when it's time
to work, I'll have work. That when I'm tired, I can
rest. Just those things. Shouldn't they belong to us?

DALTON: What do you want from me?

PACE: I want you to watch me, to tell me I'm here.

DALTON: You're here. You don't need me to tell you.

PACE: Yes I do. So watch me. Whatever I do. Take a good
look. Make some notes. 'Cause one day I might
come back here to find out who I was—and then
you're going to tell me.

DALTON: I don't. Damn it. I don't know what you mean.

PACE: Look, it's simple—

DALTON *(Interrupts)*: Stop it. Every time we meet, afterwards, it's like pieces of me. Keep falling off. It shouldn't be that way, Pace. Something's got to come clear. To make sense. I keep waiting. I can't do it anymore.

PACE: All right. Then tonight we'll run her.

DALTON: No. Not tonight.

PACE: Tonight.

DALTON: That's not what I'm waiting for. It's just a train.

PACE: Yeah. Well it's going somewhere. And it doesn't look back. Tonight, goddamn it. You'll run it tonight.

DALTON: No. Not me. That was just a game.

PACE: We've been working on this for weeks. You can't back down. It's time. I can feel it. Everything's quiet. Everything's waiting. Listen? Here how quiet it is—

DALTON *(Interrupts)*: It's just talk, Pace. Just talk. This used to be fun. That's gone. You're gone. I don't know where but you're gone.

PACE: I could hurt you. *(Takes out her knife)*

DALTON: I'm not afraid of your knife. You could cut me open but I'd still leave.

(Pace jumps him and knocks him down. She sits on him.)

PACE: What's the matter with you?

DALTON: You said you'd change me. You did, goddamn it. Now change me back.

PACE: I can't.

DALTON: Yes you can.

PACE: How. Just tell me how.

DALTON: I don't know. How the hell am I to know? I didn't do it. You did it. You brought me here. You talked and talked. You put your hands inside my head. You kissed me without kissing me. Tonight. Finally tonight. But not like a girl should. You fucked me but I wasn't even inside you. It's ridiculous. This isn't how I want to be.

PACE: How do you want to be?

DALTON: Normal. Like any other kid. And satisfied. Like I used to be. Just satisfied. And now. Now I want everything. You did this to me.

PACE: Say it.

DALTON: No.

PACE: Say it.

DALTON: No.

PACE: I hate you, Pace Creagan.

DALTON: Yeah. I do!

(Beat. He's quiet now.)

And there are times I've never been happier; I can't forgive you for that.

(Pace touches his face gently, then gets off of him. She starts to leave.)

Where you going? Pace. Hey. Pace.

(She leaves.)

SCENE FOUR

Dalton in his cell, still on his back. Dray enters, quiet and bewildered. He carries a small pillow. At first, Dalton tries to ignore him; he doesn't look at Dray as they speak.

DALTON: I was just going to sleep.

DRAY: Yes. I know it's late.

DALTON: Why did you come?

DRAY: Isn't it natural a father would come?

DALTON: You've hardly left the house in months.

(Dray holds out the pillow to Dalton.)

DRAY: I brought you your pillow.

(Dalton doesn't take it.)

DALTON: That's not my pillow.

DRAY: It's not?

DALTON: I haven't used it for years. The feathers are poking out of it. I used to wake up in the night and my face felt like it was full of nails.

(Dray runs his hand over the pillow. He finds a feather and pulls it out.)

DRAY: Yeah. There's one. *(Finds another)* Here's another.

(Dray continues to gently comb and search the pillow and pull out a feather here and a feather there, sparingly, as the scene continues. Dalton watches this strangely tender exercise. Dray looks at each feather he removes, then forgets it as he goes on to another. The feathers float unnoticed to the ground.)

DALTON: I don't sleep much in here anyway.

(Dalton watches Dray pull the feathers.)

So are you going to roast it after you pluck it?

DRAY: Not as bad as I thought it'd be. Walking the street again.

DALTON: It's about time.

DRAY: 'Course I did have this pillow to hide my face in. You think anyone saw me?

DALTON: I hope not.

DRAY: There's something I want you to do for me.

DALton: You think I killed her.

DRAY: I want you to touch me.

(Dalton does not respond.)

Does the thought. Disgust you?

DALTON: You haven't let me. In a long time.

(Dray advances. Dalton is suddenly furious.)

Stop right there. Don't, goddamn it! *(Beat)* You think you can come. In here. *(Rips the pillow out of Dray's hands and throws it aside)* After all this time with this fucking pillow and everything's going to be okay? Yeah. It disgusts me. You disgust me. Like a little fucking kid sitting in your corner week after week waiting for the world to stop. Well it did, Father. At least for me. No. I don't want to touch you. What difference could that make now? To me, you're just a noise in the corner. I won't even notice when you go.

(They are quiet some moments. Dray does not move to leave.)

Stay with me.

DRAY: I don't want to live. Like this.

DALTON: How?

DRAY: Unchanged. Your skin's warm. I can feel it from here. So close to me you smell of. Berries. I don't know. Gasoline. And somewhere behind it all something like, something like. I don't know. I don't— All my life I wanted to say something that mattered. *(Beat)* I don't know why. I don't know why. I came.

DALTON: To bring me my pillow. *(Beat)* Go home.

(Dray sits.)

DRAY: What happens when we die?

DALTON: They're going to hang me. Do you understand? I told them I killed her.

DRAY: Did you kill her?

DALTON: I don't know.

DRAY: I think when we die, we just. Disappear. A few handfuls of nothing maybe. And that's it. What do you think?

(Dalton sits down beside him, but not that close. Dalton shrugs.)

DALTON: We just lie down and we don't get back up.

DRAY: Will it be terrible?

DALTON: Some people think there's a light. Some say it comes from above. I don't believe it. If there's anything at all, it'll come up from under the ground.

Where we don't expect it. A light. A warm light and it'll cover us.

DRAY: What color is the light?

DALTON: Who knows.

DRAY: Red. I think it should be red.

DALTON: Yeah. Like the sun, when you look at it with your eyes closed. *(After some moments)* I'll touch you now. If you want.

DRAY: I'm going to close my eyes.

DALTON: Why?

DRAY: So no one will see us.

(Dray closes his eyes. Dalton awkwardly rests his head on his father's shoulder or knee. It is a small gesture. They sit this way together some moments. Then Dalton lifts his head away again. After some moments of silence Dray gets to his feet.)

DALTON: Wait a minute. I want you to show me how to make a shadow on the wall. Anything. I don't care what.

(Dray takes the pillow with him.)

DRAY: It'll take too long.

DALTON: I got the time.

DRAY *(Looking at the small bunch of feathers on the floor)*: As though a bird had died here.

(Dray leaves.)

DALTON: Wait a minute. Wait.

(Dalton looks, surprised, at the floor around him. The feathers stir as though a breeze had passed through them.)

SCENE FIVE

Dray meets Chas as he leaves the cell. They stop and stare at each other. Elsewhere on stage, a feather falls on Dalton, though now

Dalton does not seem to notice. A few more fall as the scene progresses.

CHAS: Never stops talking about you. Thinks you're a hell of a guy.

(Dray doesn't respond.)

Way a son should. Just like mine.

DRAY: He's dead.

CHAS: Looks pretty lively to me.

DRAY *(Interrupting)*: Yours. I mean.

(There is an awkward silence.)

CHAS: You're out of work. I've got this job.

DRAY: Your son was on the track team.

CHAS: I trained him. Out the old road to the cutoff in Eastwood.

DRAY: I've got to go.

CHAS: He says you do shadows.

DRAY: What of it?

CHAS: Hey. What's this? Your son never guessed it.

(Chas imitates a plane doing a perilous landing. No sound. Dray considers him carefully.)

DRAY: Baby elephant.

CHAS: Elephant? Like father like son. Wrong, but close. An airplane. Motor gone dead. Doing a dead-stick landing. In slow motion of course.

DRAY: Okay. This?

(Dray acts out a camel. With full conviction. Chas circles him, studying Dray's every movement. Dray seems to come alive in this charade, in a way we haven't witnessed before.)

CHAS: Nothing else but a camel, probably a dromedary.

(Dray stands stunned.)

DRAY: Yeah.

CHAS: Not bad at all. Can you do a windmill?

DRAY: I got to go.

CHAS: Wait, wait, we just started. I could teach you. I'm teaching your son.

DRAY: Save it for your own. Good-bye. *(He doesn't move)*

CHAS: I'm sort of practicing. For him. You know?

DRAY: You're pretty good.

CHAS: He was asking for that pillow.

DRAY: It's not his.

> *(Dray leaves. We hear the sound of someone blowing air, as though someone were blowing out matches, but more gently.)*

SCENE SIX

Pace and Dalton are sitting together, a few feet apart. Pace is blowing on a small feather. We hear the sound of her breath in the silence.

Pace blows the feather into the air, and keeps it above her head, blowing on it, just a little, each time it descends. She lets it land on her upturned face.

Dalton watches Pace. Pace sees him watching her. She gives him the feather. He tries to copy her. He does so, but badly. Pace just watches. And laughs. They are enjoying themselves.

Then Dalton "gets" it. He knows how to do it. He blows the feather up and keeps it in the air. Pace watches him. Then he lets the feather float slowly down between them.

They are both quietly happy. Because they no longer feel alone. Because they are watching each other just being alive.

SCENE SEVEN

Chas is sweeping up the feathers in Dalton's cell. Dalton's back is turned.

CHAS: What do you expect? A hotel or something. There's holes in the roof. Sometimes they build a nest up there. It's the way of the world. They're moving you tomorrow. The trial'll start. It'll be the last of us. Empty cell. Might never get filled, then I'd have to find something else. Move to another jail. Might be no more criminals, not even a rich man who thinks he's a crab. Scuttlin' back and forth. Makes sweeping a devil's job. I can tell you. Still. *(Pokes the broom into Dalton's turned back)* You gonna tell them the truth this time? Only witness was you. Huh, huh? No explanation. No defense. Look, kid. If you talk, if you give them something to make them think you're crazy or sorry or scared, they might not hang you. If you don't talk, they will. Those are the facts.

(Dalton doesn't respond. Chas tut-tuts at him.)

A nice-faced boy like you. I had a nice-faced boy. *(Keeps poking Dalton in the back)* There was no substance to him. I could knock you down and sweep you up like you were nothing but a scrap of dust.

(Suddenly Dalton turns and grabs the broom.)

DALTON: Hey. Guess what this is?

(Dalton slaps himself in the face. Then again. Then he starts to pull his own hair and hit himself, as though someone else is hitting him. He beats himself to the ground in an ugly, violent and awkward manner. Chas watches. Slowly he backs away. They are silent.)

CHAS: I've been good to you.

DALTON: Yeah. Brett was a nice boy. He used to hit himself. I saw him do it. Why was he like that? He was a fucking loon, that's why.

CHAS: Brett wasn't a loon. *(Beat)* Sometimes. Well. I hit him. In the mornings, right before he went to school. Just about the time he'd start on a bowl of cereal. And a lot of the time, she'd be there. Pace. Your Pace. But I'd hit him anyway. Brett liked her to see it. After I hit him, Brett would take Pace aside and ask her if she saw it. Of course she saw it. She was standing right beside him! But Brett wanted to make sure. Then one morning I'm just about to hit him when he says, "Wait a minute, Dad. You've got a headache so you just sit back down and take it easy. I'll take care of it." So Brett hauls off and hits himself in the mouth. And I mean hard. His lip busts and starts bleeding. I'm so surprised that I sit back down and just stare at him. Next morning, the same thing. Brett stands in front of me and hits himself in the face. Twice. I don't say a thing. I just watch. Sometimes him doing it himself, instead of me, made us laugh. Together. The only time we did that. Laugh. *(Beat)* I knew Brett ran that train. It wasn't the first time. Maybe it was fate.

DALTON: It wasn't fate. It was a train. Five hundred and sixty tons of it.

CHAS: He was. My son. He was waiting. For me to give him something. I couldn't stand it; I didn't have anything to give him. A key to a cell, maybe. A broom to go with it. Is that what you give your child when he grows up? I didn't have anything to give him. So I hit him. I could give him that.

(Dalton puts his hands in the feathers. He looks up.)

DALTON: How do the birds get in? There's no hole in this roof.

CHAS: What do we do afterwards? I loved him. Years from now?

DALTON: What we wanted. It was to live. Just to live.

(Chas begins sweeping again. As he sweeps up, he drags the broom across Dalton's hands.)

CHAS: I got to finish up here. Word is there's gonna be trouble down at the Plate Glass factory. Might be some new guests to replace you any day now.

DALTON: About your son. I'm sorry.

CHAS: Ah. It seems so long ago now; it's all I think about. *(Beat)* Hey, last chance, kid. Guess what I am? *(Sweeps the broom a little wider, almost a figure eight motion, but without much effort)*

DALTON: A giraffe. Grazing. The broom's your neck.

CHAS: No. Just an old man. Sweeping the floor of his cell.

(Dalton stops the broom with his hand.)

DALTON: Tell them I'm ready to talk.

CHAS: We're all asleep. It'll have to wait 'til morning.

(He leaves.)

DALTON: Hey. I want to talk now. Open the door. Open up the fucking door! I got something to say.

(At first he shouts to Chas, who is offstage, then he speaks to himself and finally, he is telling us, as though we were the jury, what happened:)

(Shouting) Pace wanted to make the run that night. I wouldn't do it. I was afraid. No, I was angry.

(Pace appears. Dalton doesn't see her but sometimes senses she might be there.)

PACE: You messed all over my dress!

DALTON: But I didn't touch her! I was. Upside down. I was. Goddamn it—

PACE: You don't know what you were.

DALTON: I told her to run it alone.

PACE: You dared me.

DALTON: Pace never could say no to a dare. She stood on the tracks. She was covered in sweat. I stood below the trestle. She looked small up there, near a hundred feet above me. But until she started to run, I never thought she'd do it without me.

PACE: I had it made. Bastard. I needed you to watch—

DALTON: I could hear her footsteps. Fast, fast—

PACE: Because we can't watch ourselves. We can't remember ourselves. Not like we need to.

DALTON: Christ, I didn't know she could run like that! She was halfway. She had it crossed. But then I.

PACE: Turned around. You just. Did it. *(She disappears)*

DALTON: Then I. Just did it. I turned. Around.

(Dalton is propelled into the past moment. Now he can see Pace. But where he looks to see her, high up, we see nothing. The Pace that Dalton sees we cannot see, and the Pace we see is not the Pace that Dalton sees. Elsewhere, we see Pace climbing up the trestle. Dalton shouts at the Pace we can't see.)

No! No way! I won't be your fucking witness! You're warped. That's what you are. Everybody says it. *(Beat)* Stop. You better stop!

(Pace reappears, very high up on what might be a piece of track. She calls to Dalton:)

PACE: Dalton. Watch me. Hey! Watch me.

DALTON: No. Damn you.

(Dalton turns around, so that his back is to both the Pace we can see, and the other Pace we cannot see.)

PACE: Dalton. Turn around. Watch me.

(Dalton is furious and torn. He covers his ears and shouts:)

DALTON: Goddamn you, Pace Creagan!

(Now he is back in the present, and he speaks to us. Pace remains very still on the track.)

But I wouldn't turn around. Pace must've slowed down. And lost her speed, when she was calling to me. Pace started to run back but she knew she'd never make it. And then she turned. Even from where I was at, I could see she was shaking her head. Back and forth, like she was saying: No. No. No. *(Beat)* She didn't want to die.

(Pace puts her arms over her head, like she is going to dive.)

And then she did something funny. Pace couldn't even swim and there was no water in the creek, but she was going to dive.

PACE: Watch me. Dalton.

DALTON: And this time. I watched her.

(This time Dalton turns around, and for the first time looks at the Pace that we can also see. We all watch Pace. She moves as if to dive; there is the tremendous, deafening roar of a train that sounds almost like an explosion, different from the other train sounds we have heard. Then Pace is gone and we see nothing more of her. Dalton is alone and speaks quietly:)

Pace lay beside the trestle. She wasn't mashed up from the fall. Only the back of her head. I started to shout at her. Called her every name I could think of. Even a few she'd taught me herself. *(Beat)* And then. And then I did something. Something I can't. I don't know. It was. Maybe. It was. Unforgivable. I knelt beside her. Pace never let me kiss her, like that. So I did. And she didn't try to stop me. How could she? That's what I can't forget. She once said to me: "Dalton, you can't take anything from me I don't want to give you." But then she opened her mouth. She was dead. But she opened her mouth. And I kissed her, the way I'd always wanted to. And she let me. *(Beat)* She let me. *(Beat)* I have to believe that.

(A moment later, we see Chas. He lets Dalton out of his jail cell. We know Dalton is freed.)

SCENE EIGHT

Gin appears and watches Dray. Dray is still. Gin is holding a large piece of glass in her hands, which has a small break on one side.

GIN: We've swept the place out. Most of the machinery's all right. Glass everywhere. Like hail. We scooped it up. By the bucketful. Three girls from my work are with me. About thirty others. From all over. We threw lots of this out. Thought I'd bring some home. We can use it in the back door. *(Calmly)* Put that away.

(Now we see that the shadow Dray is making is a gun. And the gun is not a shadow.)

DRAY: I went to see Dalton. He said at night when he slept, his face was full of nails. All these years. And I didn't know. *(Beat)* Come here.

GIN: I've got to get back to the plant. Are you coming with me?

DRAY: Just come here.

(Gin stands by him.)

Here.

(He gives her the gun. She just stands there with the gun hanging at her side, ignoring it.)

GIN: Almost a shame to sweep up that glass. It was so bright in there. The sun through the windows, hitting the glass on the floor—

(Dray turns to Gin and lifts her hand so the gun is at his forehead.)

DRAY: Ginny.

GIN: —like we were standing on a lake of ice that was turning to fire right under our feet.

DRAY: Change me.

(*Gin does not respond.*)

Please. Please. Change me.

(*Some moments of silence.*)

GIN: No. Not like that.

(*She puts the gun down between them and moves away.*)

Dray. Are you coming with me?

(*Dray doesn't answer. Dray makes a shadow on the wall.*)

DRAY: What is it? A horse? A dog? I don't know anymore.
GIN: This is the last time I ask you: are you coming with me?
DRAY (*Dropping his hands*): Shadows. Just fucking shadows.

(*Gin leaves. Dray stands up, knocking over his chair as he does so. He looks in the direction of Gin's exit and speaks softly:*)

Yes. I am.

SCENE NINE

Dalton is making shadows on the wall, as in the Prologue. He is in a place that is both the past and the present at the same time. Pace appears behind him. She is dressed in her brother's clothes. She carries her dress. She lays it on the ground and spreads it out carefully.

PACE: That's a bird, stupid. A pigeon.

(*Dalton slowly turns around.*)

Like the kind that live under the trestle. Haven't you heard them? At dawn they make a racket.

(*She's finished spreading out the dress. She stands back.*)

Lie down on it.

DALTON: Why?

PACE: Just do it. Or you'll be sorry. Last chance, Chance.

(Dalton kneels down on the dress.)

DALTON: What're you gonna do?

(Pace jumps up onto a higher level. She is exhilarated.)

PACE: Make something happen!

DALTON: Are you going to kick me? Are you mad at me?

PACE: Open your shirt.

DALTON: What?

PACE: Just shut up and do what I tell you. Open your shirt.

(Dalton opens his shirt. Throughout their dialogue, Pace never touches herself nor looks at Dalton.)

Now. Touch me.

(Dalton makes a movement toward her but she cuts him off.)

No. Stay still. Right there. And do this. *(She puts her own hands near her chest, though she doesn't touch herself)* Go on.

(Dalton copies her.)

Right. Now close your eyes. And touch me. It's simple.

(Dalton hesitates, then he closes his eyes and touches his own bare chest. Pace is very still, her arms at her side.)

Yes. There. You won't hurt me. *(Beat)* Go on.

(Dalton touches his nipples.)

That's right. You're touching me. I want you to touch me. It's going to happen. To both of us. Go on. Open your legs. *(Beat)* Do it.

(Dalton lies down, and opens his legs.)

Now touch me. There. Just touch me.

(Dalton touches himself.)

Can you feel me? I'm hard.

(Dalton moans. He turns over onto his stomach. Pace never looks at him, though she is just as involved as before.)

I want to be inside you.

DALTON: Pace.

PACE: Let me inside you.

DALTON: Go on. *(He takes a sharp intake of breath)*

PACE: Does it hurt?

DALTON: Yeah.

PACE: Good. I can't stop.

(Dalton moans again, as though in both pain and pleasure.)

Now. Yes. *(Raises her arms in the air)* Can you feel me?

DALTON: I'll make your dress wet—

PACE: Can you feel me?

DALTON: Yes.

PACE: Where? Tell me. Where can you feel me?

DALTON: Inside. Everywhere. Pace. *(Beat)* You're inside me.

(Dalton comes. They are quiet some moments.)

PACE: There. We're something else now. You see? We're in another place.

(Both are quiet and still for some moments. Then Dalton opens his eyes. He slowly stands up.

Pace moves toward the candle. For one moment, Pace and Dalton look at one another.

Pace crouches over the candle. Dalton makes a slight movement, as though touching his mouth. Then he raises his arms, as though welcoming her vision.

Pace blows out the candle; at the same moment Dalton seems to do the same. We hear the sound of the candle going out.

Blackout.)

END OF PLAY

NAOMI WALLACE is from Kentucky. Her play *One Flea Spare* was commissioned and produced in October 1995 by the Bush Theatre in London. It received its American premiere at the Humana Festival and was awarded the 1996 Susan Smith Blackburn Prize, the 1996 Fellowship of Southern Writers Drama Award, the 1996 Kesselring Prize, and the 1997 OBIE Award for best play. It was produced by The Joseph Papp Public Theater/New York Shakespeare Festival in March 1997, and is being produced for film. *The Trestle at Pope Lick Creek* was commissioned by the Actors Theatre of Louisville, where it premiered in 1998. It was later produced at New York Theatre Workshop (1999) and the Traverse Theatre in Edinburgh, Scotland (2001). *Birdy*, an adaptation for the stage of William Wharton's novel, opened on the West End in London at The Comedy Theatre in March 1997 and on the West End in Athens, Greece, at the same time. *Slaughter City*

was awarded the 1995 Mobil Prize, and received its world premiere in January 1996 at the Royal Shakespeare Company, and later that year at the American Repertory Theatre. *In the Heart of America* received its world premiere at the Bush Theatre, and subsequently was produced at the Long Wharf Theatre and in Dortmund, Germany. It was published in *American Theatre* magazine and was awarded the 1995 Susan Smith Blackburn Prize.

Wallace was a 1999 recipient of the prestigious MacArthur Fellowship, the grant popularly known as the genius award.

A published poet in both England and in the U.S., she has also received grants from The Kentucky Foundation for Women and The Kentucky Arts Council, and a 1997 NEA grant for poetry. Her book of poetry, *To Dance a Stony Field,* was published in the U.K. in May 1995.

Her film *Lawn Dogs,* produced by Duncan Kenworthy, opened successfully in Great Britain and the U.S., and has won numerous film awards. She is currently writing a screenplay with her partner Bruce McLeod and the historian, Howard Zinn.

At present, Ms. Wallace is under commission by the Royal Shakespeare Company, The Joseph Papp Public Theater/New York Shakespeare Festival and Actors Theatre of Louisville.